Corporate Restructuring

A Guide to Creating the Premium-Valued Company

Milton L. Rock
Robert H. Rock

Editors in Chief

with James Kristie

McGraw-Hill Publishing Company
New York St. Louis San Francisco Auckland Bogotá
Caracas Hamburg Lisbon London Madrid Mexico
Milan Montreal New Delhi Oklahoma City
Paris San Juan São Paulo Singapore
Sydney Tokyo Toronto

For Caro

Library of Congress Cataloging-in-Publication Data

Corporate restructuring: a guide to creating the premium-valued
 company/editors in chief, Milton L. Rock, Robert H. Rock, with
 James Kristie.

  p.   cm.
  ISBN 0-07-053351-2
  1. Organizational change—Management. 2. Consolidation and merger
of corporations—Management. 3. Corporate reorganizations—
—Management. I. Rock, Milton L. II. Rock, Robert H., date.
III. Kristie, James.
HD58.8.C658   1990
658.4′063—dc20   89-36429
                                                                          CIP

1234567890   DOC/DOC 895432109

ISBN 0-07-053351-2

*The editors for this book were Barbara Toniolo and Georgia Kornbluth, the
designer was Naomi Auerbach, and the production supervisor was Richard A.
Ausburn. This book was set in Baskerville. It was composed by the McGraw-Hill
Publishing Company Professional & Reference Division composition unit.*

Printed and bound by R. R. Donnelley and Sons Company.

*For more information about other McGraw-Hill materials,
call 1-800-2-MCGRAW in the United States. In
other countries, call your nearest McGraw-Hill office.*

Contents

Part 3. Related Issues

Contributors

Edward H. Bowman is Reginald Jones Professor of Corporate Management at the Wharton School of Business, University of Pennsylvania. (CHAPTER 1)

Roberts Wyckoff Brokaw III is a managing director in the Investment Banking Division of Merrill Lynch Capital Markets, New York. (CHAPTER 14)

Hobson Brown, Jr., is president of Russell Reynolds Associates Inc., New York, the worldwide executive recruiting firm. (CHAPTER 15)

Robert Bruner is associate professor of business administration at the Darden Graduate School of Business, University of Virginia. (CHAPTER 7)

Barbara Moakler Byrne is managing director of the Investment Banking Group of Shearson Lehman Hutton Inc., New York. She is a specialist in corporate restructuring. (CHAPTER 10)

Andrew Capitman is a managing director of mergers and acquisitions at Bankers Trust Co. Based in London, he leads the bank's U.S. merger and acquisition cross-border efforts. (CHAPTER 6)

James F. Carey is a partner in the law firm Jones, Day, Reavis & Pogue. He is based in Dallas, and his area of specialization is employee benefits. (CHAPTER 13)

Peter T. Chingos is national practice director of Compensation/Human Resources Consulting Services for KPMG Peat Marwick, New York. (CHAPTER 16)

Peter J. Clark is a managing director of U.S. operations of Maplestar Consulting Group, a U.S.-Canadian corporate transition consulting organization with offices in New York and Montreal. He was formerly with Coopers & Lybrand. (CHAPTER 11)

Michael R. Cooper is a strategy consultant in private practice. He is the former president of Hay Research for Management, a division of the Hay Group Inc. consulting firm. (CHAPTER 17)

Carl Ferenbach is general partner of Berkshire Partners, Boston and New York, an investment firm which organizes and invests in leveraged buyouts. (CHAPTER 12)

Stephen B. Flood is a partner of Willkie Farr & Gallagher, New York, as well as head of the mergers and acquisitions department. The law firm has a prominent practice in the mergers and acquisitions field. (CHAPTER 3)

Duane R. Kullberg is senior partner of Arthur Andersen & Co. He is the former managing partner and chief executive officer of the Chicago-based accounting and consulting firm. (CHAPTER 19)

W. Walker Lewis is chairman of Strategic Planning Associates Inc., a firm with headquarters in Washington, D.C., which provides strategy and management consulting services. (CHAPTER 4)

Philip E. Lippincott is chairman and chief executive officer of Scott Paper Co., Philadelphia. He joined the company in 1959 as a retail salesman in the San Francisco area. He was elected CEO in 1982 and chairman in 1983. (CHAPTER 22)

James M. McTaggart is chairman and chief executive officer of Marakon Associates, Greenwich, Connecticut, a management consulting firm that has pioneered the development of value-based approaches to strategic management. (CHAPTER 5)

John A. Marzulli, Jr., is a partner in the law firm of Shearman & Sterling, New York. He specializes in mergers and acquisitions. (CHAPTER 9)

Donald W. Mitchell is managing director of Mitchell and Company, Weston, Massachusetts, a management consulting company that specializes in the effects of corporate decisions upon stock prices. (CHAPTER 8)

Robert K. Mueller is a director of Arthur D. Little Ltd. and former chairman of Arthur D. Little Inc., the international management and technology consulting firm. (CHAPTER 2)

Sean M. Pattwell is president of the Professional Liability Division of National Union Fire Insurance Co., the leading underwriter for directors' and officers' liability insurance. (CHAPTER 21)

Charles J. Plohn, Jr., is a managing director of Merrill Lynch Capital Markets, New York, and head of the Special Equity Transactions Department. (CHAPTER 14)

Steven B. Potter is a managing director of Russell Reynolds Associates Inc., New York. He specializes in recruiting executives to leverage buyout companies. (CHAPTER 15)

Judson P. Reis is executive vice president and managing director of investment banking at Kleinwort Benson Inc., New York, the U.S. subsidiary of the British merchant bank Kleinwort Benson Ltd. (CHAPTER 7)

Albert A. Remeikis is a principal in the National Tax Services Office of Price Waterhouse in Washington, D.C. He is the firm's leading specialist in mergers and acquisitions taxation. (CHAPTER 20)

Michael A. Schwartz is an associate in the law firm of Willkie Farr & Gallagher, New York. He specializes in mergers and acquisitions. (CHAPTER 3)

John Sifonis is vice president in the New York office of Temple, Barker & Sloane Inc., a firm specializing in strategy, organization analysis, and information technology consulting. (CHAPTER 18)

Harbir Singh is associate professor of management at the Wharton School of Business, University of Pennsylvania. (CHAPTER 1)

Ralph A. Walter is an associate on the mergers and acquisitions team at the law firm of Shearman & Sterling, New York. (CHAPTER 9)

Tina Winfield is an assistant treasurer of Bankers Trust Co., New York, with responsibilities for the bank's corporate finance marketing and communications activities. (CHAPTER 6)

Editors

Milton L. Rock, Ph.D., is chairman of MLR Enterprises Inc., a publishing and information services company based in Philadelphia. He is the former chairman and chief executive of The Hay Group, a worldwide management consulting firm. He has written extensively for both professional and business publications in his 40-plus years in the consulting profession and is the editor of *The Handbook of Wage and Salary Administration* and *The Mergers and Acquisitions Handbook*, both published by McGraw-Hill.

Robert H. Rock, D.B.A., is president of MLR Enterprises and serves as publisher of the firm's two flagship publications, *Mergers & Acquisitions*, the authoritative journal of the profession, and *Directors & Boards*, the leading journal of corporate governance policies and practices. He also served as chairman and CEO of The Hay Group. He is the author of *The Chief Executive Officer* and writes regularly on corporate restructuring issues.

James Kristie is editor of *Directors & Boards*. He has been a business writer and editor for 15 years.

Preface

We are witnessing a battle for control of corporate America. Takeovers and makeovers are drastically altering the structure, ownership, and management of American business. During the past decade, changes in global competition and in capital markets have opened the floodgates to a torrent of corporate restructurings. Restructuring has become an ongoing requirement and challenge for American business leaders. In this book we examine the implications of restructuring for members of top management and their senior advisers.

This book surveys the broad range of restructuring transactions from the different perspectives of the varied stakeholders. We examine these transactions in terms of valuation, strategy, legal issues, tax and accounting considerations, human resources, financial engineering, and corporate governance. This book focuses on strategic concerns and policy issues. Each chapter is written by an expert in a particular aspect of restructuring.

The book evaluates the effectiveness of the restructuring process in enhancing shareholder value and in maintaining corporate control. The overall objective is to demonstrate how this process can not only help a company to gain a short-term boost in stock price but also help it to secure a lasting advantage in competitive position. We hope and expect that the reader will find the book both enlightening and useful.

Milton L. Rock
Robert H. Rock

ACKNOWLEDGMENTS

We thank James Kristie, editor of *Directors & Boards,* for developing the concept of the book and for editing its chapters. He also worked directly with the contributors to ensure a useful and readable product. And, of course, we are greatly indebted to the individual contributors who shared their expertise and experience.

For their assistance in the production of the finished manuscript, we thank Louise Krupak, Martin Porter, and Anne Pryce.

Introduction

Milton L. Rock
Chairman, MLR Publishing Co.

Robert H. Rock
President, MLR Publishing Co.

Many top executives are ballyhooing their restructurings as ways to enhance shareholder value while preserving corporate independence—and not coincidentally their own jobs. Through restructuring, they hope both to protect against unsolicited takeovers (by reducing the premium over market that a potential raider can afford to pay) and to secure continued independence (by increasing the percentage of their company's voting securities under their own or their allies' control).

Corporate restructuring can encompass a broad range of transactions but generally alludes to substantial changes in a firm's business portfolio and/or financial structure. Restructuring radically alters a firm's capital structure, asset mix, and/or organization so as to enhance the firm's value. These alterations have a significant impact on the firm's balance sheet by redeploying assets (through acquisition, divestiture, and/or work-force reduction) or by exploiting unused financial capacity (through leveraged recapitalizations, tax shields, and/or share repurchases).

Historical Perspective

Declarations of the decline in U.S. competitiveness have been echoing throughout corporate boardrooms, university classrooms, and Capitol Hill hallways. The assertion that the United States is falling behind its

1

major economic competitors is supported by certain incriminating statistics: in 1950 the U.S. accounted for 50 percent of the world's GNP; in
1960, 40 percent; in 1970, 30 percent; and in 1980, 20 percent. When
America's preeminent competitive position was challenged, many U.S.
firms responded by restructuring. According to some estimates, nearly
half of all large U.S. corporations have restructured in the last decade.
These companies have undertaken a wide range of restructuring transactions, including acquisitions, divestitures, spin-offs, share repurchases, exchange offers, joint ventures, initial public offering (IPO)
split-offs, leveraged buyouts, and recapitalizations. Typically a restructuring program includes a number of these transactions occurring over
a period of years.

Since 1982, U.S. companies have doubled their debt to nearly $2 tril-
lion, while retiring over $400 billion worth of their equity. Today,
nearly one-quarter of corporate cash flow is used to service debt. So far,
the increased debt load has been softened by favorable economic conditions, including steady growth, low inflation, and stable interest rates.
Moreover, debt can be a strict disciplinarian, demanding tough decisions regarding worker layoffs, plant closings, and overhead reductions.
Under the lash of interest payments, managements of restructured
companies refocus their activities through sell-offs and redouble their
efforts through incentives. Given the current U.S. tax laws, it makes
sense to substitute debt for equity. In fact, to reap high profits, leveraged buyout (LBO) operators need not undertake the painful process
of turning around the acquired company, or even of improving its operations. Instead, they can merely exchange debt for equity.

Fear and greed will continue to drive the leveraging of corporate
America: management's fear of a takeover, and investors' and their advisers' greed for big profits and hefty fees. These motivations are powerful drivers and invariably will lead to some excesses. The biggest potential problem associated with highly leveraged transactions is the
limited flexibility with which management can maneuver in the event of
a recession. Management's fear may prove to be well founded as the
economic expansion abates.

Impact of Restructuring

Corporate restructuring should be more than financial restructuring.
The purpose is not only to gain a short-term stock price boost but also
to secure a lasting competitive advantage. Therefore, restructuring
should not be a one-time event but an ongoing process. This process

requires rejuvenating technologies, redesigning products, and reshaping markets. That takes time and commitment.

Successful firms are those that continually undergo strategic repositioning. Techniques include acquisition of related businesses, divestiture of noncore activities, sale of equity to third parties, joint venture with complementary partners, licensing and minority investment in new technologies, and reorganization of management, as well as realignment of capital structure. All actions are within a framework of long-term strategic direction. The managements of these successful firms realistically evaluate the economic viability and market value of existing and potential businesses and capitalizations, and then choose the restructuring options that increase shareholder value.

The goal of many restructurings is a "lean-and-mean" pure play, highly focused in the market and easily understood by investors. By unbundling, management can rivet its operating attention on the business or businesses in which the company is the strongest. But once a company sheds peripheral units and strengthens its balance sheet, the challenge is to achieve all-weather growth and profitability.

In today's topsy-turvy world, revamping, streamlining, and consolidating (with their concomitant write-downs, plant closings, and employee layoffs) are heralded as bold management decisions and rewarded with stock "buy" recommendations. The bigger the restructuring, the better. With one stroke of a pen, managers believe they can do away with losses from underperforming assets. "Rationalize" is a palliative for "shrink," and "redeploy" is a palliative for "simplify"—and for "slash" and "burn" as well.

Some managements restructure to thwart hostile takeovers. They are targets because bidders believe that their stock prices do not reflect values achievable through restructuring. The starkest example is the disparity between going-concern and break-up market values. Ironically, break-up often involves sale of unsuccessful acquisitions, particularly diversification from core businesses. Thus, many trumpeted makeovers are atonements for past sins—attributed, of course, to prior regimes.

Depending on the particular situation, the specific impacts of restructuring can range from enhanced competitiveness, higher stock prices, and increased personal wealth to slashed investments, reduced employment, and heightened risk. Are the restructuring entrepreneurs princes or pirates? Had the U.S. economy not created 18 million net new jobs in the past six years, there might have been a greater public outcry against the restructuring phenomenon. (Perhaps this phenomenon helped to spawn the entrepreneurial spirit that produced this unprecedented period of job creation.)

Stakeholders in a Restructuring

Enhancing shareholder value through corporate restructuring has become the battle cry of many top managements and their advisers. For the past decade we have seen the stockholder reemerge as the dominant stakeholder. This reemergence has reversed the prior 50-year trend in which ownership and management were separated, with the latter exercising corporate control. With the recent wave of restructuring, ownership and management are again being combined for their mutual benefit—namely, enhanced shareholder value.

However, value can be seen from a variety of perspectives. Stakeholders in a restructuring can include stockholders, bondholders, creditors, directors, top executives, middle management, nonmanagerial employees, union members, retirees, suppliers, customers, communities, and government. Moreover, each of these stakeholder groups may be composed of a number of differing interests and influences. For example, the power of securityholders with direct ownership (e.g., raiders) can be significantly greater than the power of those with only indirect ownership (e.g., pension funds).

Each stakeholder bloc has its own indicators, measures, and time frames for gauging the success of a restructuring. Restructuring is aimed at achieving personal, financial, strategic, and/or operating objectives. Many top executives, for example, judge success in terms of share price, corporate control, and job retention. These measures are personal and financial indicators reflecting ownership, power, and return. However, restructuring also should affect strategic and operating objectives, as evidenced in improved competitive position, market share, and corporate productivity. Too often, these objectives are relegated to secondary considerations.

Responsibility for decisions concerning corporate structure and ownership are legally reserved to boards of directors. Traditionally, state corporation laws have focused directors' fiduciary duties only on the interests of shareholders, although recently a few jurisdictions (including New York and Illinois) have broadened the board's considerations to include the interests of other constituencies. Directors and top management need to consider and manage all stakeholder interests and issues. Although they may need to think like raiders in identifying and surfacing value, they should behave like high-principled public servants in trading off among the competing claims of the varied stakeholder groups. The legitimate interests of all should be given fair and thoughtful recognition when top management undertakes restructuring for strategic, financial, and personal objectives.

The number and size of deals have attracted the attention of state and federal governments. In an effort to protect jobs and taxes, governments have enacted some laws and regulations (and are considering others) to restrict takeovers and limit restructurings. For example, some members of Congress want to devise tax incentives that would favor equity over debt. Though there will always be clamoring for reform, governments should resist the temptation to "level the playing field." In due course the markets will correct imbalances and will discipline excesses without interference from state and federal officials.

What's in the Book

With the preceding as introduction, we are now ready to present the roster of experts who will guide the reader through the strategic underpinnings and financial frameworks of corporate restructuring. The advisers in this book will demonstrate, typically through actual examples, how to unlock and enhance value—i.e., how to turn your company into a premium-valued company.

In Part 1, Stakeholders and Restructuring Forces, you will find analyses of the central roles being played in the restructuring movement by a corporation's multiple constituencies, including the critical position of the board in orchestrating the process of value maximization. This section will also examine the nature of the relationship between restructuring and value enhancement, an understanding of which will help in a realistic assessment of corporate potential.

Part 2, Restructuring Alternatives, will brief you on the battery of restructuring alternatives that can be deployed to achieve that corporate potential. Whether you are with a Fortune 500 company or with one much removed from that august list, these techniques can be applied in a distinctive way that will be right for your company. After all, the value gap—the difference between what a company is selling for and what it is perceived to be worth (in management's eyes or in the eyes of some other interested party)—is not limited to the major industrial or financial conglomerates. Every company is afflicted to some degree with a value gap. In our experience, no chief executive officer (CEO) is satisfied with his or her company's stock price; yet, the sheer complexity of restructuring options can overwhelm a CEO. This section dissects the "deal technology" being applied to make business operations and balance sheets more competitive for the world of the 1990s.

Finally, in Part 3, Related Issues, we round out the profiles of restructuring forces and techniques with a look at an array of considerations integral to the success of a restructuring. In addition to such obvious concerns as the tax and accounting implications of a particular restructuring option, we spotlight several areas, such as human resources and organizational culture, that are often ignored in the haste to complete a transaction. In a restructuring context, our experts present some advice and wisdom on management succession and development, executive compensation and incentives, information systems integration, and corporate culture.

The challenge that we issued to the authors of the chapters was to stimulate readers to look at new ways of evaluating their companies, in terms of competitive position, market perception, asset quality, and value potential. If we bolster executives' confidence and their determination to consider taking certain restructuring actions to invigorate their companies, then our objective will have been met. Welcome to the world of corporate restructuring, and may your company soon join the ranks of the premium valued.

PART 1

Stakeholders and Restructuring Forces

1
Overview of Corporate Restructuring Trends and Consequences

Edward H. Bowman
Reginald Jones Professor of Corporate Management, The Wharton School of Business, University of Pennsylvania

Harbir Singh
Associate Professor of Management, The Wharton School of Business, University of Pennsylvania

The latter part of the 1980s has witnessed a significant level of corporate restructuring, contributing to widespread debate among corporate decision makers, politicians, academics, and financial analysts about the consequences of these transactions. Discussion about the causes and consequences of restructuring has been fraught with controversy because of differing opinions of the effectiveness of restructured firms.

Proponents of restructuring argue that a leaner, more efficient organization typically results from such transactions as a result of a thorough scrutiny of the cash-generating capability of the firm's component assets. Critics assert that organizational disruption following restructuring (some of which is unanticipated) exceeds the anticipated benefits from such transactions.

The causes of the increase in restructuring are many. They can probably be traced to a combination of changes in the product markets and changes in the capital markets. The former come largely from increased foreign competition, from accelerated rates of technological change, and from more competitive pressures faced in global markets. Additionally, valuation of niche products with strong market positions in marketing-intensive industries has substantially increased.

Changes in the capital markets come largely from new debt instruments (e.g., junk bonds), and from a new tolerance for increased levels of debt in the capital structure of the firm. These changes are accelerated by institutional innovation and aggressiveness, particularly in investment banks, law firms, and financial service institutions, such as proxy firms and arbitrageurs.

One could ask why corporate restructuring has become so prevalent now. An explanation is that the simultaneity of changes in product and capital markets has been conducive to such transactions. With heightened competition from other countries, particularly Japan, American firms in many cases must restructure their assets to survive. The impetus for restructuring may originate from external parties, such as raiders, or internal people, such as top officers or corporate planning and development groups.

A Radical Change

Restructuring can encompass a broad range of transactions, including selling lines of business, changing the capital structure through infusion of high levels of debt, going private, and even restructuring the internal organization of the firm. As the term suggests, restructuring alludes in general to a radical change in the portfolio of businesses or in the financial structure of a firm.

More specifically, restructuring can be conceptualized as change along one or more of three dimensions: assets, capital structure, or management. Asset restructuring involves the sale of lines of business of the firm that are seen as peripheral to the long-term strategy of the firm. Restructuring can also involve a sequence of acquisitions and divestitures to develop a new configuration of the lines of business of the corporation. Capital structure changes usually involve the infusion of large amounts of debt either to finance leveraged buyouts, to buy back stock from equity investors, or to pay large one-time dividends. Management restructuring is designed to increase the efficiency and effectiveness of management teams through significant changes in organizational structure. Management restructuring has typically been done in conjunction with asset restructuring or capital structuring, but is relatively infrequently the sole dimension of change in corporate restructuring.

Not a New Idea

Although restructuring has gained great salience in recent years, the sale of businesses or acquisitions of other corporations is clearly not new to corporate America. Indeed, the United States is currently in the midst of its fourth merger wave since the beginning of this century. The first merger wave—from 1896 to 1902—composed primarily of horizontal transactions, amounted to restructuring of productive assets at the industry level. The second merger wave—from 1926 to the Depression—consisted mainly of vertical integration, while the third merger wave of the late 1960s consisted of conglomeration.

In each wave, large corporations acquired significant numbers of small corporations. The principal difference between the wave of mergers and previous ones is one of scale: In this merger wave, the target for takeover has often been the large corporation, and the rationale advanced for many transactions has been the search for greater efficiency through downsizing the firm. Although estimates vary, many indicators suggest that 30 percent of the largest 1000 companies in the United States have undergone asset-based restructuring since the early 1980s. An important distinguishing feature of the current wave of restructuring is its pervasiveness in the more visible corporations of the economy.

Restructuring has usually been accompanied by corporate rhetoric about the motives behind the somewhat drastic action. This rhetoric typically cites productivity enhancements, cost controls, and other measures designed to maximize shareholder wealth. The financial press provides high visibility to such assertions, as evidenced by feature articles in popular business publications. The sources of gains in the postrestructuring phase may be caused by the sale of peripheral assets or by operational efficiencies, or at times may be attributed to a new conception of the business. An example of the latter idea of redefinition of the business exists in the retailing industry, where acquirers such as Campeau Corp. have valued companies in part based on their real estate holdings—yielding considerably higher valuations than those obtained through the discounted stream of future cash flows from traditionally defined retailing operations.

However, this rhetoric about newly discovered sources of shareholder benefit is challenged by skeptics, who adopt the position that if managers as agents of stockholders were performing their roles effectively, such pockets of undervaluation would not be as pervasive as the frequency of restructuring activity indicates. Capital gains arising from the sale of assets to more synergistic or related acquirers than the parent corporation appear to be a less controversial source of gain in restructuring than claims of new-found operational efficiency. This has led to the argument that the firm should only control assets of businesses at which it excels because of a shared core competence or other specialized resource.

Trends In Restructuring

This discussion of trends in corporate restructuring will first address portfolio restructuring and then financial restructuring. It should be noted that organizational restructuring often accompanies changes in the other two dimensions. Cases involving internal reorganization have a more diffused impact on the external market, partly because information about specific steps in an internal reorganization is released incrementally to external constituents of the firm. Thus, information released about each step in a reorganization may be underestimated by the external market because its significance in a larger plan is not apparent. Internal reorganization does not receive the detailed external monitoring given to financial restructuring, partly because of its incremental nature and partly because disclosures of such steps are not mandated by regulatory agencies such as the Securities and Exchange Commission (SEC).

Organization restructuring can take many forms, and has been a part of our industrial culture for much of this century (Chandler, 1962). However, it is the size of these changes and their number that is unusual today. Some changes may be aimed largely at corporate culture, some may be aimed at processes and systems, some at the number of basic employees, and some at levels and numbers of managers, especially middle managers and professionals. When the organizational restructuring is driven by outsiders and combined with portfolio and financial restructuring, *all* these organizational changes are to be expected.

Portfolio Restructuring

Portfolio restructuring refers to changes in the set of businesses comprising the corporation to create a more effective configuration of businesses. Effectiveness is enhanced by combining lines of business in areas where the firm has competitive advantage, and by shedding lines of business where it cannot obtain higher returns than its competitors. This approach is based on a 1987 argument by Professor Michael Porter of the Harvard Business School critiquing acquisition of unrelated businesses by some firms during the late 1970s and early 1980s. Peripheral businesses, either in competitive position or in their relationship to the core competencies of the firm, are candidates for sale because the corporate structure overlaying the management of the business itself rarely is uniquely valuable to the shareholder.

Portfolio restructuring can be either discrete or incremental. *Discrete restructuring* refers to a major shift in the corporate portfolio through a single transaction. An example of discrete restructuring was the proposed breakup in the summer of 1988 of Macmillan Inc., a publishing and information services firm, into two separate firms and the issue of a large dividend to shareholders expressly to fend off hostile bids from Robert Bass and Robert Maxwell. The restructuring plan proposed by management would have segregated Macmillan Inc. into Macmillan Publishing and Macmillan Information Inc., reflecting its two principal businesses. The assumption of very high levels of debt would have accompanied this transaction, acting as a deterrent to a future hostile acquirer.

Discrete restructuring occurs through the sale of businesses often precipitated by the threat of takeover by either a raider or a hostile acquirer. Responses of the oil industry to raiding activity led by investors such as T. Boone Pickens have included sales of assets, spin-off of downstream operations, stock repurchases, and other forms of restructuring. These discrete and far-reaching changes were made in direct response to external threats to the control of the firm and have resulted in significant increases in shareholder value (Jensen, 1986). Analogous to the proposed restructuring plan by Macmillan was the restructuring of Sun Co. into two distinct entities—one in petroleum refining and marketing and the other in petroleum production. This plan was driven by the recognition that the economic fundamentals underlying these businesses are sufficiently different to result in a value-enhancing breakup. Another innovative restructuring at the time of this writing is the proposed breakup of Mellon Bank into two entities—one that would bear the major share of risk for questionable loans carried by the original bank, and the other composed primarily of more economically stable businesses. This restructuring would protect the productive assets of the bank in the event that the questionable loans do indeed result in high losses.

Incremental restructuring occurs through a series of moves that amount collectively to a major shift in the configuration of the corporation. An example of incremental restructuring is its sale of its consumer electronics business by General Electric after the acquisition of RCA, which followed the sale of the natural resources unit, Utah International, for a significant capital gain. This appears to be much more a voluntary set of moves created by GE's top executives than precipitate actions in response to a raider. Such moves as part of a longer-term incremental strategy are quite widespread, as is clear from the fact that some of the frequent divestors of years past are among the most visible corporations today.

Research on Portfolio Restructuring

As is apparent from the examples provided earlier, portfolio restructuring is effected through a series of transactions involving the sale of particular assets and acquisition of more desirable or economically attractive lines of business. The phenomenon of corporate restructuring is too new for systematic evidence to be available on its consequences for the various major constituencies of the firm. There has, however, been a significant amount of academic research on components of restructuring—i.e., acquisitions and divestitures.

An important component of portfolio restructuring is divestiture of businesses that are considered peripheral to the longer-term strategy of the firm. Such businesses may often be high performers, but may have higher synergies with another corporate buyer or could perform even better if bought out by management. As Table 1-1 suggests, there is a very significant level of activity in divestiture of business units by public corporations. Many of these units are smaller and less diverse than public acquisitions, making them more attractive to corporate acquirers because the focused nature of the divisions often simplifies the knotty problem of integration. The nature of the transaction (private, negotiated sale) also provides the acquirer with more opportunities for due diligence and a concomitant reduction of unpleasant surprises after the acquisition.

Divestiture can be an attractive option both to buyers and sellers because a unit with limited strategic importance to the seller can be sold to a corporate buyer or investor group with a more focused strategy or

Table 1-1. Portfolio Restructuring

Divestitures as a Percentage of Merger and Acquisition (M&A) Transactions

Year	Number of M&A transactions*	Number of divestitures	Divestitures as percent of M&A transactions
1979	1530	36	2
1980	1560	104	7
1981	2329	476	20
1982	2298	562	24
1983	2391	661	28
1984	3164	791	25
1985	3437	1028	30
1986	4380	1394	32
1987	3915	1192	30
1988	3656	1151	31

*Number of transactions includes divestitures.

SOURCE: *Mergers & Acquisitions Data Base,* MLR Publishing Co., Philadelphia, 1988.

synergistic assets to create value through the transaction. In spite of the high frequency of divestiture activity and its apparent gain to shareholders of the selling firm, this option receives less public attention than conventional acquisitions of publicly held corporations. An important reason for this is the nonpublic nature of the sale. Also, a lower level of controversy typically surrounds these sales, as the buyer can more likely avoid the spotlight of the auctionlike atmosphere of a public acquisition.

The acquisition element of corporate restructurings involves the purchase of new businesses that can enhance the core of the firm. In general, the restructuring wave has led to more divestitures than acquisitions by large corporations. The emphasis is on enhancement of competitive advantage in the core lines of business of the firm. Acquisitions would, therefore, focus on particular skills, technologies, or market positions that when acquired can be enhanced or may in turn enhance one of the existing businesses of the acquirer. The corporate diversification literature argues that a useful way of creating value through acquisition is to seek targets related in key technologies or markets and with a strong competitive position (Salter and Weinhold, 1979).

Acquisition research has been very extensive in the academic world. A large number of studies, numbering in excess of 40, have examined the effects of acquisitions on stockholders of the acquirer and the acquired firm. The evidence is very clear that acquisitions create value in the aggregate for stockholders of the combined entities (Jensen and Ruback, 1983). It is also very clear that stockholders of the acquired firm do very well in terms of their stock returns. Stockholders of the acquiring firm, however, do not have significant positive excess returns at the announcement of the acquisition. The nonsignificant excess returns, after accounting for the premium paid, suggest that acquisitions are considered equivalent to other investments in which acquiring managers would otherwise have engaged. In summary, acquisitions are good for stockholders of the combined entities (Bradley, 1980; Jensen and Ruback, 1983; Singh and Montgomery, 1987).

Related Diversification

A factor that has gained considerable attention in the current merger wave has been the notion of relatedness between the acquirer and target in the core businesses. Related diversification has been the hallmark of the industrial diversified firm and a contributor to its superior performance vis-à-vis the conglomerate (Rumelt, 1974). In the context of acquisitions, relatedness in technologies and markets between the core businesses of the target and acquirer has been found to contribute to higher synergistic gains measured in terms of the combined market valuation of the target and acquirer (Singh and Montgomery, 1987). Additionally, Lubatkin (1987) has found that vertical integration in particular results in higher returns to stockholders than unrelated diversification. Research in this area underscores the need for firms to concentrate their businesses in areas where they enhance their core business.

Although research has been less extensive on divestitures than on acquisitions, the general consensus is that divestitures create value for stockholders of the selling firm. In particular, those divestitures that are seen to be peripheral to the longer-term strategy of the selling firm are viewed very favorably by stockholders of the selling firm (Montgomery, Thomas, and Kamath, 1984). On the other hand, divestitures that cannot be clearly coded as sales of businesses that do not fit the strategy or core skills of the selling firm are not as well received by the investment community.

Consistent with these results, the high-flying conglomerates of the 1960s have, in the 1980s, been steadily shedding many of the lines of business they acquired in the frenzy of the previous merger wave. Particularly dramatic have been the divestiture strategies of Gulf and Western Inc. and ITT Corp., which have created excess returns of more than 25 percent versus the market in the years 1982 to 1985. Not all of this movement "back to the core" by conglomerates has been incremental. Some has been a response to takeover threat, as in the case of the defensive merger of Textron Inc. and Avco Corp. (followed by large divestitures), and other moves have been precipitated by CEO changes, as in the case of Gulf and Western following the death of Charles Bludhorn.

Although discrete restructurings of corporate assets, such as the breakup of Allegis Inc. (now UAL Corp.) into separate entities in response to shareholder activism, attain high visibility, examples of very deliberate and incremental restructuring through acquisition and divestiture do exist. Good illustrations of incremental restructuring are available in the U.S. tobacco industry, in which two of the most visible players, Philip Morris Cos. Inc. and RJR Nabisco Inc., have steadily engaged in a program of asset reconfiguration to reduce their dependence on the cash-rich but declining tobacco industry (Miles, 1981).

Financial Restructuring

In contrast to portfolio restructuring, financial restructuring mainly involves changes in the capital structure of the firm. Financial restructuring has usually meant the infusion of high levels of debt to increase the leverage of the company and thereby reduce the likelihood that the firm will be a takeover candidate.

The most frequent method of financial restructuring is the leveraged buyout (LBO). The LBO involves the purchase of the firm by a group of investors who typically incur debt-to-equity levels as high as 10 to 1 in the process of financing the transaction. As Table 1-2 shows, the 1980s witnessed a dramatic rise in the incidence of this type of transaction. Interestingly, LBOs have been consummated at premiums equivalent to that paid in a conventional acquisition. This raises questions about the sources of postbuyout gains that might offset or exceed the nominal premiums of 35 to 40 percent paid to take the firm private. The ques-

Table 1-2. Financial Restructuring: Leveraged Buyouts

Year	Total number of LBOs	Number reporting price	Average purchase price ($ million)	Number of LBO divestitures
1981	100	51	75.9	70
1982	164	72	47.9	116
1983	230	87	51.9	179
1984	253	125	149.6	156
1985	254	121	162.3	165
1986	335	142	318.0	240
1987	268	111	323.0	188

SOURCE: *Mergers & Acquisitions Data Base,* MLR Publishing Co., Philadelphia, 1988.

tions about the long-term viability surrounding such transactions intensify when we recognize that the same management team is in place after the transaction.

Although such concerns appear plausible, the evidence on stockholder reactions to buyout proposals is consistent with that on conventional acquisitions, with risk-adjusted abnormal returns of 28 percent due to the buyout announcement (DeAngelo, DeAngelo, and Rice, 1984). And although concerns about the high levels of debt incurred in such transactions may well be justified (if interest rates rise to unexpectedly high levels), the payment record of firms that have gone private has been good.

An important source of success in management-led buyouts is the management team itself, in a new regime with a radically changed but more appropriate incentive structure. Typically, participating managers in buyouts stand to own stock on average five times as high as the amount invested by them at the time of going private (Lowenstein, 1985). This prospect of personal gain tied to the success of the venture is a significant source of gain after the buyout. Another source of gain in buyouts is the sale of business units that may be attractive to a corporate buyer and are not central to the core of the new firm.

An extreme example of extensive asset sales postbuyout is Beatrice, in which the sale of assets postbuyout provided the principal source of gain in the transaction. Such transactions have precipitated debate about agency problems: Are management teams exploiting private information about the true value of the assets or really creating value through operational efficiencies after the transaction?

Financial restructuring of the firm is motivated by a relatively new view of the motives behind infusion of debt in public corporations. According to this new view of the firm, the existence of high levels of cash reserves in the company is a signal of management incompetence in investing capital in its various projects, and increases the vulnerability of the company to takeover (Jensen, 1986). This argument rests on the premise that management is often reluctant to redistribute free cash flows to stockholders if investment opportunities in the base business are not economically justified vis-à-vis the cost of capital.

Instead, as argued by Michael Jensen of Harvard University, managers of public corporations invest free cash flows in marginal operations or ill-advised growth, imposing in effect an "agency cost" on their stockholders. This implies that the high levels of debt have a disciplining effect on corporate management and that the primacy of interest payments focuses attention on generating more cash from operations. This argument assumes that management does not judiciously invest slack resources created by successful base businesses. Evidence in support of

this argument is drawn from the U.S. oil industry, in which considerable value was created through corporate restructurings mostly
prompted by raids from individuals such as T. Boone Pickens. This theory is clearly consistent with the mergers and restructurings in the oil
industry. However, extrapolating the theory to other environments may
be unwise.

Benefits from Financial Restructuring

Quite simply, benefits from financial restructuring probably arise from
a careful audit of the cash-generating capability of individual divisions
in a corporation, from the attendant need to service high interest payments after the transaction, and from the incentive structure developed
for managers. The potential cost of this focus on cash generation is a
possible compromise of long-term investments in favor of short-term
cash generation. For example, research and development (R&D) investment is risky and can require large amounts of cash in the short term in
hopes of future capital gain. This potential can be compromised if the
focus is on current-period returns.

Although there will be ongoing debates among academics and other
observers about the long-term effect of financial restructurings, investors have greatly stepped up their activity in this area. Investors such as
Kohlberg Kravis Roberts & Co. are pioneers in the leveraged buyout
business and have enjoyed spectacular returns on their earlier investments. These returns have produced the market confidence necessary
to raise investable capital for more transactions to the level of $40 billion
in 1988. Other investment firms have also begun to buy equity in LBO
opportunities, notable among these being Merrill Lynch and Morgan
Stanley.

Besides leveraged buyouts, there are other forms of financial restructuring, such as leveraged recapitalizations and debt-financed stock repurchases. Leveraged recapitalizations parallel buyouts to the extent
that high levels of debt are incurred to increase management holdings
in the company. Debt-financed capital is used to compensate public
shareholders for the dilution resulting from management ownership.
An important difference between the leveraged recapitalization and the
buyout is that the firms continue to be publicly traded after restructuring. Stock repurchases are another form of financial restructuring. In
this case, firms with high levels of free cash flow but with limited growth
opportunities and possible stock undervaluation may seek stock repurchases to use the cash flow to buy back stock with debt financing, and

return capital gains to stockholders while forestalling threat of takeover. The increased debt levels with all these alternatives can be troublesome for firms that have high capital intensity, but would be less important to firms with high cash flows but low-growth markets.

These developments suggest that restructuring on average has been positive in its payoff not just to prior stockholders, but also to investor groups willing to take the risk of investing in a firm through high levels of debt, with the intention of "cashing out" at a later stage (typically five years).

Effects of Restructuring

The effects of restructuring are experienced differentially by the stakeholders of the firm. A short list of these parties includes stockholders, managers, and employees. It is very clear that restructurings can be far-reaching enough to have effects on other stakeholders in the firm, such as suppliers and customers, but systematic patterns in this area are not apparent. We will, therefore, focus on the effects of restructurings on shareholders, managers, and employees.

By far the most visible constituency of the firm in the context of restructuring is the stockholders. Rhetoric surrounding restructurings has strongly emphasized shareholder value as the primary motive underlying the transaction. It is clear from the evidence that restructuring brings value to stockholders in the near term. In an efficient capital market this would be consistent with longer-term value creation as well. The only controversy surrounding shareholder interests pertains to the possibility that selling shareholders in leveraged buyouts may not receive the best price for their stock if the firm makes disproportionately high gains after going public again. However, because restructurings are accompanied typically by increases in shareholder value, it is clear that given a choice between restructuring and no change, shareholders would prefer restructuring, barring exceptional cases.

Effects of restructuring on management can be discussed at two levels. First, what has been the impact of the restructuring trend on corporate decision making? Second, what effect has restructuring had on managerial commitment to the firm and the willingness to make personal investments that are dedicated to the firm itself? Although systematic research has not been completed on the effects of the current trend of restructuring on managerial decision making, it is clear that managers now view their firms from an increasingly asset-based perspective, as distinct from a product/market-based perspective. This is particularly true at the corporate level. Incentive and control systems in several large corporations now also include measures of value creation at the divisional level as a performance indicator. This has led managers to make more financially oriented decisions with respect to new investments or alternatives in corporate growth. It may well be that the high frequency of divestitures in this merger wave indicates that many decisions to sell units have been prompted by an asset-based reassessment of the firm.

The effects of restructurings on employees are as yet very mixed. Employees, who are not privy to the decisions that underlie restructuring, may bear the brunt of the radical cuts in work force these transactions sometimes necessitate. If the cuts are inevitable but have been accelerated through these transactions, then the criticism may be less strong. However, there is little doubt that employee commitment is affected by radical layoffs related to financial necessities created by restructuring. These are "negative externalities" that are not easily measured in research focusing on stock prices.

Similarly, the distinction between an "inevitable" cut in work force that is merely accelerated by restructuring and an "excessive" cut in work force is blurred and potentially controversial. This has engendered calls for managers to exercise good judgment over the extent to which employee cooperation is compromised by radical layoffs or renegotiation of benefits as a result of restructuring. The saga of Frank Lorenzo, CEO of Texas Air, with Eastern Airlines' and Continental Airlines' employees underscores the need for careful analysis in this area.

The effects of restructuring on people and communities may also resemble a wealth transfer, but in these cases it is thought of as negative externalities. Although stockholders may gain from such transactions, losses may be borne by some parties in areas where the stockholders are unaffected. Especially with organizational restructuring, as illustrated by layoffs and management elimination, it can be argued that the costs paid by parties other than stockholders were necessary and would have happened anyway, although over a longer time period.

What is missed is that the abruptness of the changes may largely affect the size of these social costs, or negative externalities. With more time and planning, the costs might be ameliorated, though each case may be different. A potentially important type of social cost associated with restructuring is that bad times for the company *may* cause many highly leveraged firms to fail. If this failure is widespread enough, it could have cascading effects across a number of sectors and institutions unprepared for this impact.

A party affected by restructuring that is now starting to surface in the press and in the courts is the bondholder. Institutional investors, such as state pension fund managers, are recognizing the negative effects that restructuring *may* have on bond values. Professor Stewart Myers (1977) wrote an interesting paper on the "transfer of wealth" that takes place between stockholders and bondholders through financial restructuring. Similarly, Bowman (1982), in a study of firms in financial difficulty, was concerned about the potentially adverse effects of increased financial risk on the interests of bondholders. There is at least the possibility in some cases that a firm's own pension plans and pensioners may be similarly affected.

Altered Concept of Managing the Corporation

Whatever the long-term outcome of the current trend of corporate restructuring, it is clear that the concept of managing the modern corporation has altered, along with the wave of restructuring. The range of alternatives in corporate growth or retrenchment available to managers of multibusiness enterprises has increased to include not just diversification but divestitures, recapitalizations, and stock repurchases. The possibility of sale of business units may well limit the tendency toward unbridled growth that corporations showed in the 1960s and 1970s. And although reactions to restructurings vary across different stakeholder groups (as elaborated in the following chapter), the potency and immediacy of these transactions are to be appreciated as valuable tools for managers to make a major impact on the corporation and its stakeholders.

Bibliography

Bowman, E. H. "Risk Seeking by Troubled Firms." *Sloan Management Review,* Summer 1982.

Bradley, M. "Interfirm Tender Offers and the Market for Corporate Control." *Journal of Business,* vol. 53, no. 4, 1980.

Chandler, A. D. *Strategy and Structure.* Cambridge University Press, Cambridge, Mass., 1962.

DeAngelo, H., L. DeAngelo, and E. Rice. "Going Private: Minority Freezeouts and Stockholder Wealth." *Journal of Law and Economics,* October 1984.

Herman, E., and L. Lowenstein. "The Efficiency Effects of Hostile Takeovers." Working Paper, Rodney White Center for Financial Research, The Wharton School of Business, 1986.

Jensen, M. C. "The Agency Cost of Free Cash Flow." *American Economic Review,* Summer 1986.

Jensen, M. C., and R. P. Ruback. "Takeovers: The Scientific Evidence." *Journal of Financial Economics,* March 1983.

Lowenstein, L. "Management Buyouts." *Columbia Law Review,* May 1985.

Lubatkin, M. L. "Merger Strategies and Shareholder Value," *Strategic Management Journal,* March–April 1987.

Mergers & Acquisitions Data Base. MLR Publishing Co., Philadelphia, 1988.

Miles, R. "Learning from Diversifiying," Harvard Business School Case, No. 9-481-060, 1981.

Montgomery, C. A., A. Thomas, and R. Kamath, "Divestiture, Market Valuation and Strategy." *Academy of Management Journal,* December 1984.

Myers, Stewart. "Determinants of Corporate Borrowing." *Journal of Financial Economics,* 1977.

Porter, M. E. "From Competitive Advantage to Corporate Strategy." *Harvard Business Review,* May–June 1987.

Rizzi, Joseph L. "What Restructuring Has to Offer." *Journal of Business Strategy,* Fall 1987.

Rumelt, R. P. *Strategy, Structure, and Economic Performance.* Harvard Business School Press, Cambridge, Mass., 1974.

Salter, M. S. and W. Weinhold. *Diversification via Acquisition: Creating Value.* The Free Press, 1979.

Singh, H., and C. A. Montgomery. "Corporate Acquisition Strategies and Economic Performance." *Strategic Management Journal,* July–August 1987.

2

Stakeholder Strategy in a Corporate Restructuring

Robert K. Mueller

Director, Arthur D. Little Ltd.

"When Paris sneezes, Europe catches cold." So said Clement Metternich, Austrian diplomat and chancellor, in 1830. An updating of Metternich's metaphor for this era of corporate restructuring might go like this: "When corporations sneeze, societies catch cold." It may stretch the analogy a bit, but the Metternichian metaphor acknowledges both the acute and the chronic consequences of corporate conduct, particularly as played out by a restructurer or restructuree. When a corporation restructures—or, as with some large firms, merely shifts its weight around—external interests may be affected. Many individuals and institutions can have an indirect stake in various corporate happenings. A restructurer's normative strategy (described later) would not deal insensitively with adverse potential social or political impact of corporate restructuring. Rather, responsible, explicit advance plans should be made by corporations when or before a restructuring takes place—for example, to cushion negative impacts on community tax revenue, to provide assistance in relocating redundant employees, and so on.

For that matter, any dislocation or discontinuity of corporate activity should be carefully considered in the trade-off decisions that must be made to keep the corporation economically viable and competitive. Being sensitive to these kinds of considerations is what we term "stakeholder consciousness"; and while such stakeholder consciousness exists in many companies and in many regions of the world, the broader stakeholder concept has yet to be fully developed as an integral element of corporate strategy.

The Stakeholder Concept

In times of feudal dynasties, the privileged class granted stakes, or a partial sharing of the agricultural yield of land, to tenant farmers—persons whose livelihood depended on tilling the landowners' soil. Stakeholders were also identified in those times as persons who held stakes for others until ownership was determined, as in a wager or a business transaction. Later, the serfdom and gambling heritage led courts to define a stakeholder as a person entrusted with the custody of property or money that is the subject of litigation or of contention between rival claimants in which the holder claims no right or property interest.

With further growth and complexity of societies, the stakeholder notion now embraces all those interests—including equity shareowners—who are affected directly or indirectly, positively or negatively, by activities of corporations and other economic institutions. Importantly, various classes of stakeholders include parties with no equity ownership, who have little or no control over the corporation but who may be affected by its conduct or presence.

In order to consider a practical and realistic strategy for managing stakeholders as part of a restructuring, it is helpful to view stakeholders in separate classes:

- *Class 1—direct equity owners.* These owners are securities holders, individuals and institutions having title to stocks, bonds, and other such instruments indicating direct ownership.

- *Class 2—indirect equity owners.* This class of stakeholders is represented by the pension funds, mutual funds, broker-custody accounts, trusts, foundation portfolios, and networks of investor groups holding shares in various corporations. An investor holding shares of such funds has indirect equity ownership.

- *Class 3—customer and client stakeholders.* These are commercial entities dealing with the purchase of the organization's products, equipment, services, or real property; or that act as distributors, agents, licensers, debtors, or borrowers.

- *Class 4—directors, top executives, managers and nonmanagerial employees, retirees, and contract service employees.* This class embraces all human resource components, both within and external to the corporation being restructured, who may be affected.

- *Class 5—suppliers.* These are commercial services entities such as those providing advertising, tax expertise, certified public accountancy, medical, transport, legal services, plus suppliers who provide goods, real property, money, insurance, communications, and maintenance services, etc.

- *Class 6—public services.* Stakeholders in this class include those in the communities where operations of the corporation are conducted. Many supporting public services—utilities, education, protection, health care, transport, government administration—can be involved or affected by a corporation's conduct.

Roots of the stakeholder concept spring from historical ideas of economists Adam Smith in the 1700s, and Adolf A. Berle, Jr., and Gardiner C. Means in the 1930s. Apparently, the use of the term "stakeholder" in the management literature originated in an internal 1963 memorandum at the Stanford Research Institute as part of the corporate planning process involving systems theory, corporate social responsibility, and organization theory.

The Notion of Restructuring Propriety

A modern stakeholder is one who holds that which is placed at hazard. In a corporate context, as illustrated in our class subsets above, this goes beyond holding ownership shares in the company. Thus, in thinking about a stakeholder strategy it is necessary to be clear about the issue of legal accountability.

Consideration of any stakeholder interests of employees, customers, suppliers, or communities where the corporation operates is not generally indicated in the legal accountability of the board of directors. A sense of proper social responsibility of the corporation, however, should prevail from a commonsense governance standpoint. Corporate conduct is an important issue in the public mind. Perceived or actual corporate abuse of the charter granted by the state, as viewed by the public, may only bring litigation, increased regulation, and decline in business reputation, esteem, and image if social responsibility is not carefully considered when making business decisions.

The stakeholder theory rejects the Victorian idea of profit for the owners as the sole or primary consideration. However, in reducing this theory to practice, one must recognize where the legal accountabilities currently lie. Social, political, or ecological consequences are not always managed components of strategic action unless required by law, as in the case of antitrust constraints. A stakeholder's strategic perspective will include social responsiveness as an element of corporate conduct. This domain of human action is the sphere where we do what we should do, though not obliged to do so by law. Corporate leadership is the initiative needed to minimize disruptive effects.

In thinking about restructuring-driven impacts, it is useful to review a few of the rationales for restructuring (not in any rank order):

- To alter ownership patterns by way of public and private spin-offs, mergers and acquisitions, consolidations, joint ventures, and divestments

- To provide access to capital by going public with separate decoupled businesses

- To provide protection from liability exposure of a part of the business by separating assets into different corporations having different risk elements

- To change corporate climate—for example, to create an innovative environment by restructuring and reorganizing

- To refocus structure around a new business or strategy so as to minimize conflict with a prior business strategy

- To deal with tax and currency-exchange fluctuation considerations

- To change the image of a corporation by restructuring and reidentifying itself

- To change the nature of the corporation—for example, into a holding company rather than an operating company—for business or legal purposes

- To deal with antitrust and/or legal constraints

- To cope with organized labor threats by separating operating units and labor contracts

- To downsize, decentralize, or centralize through reorganization

- To respond to market needs with a competitive advantage by providing better services and products via a completely separate corporate configuration

- To achieve flexibility of management, permitting different compensation policies, human resource systems, and career opportunities in separate restructured organizations

- To better control and protect transfer of intellectual property such as technology, and to access local R&D through separate corporate legal entities

- To provide process mechanisms for separate joint venture arrangements, alliances, cooperatives, partnerships, commercial contracts, bartering, swaps, etc.

- To provide geographic differentiation and market segmentation

The process of restructuring a corporation (or industry) may be perceived by some to unfairly rattle the cage of the status quo. However, such restructuring can be beneficial or destructive when viewed in the long term. Certain stakeholders may receive no benefits—only damage to their position—from a corporate restructuring process. On the positive side, shaking up a corporation may be necessary for survival or to realize a greater return to equity owners and benefits to other stakeholders in the long run.

The drive for competitive advantage is one major source of corporate restructuring. The dominant criterion for success is total return to shareholders, including stock appreciation and dividends, compared to one's competitors. The effects on employees, customers, and suppliers, divested and acquired businesses, factory communities, reshuffled managers, company bureaucracy, the environment, and corporate culture and style are often harsh from a human-resource viewpoint. These components of our overall business system are seldom a formal part of restructuring strategy.

Such restructuring is ambition-driven transformation of the balance sheet by the restructurers. This is characteristic of the American private enterprise system and a business's pursuit of economic superiority. The drive for competitive advantage is, however, measured or traded off against long-term benefits and disadvantages not only to shareowners but to all stakeholders. The social accounting books stay open a long time. It often takes history to balance these books against the obvious economic gains and losses that are primary factors in a restructuring strategy.

The spate of mergers, acquisitions, divestments, asset stripping, and other manifestations of restructuring in the 1980s has been too often dominated by self-interest. In the case of proactive raider-restructurers, limited concern is given to strategic impact beyond antitrust constraints and economic gains and losses. These raider actions often ignore any implicit obligations or recognition of the rights and interests of others affected by a restructuring. Corporate restructurers of the raider variety have shown an insensitivity to the impact on other affected parties, despite the role of our legal and political system of chartering corporations in their social context. The American public corporation can no longer be viewed as existing solely for the benefit of trading profits on the part of short-term holders of its securities. Directors must, in response to a hostile initiative, be fully authorized to give fair and thoughtful recognition to the legitimate interests of all corporate constituencies, i.e., the stakeholders. A number of states have enacted legislation to codify such authorization, and others are considering doing so.

Restructuring has rekindled strong interest by some corporations in their stakeholders. NCR Corp. has taken an unusual public relations view by openly indicating that it does not think there is any fundamental conflict among stakeholders. NCR's chairman and chief executive officer, Charles E. Exley, Jr., addressed the First International Symposium on Stakeholders, held in Dayton, Ohio, in 1988, promoting NCR's notion that the great wide world in which the company operates deserves as much consideration as corporate owners.

NCR is not alone in the American corporate world, where directors of publicly listed companies are becoming more concerned with corporate responsibility to a wider public than just its shareholders. Companies currently seeking to serve the interests of their stakeholders are known as "vanguard" companies, and this group includes Control Data Corp., Johnson & Johnson, Deere & Co., McDonald's Corp., and Motorola Inc. Vanguard companies start from the assumption that there is no general distinction between individual and corporate ethics. Professor James O'Toole, of the University of Southern California's business school, has written in his book, *Vanguard Management,* (Doubleday and Company, New York, 1985), that his research indicates that companies obsessed with profits to the exclusion of everything else may do better over a few years but not over the long term.

Stakeholder Consciousness

To develop an overall philosophy of a stakeholder strategy in corporate restructuring involves three stages of consciousness raising about stakeholders. One way of viewing this progression is to look at the broadening scope of the stakeholder concept that a company chooses to address.

The *first* stage is when a company restructurer can be characterized by the desire to tread water and stay out of trouble. Such strategy focuses on immediate economic effects of restructuring on stockholders. The objective is to avoid unnecessary litigation by giving limited concern to adverse impact on stakeholders. This strategy is a nonformal one, with any consideration of stakeholders lying with the lawyers and addressing only the necessary laws and regulations in the local environment. This stage deals only with those public constraints that leave no room for interpretation.

A *second* stage occurs when restructuring complies in a more formal way with legal or regulatory constraints and public-social concerns. This approach on the part of restructurers includes a desire to better manage selected stakeholder relationships prescribed by company policy, laws, or regulations. The principal focus is on the stockholder, the employee, the environment, and community relationships. Restructuring strategy maintains a desired level of compliance with various social and legal requirements. The strategy includes some recognition of potential impact of restructuring on various stakeholders however they may be perceived by the restructurer. Stage 2 is a restructuring-with-compliance model.

There is a *third* stage: restructuring with stakeholder assurance. The basic philosophy is that the full range of potential effects of restructuring by the corporation is identified and carefully considered, and trade-off decisions are then made. This stage includes both internal and external components of the broad economic, political, and social system in which the corporation is restructured, and addresses such components from a strategic standpoint. Regulations and statutes impose certain compliance-related requirements and identify risks to be taken by the restructurers. However, there are other, relatively remote risks and potential effects, both beneficial and adverse. These may not be covered adequately by regulatory or statutory requirements or existing social norms but are also carefully recognized in the business decision process.

One of the purposes of developing a third-stage stakeholder strategy is to minimize surprises resulting from restructuring. Each restructuring situation is specific to the organization restructured and its environment, both external and internal. Because the external environment is increasingly complex and hard to evaluate, new tools are needed to avoid the consequences of failure to act, or the consequences of uninformed actions on the part of the restructurers.

Stakeholder Strategies

Various scholars and consultants have proposed more sophisticated approaches to detecting, defining, and understanding the implications of external forces and developments for any type of corporate activity, including restructuring. Their basic approach is *stakeholder analysis for effective issues management.* This is a logical, step-by-step process to identify all stakeholder groups and to consider the reasons why an affected group might mobilize around any element of the issue.

The principal focus of "third-stage restructuring with stakeholder assurance" is creating a restructuring strategy that embraces the perspective of the entire environmental system. The decisions made—which are trade-offs in the light of economic, social, and political realities—acknowledge the fact that the corporation exists primarily as an economic entity and is not an instrument of social reform or a means to achieve sociopolitical objectives.

This focus requires anticipating both the positive and negative effects, as well as managing any risks involved in the restructuring process. Not many restructurers take such a stage 3 approach. To do so may involve the following sequence: issue identification, risk evaluation, risk management, and compliance with subsequent verification.

One stakeholder analysis tool for effective issues management involves a systematic modular approach to detecting, defining, and understanding the implications of external forces and developments. The stakeholder analysis module uses a matrix approach to depict probable responses to each issue.

Former business school professor Frederick D. Sturdivant, now senior vice president, The MAC Group Inc., approaches stakeholder management in a pragmatic way. Because stakeholders often have conflicting needs and expectations, he recognizes that company leaders are unlikely to possess either the ability or the will to find optimal solutions. Sturdivant proposes a four-step process:

1. Objectively assess senior management commitment.

2. Generate a comprehensive list of stakeholders.

3. Shorten the list by grouping stakeholders based on similar needs and expectations.

4. Assess each subset's power.

This last step is the disciplined, tough-minded sorting out of stakeholder subgroups on the basis of their power and, therefore, the degree of attention/responsiveness they will receive. "Ultimately, it is an economic concept; and, like it or not, unless stakeholder management can be cast as a process that enhances the economic viability and performance of the enterprise, it will never be a widely employed concept," advised Sturdivant at the aforementioned First International Symposium on Stakeholders.

The Efficacy of Stakeholder Capitalism

Clearly there are conflicts of interest and differing expectations among groups of shareowners and stakeholders. An equityholder may perceive too great a risk over that of a bondholder for an investment in plant and equipment. However, the only direct clear legal obligation of corporate fiduciaries beyond that of obeying civil law and contractual constraints in general is to the corporate owners who pay them. Thus, only a certain class of stakeholders seems legitimate—those with the long-term view that happens to coincide with management's desire to continue the operation.

I have doubts that management or directors can or should have to act as fiduciaries to stakeholders in the real business world. Stakeholder capitalism as a rising power of ethics and accountability in corporate affairs is a seductive goal for those who are not in responsible charge of operating corporations. Moreover, it confuses legal accountability and the power of boards of directors to pursue economic goals with the power to pursue the broader public good.

While social controls on conduct of corporations are needed to a certain extent, the role of the common shareholder as the ultimate constituency of the corporation makes a great deal of sense. Unlike workers, creditors, tax collectors, suppliers, and other stakeholders, only this constituency—the common shareholder—plays for the "entrepreneurial margin." Any arrangement that keeps a noneconomic activity of the corporation continuously going purely for stakeholder relationships redistributes the loss to others and burdens other parts of the economy.

The dismantling of corporations in the name of shareholder value—junkyard capitalism—can abuse the corporate system if only short-term economic interests are recognized. Managerial capitalism can be enriched by prudent consideration of realistic and practical stakeholder interests. However, the notion that legal or regulatory mandating of managers in responsible charge of economic-driven organizations *must* act in the interests of all stakeholders does not make practical sense for the long term.

I believe the answer involves a change in attitude on the part of corporate boards of directors, management, and would-be corporate restructurers. Together they can effectively consider and manage most all stakeholder issues. This requires becoming more conscious of the ethical and moral dimensions of stakeholder interests and voluntarily mapping out plans to ease any adverse effects of a corporate action. Perhaps recognition of a basic teaching of Buddhism applies: the philosophy of interdependence. If something happens, then someone else is affected. Everything is linked and must be recognized.

3

The Role of the Board of Directors in Considering a Restructuring Transaction

Stephen B. Flood
Partner, Willkie Farr & Gallagher

Michael A. Schwartz
Associate, Willkie Farr & Gallagher

State corporation laws provide that the business and affairs of a corporation are to be managed by or under the direction of the board of directors. Many management decisions are delegated to the corporate officers who manage a corporation's day-to-day operations. Decisions about corporate structure and ownership, however, are quintessentially board-level decisions, and although senior managers (some of whom may be directors) may initiate and develop a restructuring transaction, the law makes it clear that the responsibility for these decisions is strictly that of the board.

In making decisions about corporate ownership and structure, the fundamental fiduciary duties owed by directors are the *duty of care* and the *duty of loyalty*. The duty of care requires that directors act in an informed and deliberate manner and exercise the degree of care that an ordinarily careful and prudent person would use in similar circumstances. Prior to making decisions, corporate directors must inform themselves of all material information reasonably available to them. The duty of loyalty requires that directors act in good faith and without conflict between duty and self-interest.

Traditionally, directors have owed their fiduciary duties only to shareholders. More recently, however, a few jurisdictions, including Arizona, Illinois, New York, and Ohio, have statutorily broadened the board's focus to include nontraditional concerns and constituencies whose interests directors are permitted—but in most cases are not required—to consider. To varying degrees directors in these jurisdictions are expressly authorized to consider the interests of employees, suppliers, creditors, and customers, and may consider the economy of the state and nation, community and societal concerns, and the possibility that long-term shareholder interests may be best served by the continued independence of the corporation.

The Business Judgment Rule

The courts have long recognized that business decisions are best made by businesspeople, not by judges. In order to avoid judicial second-guessing of business decisions, the courts have developed the *business judgment rule,* which is an evidentiary presumption that, in making business decisions, directors have acted on an informed basis, in good faith, and in the honest belief that the action taken was in the best interests of the corporation. Under the business judgment rule, conventional transactions are presumed valid, and decisions of a board of directors will not be disturbed by the courts so long as they can be attributed to a rational business purpose.

Where, however, a challenged decision involves the adoption or implementation of a takeover defense or involves a "self-dealing" situation where corporate fiduciaries stand on both sides of a transaction and negotiate and approve its terms, the directors are entitled to the protection of the business judgment rule only after making an initial demonstration of their bona fides. In the case of a takeover defense, the directors initially must show that they had reasonable grounds for believing that there was a danger to corporate policy and effectiveness and that the defensive measures adopted were reasonable in relation to the threat posed (e.g., *Unocal Corp. v. Mesa Petroleum Co.,* 493 A.2d 946

[Del. 1985]; the discussion of fiduciary duty in this chapter is based primarily on the law of Delaware, which is the most developed body of corporate law in this area). In a "self-dealing" situation, the conflicted directors bear the burden of affirmatively establishing to the court the "entire fairness" of the transaction [e.g., *Weinberger v. UOP, Inc.*, 457 A.2d 701 (Del. 1983)].

A Buyout and a Bear Hug

For the purpose of illustration, consider a hypothetical situation loosely modeled after one of 1988's major takeover cases, the acquisition of Macmillan Inc. Management proposes a restructuring of a company in which all shareholders would receive a substantial dividend, with the "public" shareholders receiving cash and the management group receiving an equivalent per-share amount in stock. As a result of this restructuring (and handsome stock awards to the management group to be made just prior to the record date for the dividend), management will increase its stock ownership from less than 5 percent to approximately 40 percent. The purpose of the proposed restructuring is to make the company a less attractive takeover target at a time when the company's industry has received too much unwanted attention from "aggressive" investors. Also, by giving management a significantly larger stake in the restructured entity, the board hopes to give management a strong incentive to continue the company's vigorous growth.

As the final preparations for the restructuring are being made, the chairman of the board receives a "bear-hug" letter from a bidder proposing an all-cash acquisition of 100 percent of the company's stock at a 20 percent premium to the market—but a price that is just at the bottom of the range that the company's investment banker would call "fair." The bidder states that the proposal is subject to the approval of the board of directors and that all the proposal's terms, including price, are negotiable. Two days later, the investment banker reports to the board that the per-share value of the restructuring proposed by management, after taking into account the postdividend "stub" value of the company stock, is slightly higher than that offered by the bidder. The investment banker advises the board that it is prepared to render its written opinion that the proposed restructuring is fair and that the bidder's proposal is inadequate. The company then announces that it will proceed with the restructuring, declares the dividend, and sets the dividend record date. Shortly after this announcement, the bidder withdraws the bear-hug proposal, commences a hostile tender offer at a price 15 percent higher than the investment banker's per-share valuation of the restructuring, and institutes litigation against the company to enjoin consummation of the restructuring on the ground that it is a defensive measure adopted in breach of the directors' fiduciary duties.

Determining a Reasonable Response

Analyzing the applicability of the business judgment rule in the context of this hypothetical illustration, the company's directors must demonstrate that the bidder presents a legally cognizable threat to the company's policy and effectiveness, and that the defensive restructuring is a reasonable response to the threat posed. In this case, the directors probably will not be able to make that showing. The bidder has made an all-cash bid at a price that, although not the highest price the board could obtain were it to sell the company, is within the range of fairness and is 15 percent higher than the per-share value attributed by the investment banker to the restructuring. The original bear-hug offer was subject to the approval of the company's board and was said to be negotiable. The bidder's proposal, therefore, is not considered coercive.

Were the directors to allege that the real threat posed is that the bidder wants only to put the company "in play," or that the bidder intends to "greenmail" the company, the court would likely find that merely putting the company in play, without doing more (such as trying to do so by making a bid at a nonnegotiable price well below the range of fairness), is not an actionable harm, and that a mere suspicion or allegation of a greenmail attempt does not demonstrate a threat.

The case law indicates, however, that the directors can demonstrate a reasonable belief that a threat existed by showing that they acted in good faith and made a reasonable investigation of the relevant facts. If the directors are able to show that they had looked carefully into the bidder's past and had discovered that the bidder had on several occasions successfully extracted greenmail payments from other companies, they might be able to demonstrate that they reasonably believed that the bidder presented the type of threat that would permit a strong defensive response.

If, nonetheless, the directors properly determine that the bidder presents a threat that permits a defensive response, the measure chosen must be proportional to the danger perceived. Here, assuming inadequate grounds for finding a greenmail attempt, the only legally sufficient threat appears to be that if the tender offer succeeds, shareholders might receive less than if the company had been "shopped" in an orderly fashion. Management's proposed restructuring, then, which provides less value to shareholders than the bidder's tender offer, is not a reasonable defensive response. And having determined to proceed with a management proposal that effectively puts control of the company in management's hands, the board cannot now determine that the company should remain independent rather than be sold.

At this point, the company has to choose between two alternatives:

- Calling a special meeting of shareholders to allow them to decide between the proposed restructuring and the tender offer, a choice that would be likely to result in rejection of the restructuring; negotiations with the bidder in an effort to achieve an improvement of the tender offer price; and an attempt to elicit a higher bid from the management group
- Seeking some other, more valuable economic alternative to the bidder's tender offer and management's original restructuring proposal

The Role of the Special Committee

In many restructuring transactions at least some board members, especially "inside" directors, are likely to have interests that conflict with those of the company's shareholders. A common conflict occurs when the restructuring treats management differently from shareholders at large, and when the restructuring results in a shift of control, or at least substantial voting power, to management and persons acting in concert with management. In an effort to best position the board to fulfill its fiduciary duties to shareholders, counsel generally recommends that the board appoint a special committee of independent directors to review and evaluate the restructuring proposal, to negotiate improvements in the proposal if appropriate, and to report its conclusions and recommendations to the full board. With the benefit of the special committee's efforts before it, the full board will be able to act on the proposal with significantly less concern that its judgment will be overturned by a court.

Corporate statutes, case law, and charter documents typically permit the board of directors to appoint committees of the board with authority to function as special committees. In setting up a special committee, the board must determine what its brief is to be, must invest it with the authority to carry out its task, and must authorize it to retain expert advisers. Members of a special committee are commonly indemnified by the company expressly for any liability arising out of their service on the committee.

The members of a special committee, as such and as company directors, owe a fiduciary duty to shareholders. Because the special committee is designed to permit a disinterested evaluation of the proposal, the members of the special committee should be as independent of the restructuring under consideration as possible. Absolute independence, of course, is impossible in many cases, if for no other reason than that the success of the proposal will bear on whether the directors will be able to remain on the board. However, such a "conflict," by itself, should not undermine the independence of the special committee or impeach its conclusions. [See *The British Printing & Communication Corporation PLC v. Harcourt Brace Jovanovich Inc.*, 664 F. Supp. 1519, 1530 (S.D.N.Y. 1987), applying New York law.]

The assignment of the special committee may be limited to assessing the fairness of a particular proposal or comparing competing proposals, or it might extend to negotiating the best deal possible for the company's shareholders—including seeking revisions to existing proposals and soliciting new proposals. Courts have generally recognized the value of the special committee mechanism, but in some cases have been critical of how the committee's role was limited by the board. For example, a special committee that recommends a transaction proposed by a controlling shareholder may be criticized for recommending a price that is at the low end of its financial adviser's range of fairness without attempting to negotiate a better deal for shareholders.

The Special Committee in Action

To return to our previous illustration, assume that the target company's board of directors had appointed a special committee to review management's restructuring proposal before the bidder surfaced with its bear hug. At this point, the special committee would normally be charged only with the task of evaluating the fairness of management's proposal. If the special committee were to find that the proposal was at or near the low end of the range of fairness, the committee should seek to negotiate an improvement of the proposal with the management group rather than to make (or to pass to the full board) a close decision that will likely be reviewed by a court to determine in hindsight the "entire fairness" of the transaction. If it were confident that the proposal was "fair" even though not overly generous, the special committee could, of course, determine not to negotiate with the management group and simply endorse the proposal.

Once the bidder delivers its bear-hug letter to the company, the board should revise the task of the special committee to include a comparison of management's restructuring and the bidder's proposal. If it has already endorsed management's proposal involving a transfer of control of the company to management, the board has probably hung a "for sale" sign on the company and is bound to conduct a fair auction of the company in order to obtain the best price for its shareholders, or at the very least to submit the restructuring proposal to the shareholders so that they have a chance to choose between it and the bidder's proposal.

The board cannot show favoritism for either management or the bidder and can only offer inducements, such as expense reimbursement, breakup fees, and lockup options, to the extent necessary to continue the auction process or to end it with a superior proposal at the high end of the range of fairness (e.g., *Cottle v. Storer Communication Inc.*, 849 F.2d 570 [11th Cir. 1988]). To this end, the board would be well served by directing the special committee to conduct active negotiations in addition to comparing the competing bids.

The Special Committee and Its Advisers

Whatever its mandate from the board, the special committee should retain competent advisers from the outset. Typically, the only advisers necessary are an independent financial adviser and independent legal counsel. In certain circumstances, depending on the company's business, the specifics of a particular proposal, or the familiarity of the special committee's members with the company's industry, it may be appropriate to retain appraisers, engineers, or other experts.

Since the special committee's task always involves making determinations of "fairness," it is essential that the special committee retain an experienced financial adviser, typically a nationally or regionally recognized investment banking firm. Although courts speak of "fairness" in terms of both "financial fairness" and "fair dealing," financial fairness almost always takes on greater significance than nonfinancial aspects of fairness—such as candor, control over the timing and structure of a transaction, and the fairness of any negotiations that occurred—which the special committee also has the responsibility to assure. The financial adviser should be experienced in evaluating corporate restructuring transactions and merger and acquisition transactions generally, and should be prepared to render a written opinion to serve as one of the bases on which the special committee will make its recommendation.

Throughout the process, the function of the financial adviser will be to prepare an analysis of the values inherent in the company and in the proposed transaction, to educate the members of the special committee on the relevant valuation techniques, and to develop an opinion about the fairness and adequacy of a proposal. In making a determination about fairness, the financial adviser will evaluate the effects of the proposal in relation to the company's intrinsic value. Determinations of adequacy are made with reference to other actual proposals or realistic possibilities, and a proposal may be found to be "inadequate," even though the proposal is otherwise within the range of fairness, because other proposals or realistic possibilities are viewed as superior.

The financial adviser chosen by the special committee should be familiar with the company's industry but should be independent of the company. A past working relationship with the company will not necessarily disqualify an adviser, but the special committee should look closely at past relationships for any indication that those relationships might cause the financial adviser to be beholden to, or predisposed to accommodate, the company's management. An investment banking firm previously or concurrently associated with any of the proposals the special committee is to evaluate should, of course, be avoided. In the Macmillan case, the court noted with obvious disdain that an investment banking firm had "worked with management on the proposed restructuring for over 500 hours before their 'client,' the special committee, formally came into existence and retained them."

The engagement letter providing for compensation to the financial adviser should ordinarily specify a fixed fee unrelated to the success of a particular proposal. If the special committee has been authorized or directed to conduct an auction, however, it might be appropriate to agree to pay a contingency fee related to the value realized by shareholders.

Competent legal advice is also necessary to the proper functioning of the special committee. At the outset, counsel must explain to the committee members their legal obligations under federal and state law, and this advice must continually be updated based on developing circumstances. In addition, counsel should guide the deliberations for the special committee so that its recommendations will be viewed by a court as the informed, deliberate, and dispassionate business judgment of corporate fiduciaries, entitled to the protection of the business judgment rule. Such guidance will include:

- Making sure that the special committee has adequately considered all relevant and material areas of inquiry

- Arranging (where appropriate) meetings and interviews with corporate managers and proponents of the transaction being evaluated

- Keeping a complete record of the activities of the special committee, including minutes of committee meetings, notes of meetings or conversations between the special committee and others, and files of documents reviewed by the special committee

Counsel will also be helpful in reviewing with the special committee the course of its investigation in preparation for arriving at its recommendation. Finally, counsel to the special committee will review any public disclosure document sent to shareholders to make sure that it describes all of the material information reviewed by the special committee; comports with the explanations provided by management to the special committee; and accurately describes the membership, activities, and recommendation of the special committee.

As is the case with the financial adviser, legal counsel to the special committee should be experienced with transactions of the type proposed should be familiar with merger and acquisition activity generally, and should be independent of the company. Ideally, legal counsel should be retained by the special committee before a financial adviser is chosen, so that counsel can advise the special committee on and participate in the process of selecting the financial adviser.

Special Problems in Defensive Restructurings

A defensive restructuring, which is a restructuring transaction motivated by a desire to fend off or to lessen the likelihood of a hostile takeover, may be undertaken in advance of an actual threat or in the face of a hostile proposal or bid. A defensive restructuring made in anticipation of a threat is typically designed to secure for the shareholders the "hidden" value in the company (i.e., the value that is not reflected in the company's stock price), which a corporate raider would otherwise seek to obtain solely for himself or herself.

In such a restructuring, management is more likely to be able to fine-tune the proposal to take into account long-term strategic goals than in the case where a defensive restructuring is developed in the face of a hostile bid. When there is an actual bid on the table, the development of a defensive restructuring is constrained by the pressing need to maximize short-term values for the shareholders. In contrast, when a restructuring is undertaken and allowed to be implemented prior to the existence of a hostile takeover threat, long-term considerations can be addressed with the objective of gradually enhancing the market price to more accurately reflect intrinsic value, thereby removing a raider's incentive to launch a hostile bid.

A defensive restructuring that is met with a hostile bid before it can be implemented may turn out to be a double-edged sword. Although such a defensive restructuring may ultimately defeat the hostile bid, it may have the effect of putting the company on the auction block and setting the minimum sale price. Although the courts have only recently begun to grapple with the issue, it appears that a board of directors only has a duty to conduct an auction once it takes steps that indicate the corporation will be sold, or once a sale becomes inevitable. What these steps are and what makes a sale inevitable are questions that can be determined only in the context of all the relevant facts and circumstances, but actions such as the board authorizing management to negotiate an acquisition of the company should be sufficient to change the directors' role "from defenders of the corporate bastion to auctioneers charged with getting the best price for the stockholders at a sale of the company" (*Revlon Inc. v. MacAndrews & Forbes Holdings Inc.*, 506 A.2d 173, 182 [Del. 1986]).

The Board and Defensive Restructurings

One question that has not yet been squarely answered by the courts is whether a board of directors can approve a restructuring as a defensive response to a third-party bid that transfers control of the company to management without assuming the obligation of conducting an auction. In our hypothetical illustration, the defensive restructuring would leave management with a 40 percent position in the company, an ownership level that in many cases would constitute "control." The question of change of control may depend on whether management is considered monolithic, whether there are restrictions on management's right to transfer stock, and whether there are other unrelated stockholders.

If there is a transfer of control, it is tantamount to a sale (which would trigger the duty to conduct an auction), because by permitting such a transfer the board potentially deprives shareholders of the benefit of a control premium, which clearly is an element of value that would be realized by shareholders if an auction were to be conducted to produce the highest possible price. Alternatively, the restructuring could be submitted to a shareholder vote so that the shareholders would decide between the restructuring proposal and the third-party bid. In this case, there would be no duty to conduct an auction except in the unlikely event that neither the restructuring nor the third-party bid was within the range of fair values.

In the Macmillan case, from which our hypothetical illustration is drawn, that issue was raised before the Delaware Chancery Court but was never decided because the court found preliminarily that the management restructuring proposal was not a reasonable response to the threat posed and therefore was not entitled to the protection of the business judgment rule. That restructuring proposal, the court preliminarily found, was economically inferior to the hostile bid and, because it was to be implemented by board action alone and would have the effect of precluding the hostile bid, denied shareholders the ability to choose between the competing proposals. Had the restructuring plan been found to be economically superior or had the board given shareholders the ability to choose between the two transactions, the outcome of the Macmillan transaction undoubtedly would have been different.

Directors as Reviewers and Evaluators

The role of the board in considering a restructuring transaction in which management is treated differently than public shareholders requires the appointment of a special committee composed of independent directors. With the assistance of experienced independent counsel and financial advisers appointed by it, the special committee has the function (varying depending on the circumstances) of reviewing and evaluating the restructuring proposal, comparing the restructuring proposal with any competing proposal, negotiating with management and third parties, if any, to obtain improvements in the competing proposals, and then reporting its conclusions and recommendations to the full board.

Defensive restructurings present special problems to the special committee. As a threshold matter, it is necessary to determine whether control is passing from the public shareholders to management, and if so, to determine fairness in terms of whether a control premium is being paid to the public shareholders. In case of a third-party competing bid, it may be appropriate to conduct an active auction between the proponents of the restructuring transaction and the third-party bidder. Alternatively, it would seem permissible to submit the restructuring proposal to shareholders to allow them to choose between it and the third-party bid.

4

Strategic Restructuring: A Critical Requirement in the Search for Corporate Potential

W. Walker Lewis

Chairman, Strategic Planning Associates Inc.[*]

*To keep an industry pure, you've got to keep
it in perpetual ferment."*   HENRY FORD

Nearly half of large U.S. corporations have "restructured" in the 1980s. More than 50 percent failed in their efforts. Of those who failed:

- One in five was taken over.
- Half destroyed shareholder value.

The question is, why? Strategic Planning Associates (SPA) believes that these companies were not extensive enough in their efforts nor strategic in their approach. The financial-oriented strategies that many chose not only resulted in poor odds of success but also failed to address the persistent threat of hostile takeovers. In addition, we have found that the majority of restructures were either resounding successes or crushing failures—there was very little middle ground.

Clearly, the initiation of a major restructuring program is not to be taken lightly. In this chapter, we identify the policies that have led to successful restructures, and what can be done to avoid the pitfalls of failure.

During the past decade, announced restructuring programs have varied considerably in extent, approach, and motivation. Some companies, such as Ford Motor Co. and Martin Marietta Corp., initiated restructuring in response to competitive share loss, impending bankruptcy, or takeover threat. Others, such as General Electric Corp. and Ralston Purina Co., were operating from a position of strength and acted to close the gap between actual performance and full potential. These companies restructured skillfully and were successful in their efforts. In fact, since the beginning of their restructuring programs, these four companies outperformed their industry peers in the creation of shareholder wealth by 110 percent, or $31 billion—no small sum.

However, there has been no hard evidence yet assembled to demonstrate that the majority of restructuring programs have been successful in increasing competitiveness and shareholder wealth or in making the companies involved resistant to takeover attempts.

A Restructuring Study

SPA has fielded a restructuring study focused on the experience of some 135 large American corporations. The companies represent most of the major restructurings in Fortune 300 companies during the 1980s. The largest, General Motors Corp., had 1987 sales of $101 billion. The smallest, Insilco Corp., had sales of $710 million. The 135 companies cover 26 major industries. Their aggregate market value in 1987 was $534 billion.

SPA applied three criteria to define the degree of success in each restructuring effort it reviewed:

- The company increased in value more than 20 percent over its competitors based on total return to investors from stock appreciation, dividends, and special distributions. (In the case of the automobile, food, and chemical segments that were abnormally affected by restructuring, performance was measured against the S&P 500.)

- The company increased its competitiveness in relevant markets.
- The company avoided or withstood a corporate raid.

Figure 4-1 indicates how many of the 135 companies met the first test: superior growth in shareholder wealth. Only 62 of the 135 companies—or 46 percent—were judged a success in this category. When all three criteria were applied, fewer than 20 percent were successful. As this exhibit indicates, very few companies were marginally successful or unsuccessful: 107 companies—or 79 percent—of those studied were either 40 percent above their industry performance or more than 20 percent below it.

Those who succeeded were able to increase shareholder wealth at a rate 2 ½ times greater than competitors in the same industry. Only one was raided.

Some 38 of the 135 companies studied by SPA were targeted by corporate raiders. Of these, 24 succeeded in remaining independent, although, for some, not without extensive, perhaps excessive, leverage. Those companies who fought off raiders, such as Martin Marietta, used extensive restructuring 84 percent of the time. Those who used a more moderate approach and remained independent were typically faced with a milder threat and escaped with the payment of "greenmail" (buying back only the raider's stock at a premium).

Of the 14 companies that lost their independence as a result of a raid, half failed to implement extensive restructures. These results make it

Very Few Companies Were
Marginally Successful or Unsuccessful

Figure 4-1. Very few companies were marginally successful or unsuccessful in creating value.

clear that the right kind of restructuring not only increases the market value of a company but also reduces the gap between actual and potential performance to a point where raiders see no profit in threatening to take over a company.

Indicators of Success or Failure

Success or failure in restructuring is highly dependent on both the type and the degree of restructuring. For many companies the key factor is whether change is achieved by financial restructuring alone or also includes strategic and operational changes that address the fundamentals of how a company is managed.

In the SPA study, financial restructuring is characterized by divestments, write-offs, across-the-board cost cuts, increased leverage, and stock repurchase programs. Strategic restructuring involves actions such as significant changes in market approach, extensive redirection in product development, major changes in human resource policies (extending performance-driven compensation programs and simplifying career path objectives for senior management), refocusing the business competitively, selective cost cuts, as well as financial restructuring activities to enhance the value of cash flows. Companies engaged in strategic restructuring combine the management skills of the modern CEO, who relies on focused strategies, flat organization, and lean, high-quality operations, with financial savvy to assure the realization of the value created.

The degree of restructuring that is carried out is equally important. Likelihood of success is higher if a restructure is *extensive.* Extensive restructures involve major shifts in the business focus, management approach, and financial hurdles of the enterprise. For example:

- The acquisition or divestiture of more than 40 percent of operations (American Express Co., Allegis Corp.)

- The replacement or reassignment of senior managers (Borg-Warner Corp., General Electric)

- A reduction in employee counts of 20 percent or more for a given level of sales (Armco Inc., Atlantic Richfield Co.)

- Significant debt recapitalization (Harcourt Brace Jovanovich Inc., Holiday Corp.)

By exclusion, *moderate* restructuring occurs when any lesser effort is undertaken.

The SPA study placed its 135 restructured companies into categories based on the nature of the restructuring program (financial alone versus strategic) and the degree of restructuring efforts (extensive versus moderate). The result, as shown in Figure 4-2, reflects the rate of success in each category.

Admittedly, the results of some restructures were skewed by unrelated and uncontrollable factors. For example, the disastrous gas leak at Bhopal caused Union Carbide Corp.'s stock to plunge, yet cannot realistically be attributed to the nature of its restructuring program. Bank of America's results were similarly damaged by the devaluation of the vast portfolio of Third World debt it accumulated during the 1970s—a condition for which no amount of restructuring could fully compensate. In spite of these random errors, the number of the companies in the sample and the sheer magnitude of the differences in performance allowed fairly sweeping generalizations to be drawn with confidence.

Companies that carried out strategic restructuring programs consistently outperformed those that engaged in financial restructuring alone; and extensive programs were often, although not necessarily always, more successful than moderate ones. Extensive financial restructuring succeeded only 32 percent of the time. Moderate financial restructuring—consisting primarily of financial tinkering—was rarely successful. It appears that, in general, financial restructuring was most successful when the objective was to promote a breakup. Beatrice Foods, for example, was acquired by Kohlberg Kravis Roberts & Co. following a $6.3 billion leveraged buyout. Financial restructuring was

Restructuring Rate of Success

		Type	
		Financial	**Strategic**
Degree	**Extensive**	32% – Beatrice	70% – Ford
	Moderate	13% – Viacom	41% – J.P. Morgan

46%

Figure 4-2. The greatest rate of success in creating value was achieved by companies that engaged in extensive strategic restructuring.

used to dismantle at a profit a company that had operated some 64 businesses.

The greatest success rate among the companies involved in the SPA study was achieved by the 50 companies that engaged in extensive strategic restructuring. Those companies embarked on fundamental and extensive changes in operations, finance, and management. Seventy percent achieved a shareholder return 20 percent or more above their competitors. Half of these outperformed their peers by 100 percent or more. Each, despite inevitable differences in tactics and emphasis, was able to:

- Change the fundamental operating behavior, organizational dynamics, and management culture that define corporate strategy.

- Restructure as extensively as required to bring the company to its full potential.

- Install restructuring as a permanent part of corporate life.

Performance versus Potential

It is clear that a company's current performance and future prospects are related directly to its past history. How this legacy affects current profitability and how it can be used as a base for working toward achieving full potential are critical elements in successful restructuring. For troubled companies, like Baldwin-United Corp. or International Harvester Co. after its UAW strike, this legacy may create an insurmountable barrier to survival.

It is critical to understand what is meant—and not meant—by the term "full potential." Full potential is not the same as current profitability. Current profitability is a measure of what a company can achieve as is. Full potential is the maximum profitability that can be achieved by undertaking extensive strategic restructuring. A company with high current profitability may not be operating at full potential. A nearly bankrupt company, on the other hand, may be operating at full potential. Failure to understand this can spell trouble for both kinds of companies. Even highly profitable companies may be operating at less than full potential. A few indicators include the following:

- Unrelated business diversifications that have no tangible path to paying off

- Profitability averaging that fails to separate out activities at the customer, distribution, and product level to determine which areas are profitable and which are not

- Lack of detailed analysis of competitors' economics at a given quality level
- Failure to build a "model" of the business when competitive interactions and value-added complexity require it
- Failure to keep research and development costs in proper balance with marketing capabilities
- Unchecked growth in data and information systems. What is collected is far in excess of what could ever be useful—or is not in useful form
- Hierarchical management structures that often resist the changes necessary to stay competitive
- Decentralized businesses that define their potential without strong guidance from corporate leadership
- Excessive controls that punish mistakes and dampen initiative
- Averaged resource allocation rather than allocation based on the potential profitability of a company's best components
- Budget-based compensation programs that create incentives for avoiding full potential
- Excessive reliance on management process over clear high-potential programs
- Failure to provide a proper mix of managerial elements between risk takers and risk avoiders—conservative managers versus entrepreneurs

When currently profitable companies undertake aggressive restructuring to reach full potential, the process is painful but can be rewarding. The healthy or currently profitable companies in SPA's study, as shown in Figure 4-3, were 85 percent successful when they carried out extensive strategic restructuring. Nearly half the profitable companies that restructured moderately achieved higher performance levels.

These impressive results raise the question: Why don't more profitable companies restructure? The answer may be that many companies assume that current profitability levels are sufficient. They equate current profitability with full potential. Current high profit levels often promote a "Don't fix it if it ain't broke" attitude that, in turn, creates corporate inertia. The consequences of this attitude spell as much danger for the profitable company as for the troubled company. The profitable but underachieving company may also find itself faced with a

Restructuring Rate of Success:
Healthy Companies

Type

		Financial	Strategic
	Extensive	45%	85%
Degree			
	Moderate	25%	47%

57%

Figure 4-3. Among healthy or currently profitable companies,
85 percent were successful in achieving higher performance
levels when they carried out extensive strategic restructuring.

takeover attempt. The corporate raider on the prowl often spots what
the company itself does not see: unrealized potential.

A troubled company's profit problems may not be totally attributable
to an inherited legacy of poor performance or bad practices. They may
also hinge on whether the company's businesses are faced with new
technologies or new product competition that adversely affects their
ability to survive. But the strategy for survival in this case is clearly dictated: Change or die. For the troubled company, restructuring becomes
not only totally acceptable, but mandatory.

SPA's review of some 58 troubled companies carries a discouraging
message: As shown in Figure 4-4, overall only 31 percent of the troubled companies that restructured were able to increase shareholder
wealth at a rate significantly above their competitors. Even extensive

Restructuring Rate of Success:
Troubled Companies

Type

		Financial	Strategic
	Extensive	7%	54%
Degree			
	Moderate	0%	31%

31%

Figure 4-4. Even extensive strategic restructuring produced
only a 54 percent success rate among troubled companies,
and all other strategies fared far worse.

strategic restructuring produced only a 54 percent success rate. All other strategies fared far worse. The high failure rate is not surprising in view of the fact that troubled companies had lost much of their resilience and ability to define themselves by the time restructuring began.

If raiders' assessments of unrealized potential leads them to believe they can profit by a takeover attempt, they are likely to take on a profitable company or a troubled one. What gives them added incentive is not only the enormous profit they may derive from their efforts, but also the ease with which modern corporate raiding is financed.

The Corporate Raid: Takeover Made Easy

The American public regards corporate raiding as an activity somewhat akin to evicting hapless widows and orphans. Various efforts have been made to protect the nation's corporate widows and orphans from the clutches of raiders—poison pills, changes in tax laws, judicial sanction of the Indiana antiraider law, and passage of similar legislation in Delaware. The Ivan Boesky scandal and the outrageous flaunting of wealth from "greenmail" has also helped to harden public opinion against corporate raiding.

There has been every opportunity for raiding to die out. But it hasn't. A major reason is that corporate raiding, though risky, can be extremely profitable. Raider returns are high because the equity money sits at the bottom of an enormous pile of leveraged debt. The success of the junk bond market and the continued participation of the financial giants in this lucrative market ensure the ready availability of takeover financing.

Corporate raiders have generally focused on companies with stand-alone businesses, cutting a wide swath through retailing, textiles, building materials, upstream oil, and basic manufacturing industries. We believe that complex businesses and even regulated companies are likely future targets. Raiders are now turning to downstream oil, refining and marketing, specialty chemicals, telecommunications, and regulated areas of financial services.

The gap between actual and potential performance is harder to identify in complex, integrated businesses, and the size of the gap may be even greater than anticipated. If the object of raiding is to attack companies that are operating well below full potential, then raiding should ultimately occur in any industry where such a gap exists. Since the strategy of corporate raiders is to attack where profitability and cash flow fall well below potential, one of the major tasks for both the troubled and the successful company is to determine the extent of vulnerability and what it will take to survive or boost performance to levels beyond the reach of even the most aggressive raider. The failure of many American corporations to maintain peak performance levels creates a host of tempting targets.

The stakes are large, with the consequences extending well beyond the individual companies involved. Increasing the number of companies operating near their full potential for profitability and growth will not only slow the raiding epidemic but can also help meet the nation's need for increased competitiveness. The 50 largest American companies account for 26 percent of total exports. An increase in their export share would reduce the U.S. balance-of-trade deficit substantially. On the domestic front, a deeper commitment by large companies to the pursuit of strategic restructuring as a way of life would release workers for productive employment in the robust small-company sector while simultaneously providing new jobs in the kind of major products that only large companies can undertake.

Taken to its fullest potential, strategic restructuring can deter corporate raiders and the ill-disguised brutality of their attacks. As Carl Icahn admitted in a recent interview, "The managements I won't touch are those operating their companies at close to their true value."

Successful Restructurings: The Requirements

Successful restructurings need not have a master plan. A CEO with a clear set of goals, a keen sense of tactics, and the strong support of the board of directors can achieve a great deal on an ad hoc, project-by-project basis. In fact, restructuring plans that are the result of a ponderous, decentralized, bottom-up planning process are very likely to be mediocre in character and doomed to fail. Most successful transitions to a restructuring culture are characterized by an evolving set of programs that can be summarized on one page.

The simplicity of a restructuring plan at the CEO level does not imply that restructuring is simple or that it is best done in an unplanned frenzy of activity, often described as "ready, fire, aim." What is clear is that while a successful restructuring may seem to be random and chaotic, its success lies in its selection of the right issues to focus on in the right sequence. When Michael Eisner became CEO of Walt Disney Co., he focused on the rebuilding of Disney's market share in the movie industry as a critical element of his restructuring. Since this program required up-front investment for a long-term payoff, Eisner also focused on a short-term profit program to "cover" his investments. By raising prices at the Disneyland parks, Eisner achieved an immediate increase in short-term profits, for which he was widely acclaimed. Three years later, when the movie investments began to pay off in a big way, Eisner's restructuring emerged as more than a quick fix.

The debates that range over the value of programs that clean up inefficient operations versus investments that support growth are equally wrong. Successful restructuring requires both kinds of programs in a series of waves that both improve results and win over the inevitable skeptics.

Since every chief executive is, in part, the result of personal experiences, there is a tendency to lean too heavily on one element of what has to be a comprehensive set of actions. CEOs who believe in operating efficiencies are right, but if the company's operations are trapped in industry overcapacity, operating efficiency programs must be coupled with significant asset redeployment. CEOs who believe in measurement as the best motivator of proper behavior often find that extensive restructuring requires a more activist approach to create a culture in which improved measurement can have its predicted impact. CEOs who believe in the power of compensation as a driver of performance are not wrong. When compensation stimulus is offset by a lack of knowledge of what to do to achieve the goals, the result is frustration and counterproductive politics.

The CEO who wants to close the gap between a company's actual and potential performance needs to have a clear picture of the programs with the highest impact on potential. Whether such programs are short-term or long-term in their payoff, or aimed at pruning, cleaning, growing, or building, the important issues are how much potential they contain and how to build a culture capable of implementing and evolving (see Figure 4-5).

The development of a list of restructuring programs with their potential quantified provides a picture of the rewards for an extensive restructuring. Companies with low profitability might actually have less potential from restructuring than those that already have a high level of profitability. When the estimate of potential suggests that a company's stock price can be doubled in a short-term environment or outperform the market averages by more than 50 percent in a five-year period, restructuring is clearly indicated. When a company is already operating at 80 percent of potential, change can and should be applied more cautiously. Establishing and maintaining the CEO's list of "big" ideas is a critical requirement for a successful restructuring.

A second critical requirement is to match up the CEO's expectations

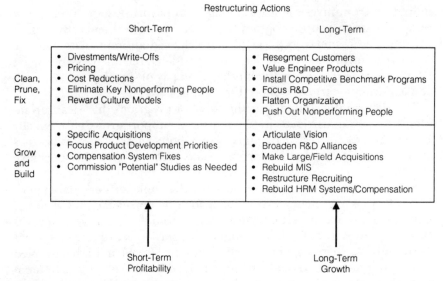

Figure 4-5. Options for the CEO who wants to close the gap between a company's actual and potential performance.

with the organization's expectations by forcing the organization to establish a "banker's forecast." Such a forecast is a tough-minded view of the likely financial results of each business. Asking each organization to augment its baseline with the incremental programs it "can see" gives the CEO an opportunity to evaluate the gap between CEO estimates and the business-level outlook.

When the CEO and the organization are close in this view of potential, a frontal assault is called for. When significant gaps exist, a CEO may have to force the issue in order to validate or invalidate management views. The sequencing of various programs in a restructuring is one of the critical skills of a successful CEO.

Focus on the CEO

It is almost a cliché that restructuring programs do not occur without a strong sense of "ownership" at the decentralized level. Of course, the concept of ownership is anything but straightforward. In a tragic attempt to achieve ownership, CEOs will endorse a flawed program because the organization has proposed it with a strong sense of ownership. CEOs must serve as activist investors who seek owners for profitable ideas rather than following a more passive approach to keep

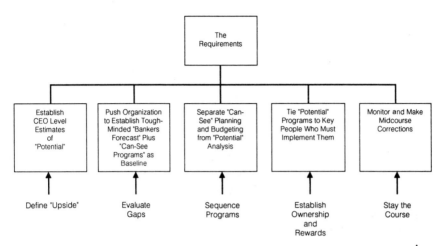

Figure 4-6. The sequencing of various programs in a restructuring is one of the critical skills of a successful CEO.

existing managers happy. When a powerful program is taken on by a strong management team, entrepreneurial compensation can seal the deal. Figure 4-6 presents an outline for management of this process.

At the end of the day, the power of the shareholders must be focused on the CEO. The CEO is the "activist" investor who can and must seize the power to monitor major trends and make midcourse corrections. Well-intentioned approaches that turn the CEO into a passive observer and "front" for a fully decentralized organization are as tragically flawed as a concept of the CEO as chief operator monitoring the details of all programs simultaneously. CEOs who flatten their organization to relate directly to their businesses will not have the time to be compulsive centralists. CEOs who combine a flat organization with an active investor's sense of ultimate authority are prepared to thrive in a continuous restructuring culture.

5
The Impact of Restructuring on Shareholder Value

James M. McTaggart

Chairman and Chief Executive Officer,
Marakon Associates

In 1988, two members of the Securities and Exchange Commission's staff estimated that roughly $162 billion of shareholder value was created by corporate restructuring between 1981 and 1986. Of this total, $134 billion came from takeovers of public companies, $22 billion from public company divestitures (excluding spin-offs), and $5 billion from eight leveraged recapitalizations. The detailed statistical analysis (B. Black and J. Grundfest, "Shareholder Gains from Takeovers and Restructurings between 1981 and 1986: $162 Billion Is a Lot of Money," *Journal of Applied Corporate Finance,* Spring 1988) served to prove what most people already knew intuitively: Despite the disruption it has caused for many individuals, the restructuring movement in the United States over the past decade has created vast wealth for society as a whole. The article, however, left unanswered two important questions:

- What specific strategies and transactions were employed to create the value for shareholders?

- Why, in most cases, was the incumbent management team unable or unwilling to take on the restructuring?

56

In order to answer these questions, we must first define what we mean by restructuring. (These observations on a definition will amplify those made elsewhere in this book.)

The Many Faces of Restructuring

Restructuring is synonymous with undertaking a major change in the way a company does business. There are many ways to restructure a company. Typically, restructuring involves decisions that both generate and deploy large amounts of cash. On the cash-generation side, there are four basic options:

- Portfolio restructuring, in which one or more businesses are divested
- Asset sales, in which underutilized or nonproductive assets, such as excess real estate, are converted to cash
- Increasing the amount of debt in the capital structure
- Significantly reducing costs, usually by eliminating overhead

On the redeployment side, there are also four basic options:

- Increasing the amount of capital committed to existing or remaining businesses
- Making acquisitions
- Returning capital to shareholders by repurchasing common stock or increasing dividends
- Repaying debt

In most cases, the overall restructuring strategy employs several options from both sides. For example, in April 1985, Atlantic Richfield Co. announced plans for a major restructuring. On the cash-generation side, all refining operations and service stations east of the Mississippi were to be sold, all non-oil mineral operations were also put on the auction block, planned capital spending was cut by 25 percent, and $5.2 billion of additional long-term debt was to be issued. On the redeployment side, dividends were increased by 33 percent, and $4 billion of common stock would be repurchased. The results, as shown in Figure 5-1, were striking. Roughly $600 million of excess shareholder value was created by the plan.

In general, the impact of restructuring on shareholder value depends primarily on the size of the company's "value gap." The value gap is de-

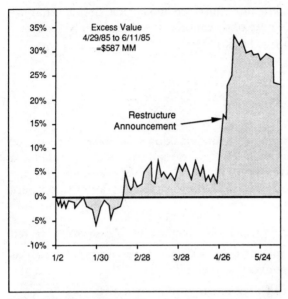

Figure 5-1. The market reaction: Arco excess returns relative to S&P 400. In the weeks following Atlantic Richfield Co.'s announcement of a major restructuring (April 29–June 11, 1985), roughly $600 million of excess shareholder value was created.

fined as the difference between the market's current appraisal of the company and the price at which its shares would trade if management pursued value-maximizing strategies. There are three management shortcomings that account for most of the gap between actual and potential market values:

- A tendency to invest too much capital in unprofitable businesses
- Poor balance sheet management
- Tolerance of excess overhead

In order to understand these causes of the value gap and how alternative restructuring strategies might close the gap, it is first necessary to examine the business fundamentals that determine the market value of any company.

Determinants of Value

Fundamentally, the value of a company is determined by the cash flow that it generates for its owners over time, and the minimum acceptable rate of return required by capital investors. This "cost of equity capital" is used to discount the expected equity cash flow, converting it to a present value. The cash flow is, in turn, produced by the interaction of a company's return on equity (ROE) and the annual rate of equity growth. High-ROE companies in low-growth markets, such as Kellogg Co., are prodigious generators of cash flow, whereas low-ROE companies in high-growth markets, such as Texas Instruments Inc., barely generate enough cash flow to finance growth.

A company's ROE over time, relative to its cost of equity, also determines whether it is worth more or less than its book value. If its ROE is consistently greater than the cost of equity capital (the investor's minimum acceptable return), the business is economically profitable and its market value will exceed book value. If, however, the business earns an ROE that is consistently less than its cost of equity, it is economically unprofitable and its market value will be less than book value. These basic principles can be seen at work in Figure 5-2, which plots the profitability of the Dow Jones Industrials, based on Value Line forecasts of ROE and Marakon estimates of the cost of equity capital.

Growth acts as a magnifier for these relationships. That is, if ROE remains constant and the growth rate of a profitable business increases, its market-to-book ratio rises. For an unprofitable business, increasing growth actually drives the market-to-book ratio lower (unless growth causes ROE to rise). And in the case where ROE is just equal to the cost of equity, growth has no impact on the market-to-book ratio. The primary reason for the scattering of the observations in Figure 5-2 is differential growth rates.

The profitability of a company is determined primarily by the profitability of its businesses. The profitability of a business is, in turn, determined by economic forces affecting supply and demand in its product markets, its competitive position, and the effectiveness of its strategy. In perfectly competitive markets, those with no entry or exit barriers, no product differentiation, and uniform cost positions, the force of competition will ensure that all businesses earn an ROE just equal to the cost of equity. Thus, earning a positive "spread" between ROE and the cost of equity typically requires gaining and holding a competitive advantage. The advantage can come in the form of lower operating costs, which increase margins; higher investment productivity, which increases asset turnover; or greater perceived product quality, which allows management to increase margins through premium pricing.

While advantage and spread are usually directly related, there are two instances in which the relationship breaks down. The first occurs when the cost or investment required to gain the advantage is larger

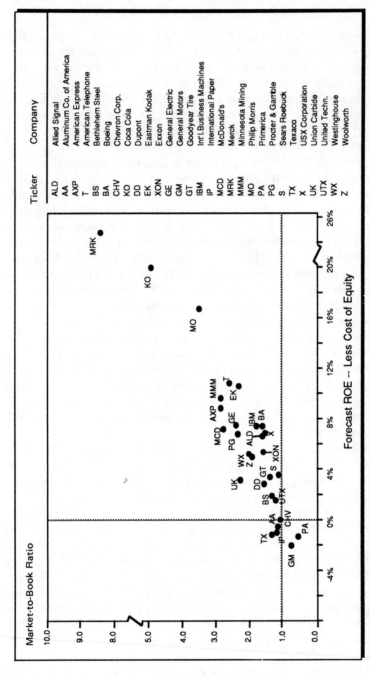

Figure 5-2. Dow Jones Industrials (February 1989). A business fundamental in any restructuring analysis: If return on equity (ROE) is consistently greater than the cost of equity capital, the business is economically profitable and its market value will exceed book value.

than the benefits produced. In this instance, profitability declines over time and value is destroyed. The second occurs when management chooses to exploit the advantage by building market share rather than improving returns. In this instance, the impact on shareholder value will depend on the terms of the trade-off between spread and growth.

The interaction of constantly changing economic forces and competitive strategies produces a wide variation in both industry and company profitability. Understanding how industry economics and competitive position determine profitability for a given business is the first step toward developing strategies to increase shareholder returns.

Value Gap 1: Inappropriate Strategies

The wide variation in industry and company profitability also occurs within a typical diversified company's portfolio of businesses. Within a company, however, the capital allocation discipline provided by creditors and investors is replaced by management policies and strategies, which can significantly magnify the variation. This magnification can occur in either of two ways. The first way occurs when management allows low-return businesses to invest too much capital, a process that can sometimes produce businesses with negative market values. The second occurs when management allows or causes high-return businesses to underinvest. Over a prolonged period, this usually results in a loss of competitive position and declining returns. In both instances, the business-unit market values are significantly lower than they would be otherwise.

This tendency to misallocate capital by allowing or causing businesses to pursue inappropriate strategies is the first of the three major sources of the gap between actual and potential market value.

A Company's Inappropriate Strategies

The business portfolio shown in Figure 5-3, based on a real diversified firm, illustrates the magnitude of the value gap that can be produced by pursuing inappropriate business strategies. This company's sales were roughly $750 million, and its common stock was trading at about 80 percent of book value. Its portfolio contained five profitable and four unprofitable businesses. The operating value of each unprofitable business, based on the prevailing strategies, was less than 50 percent of its book value. All told, the four operating values totaled $115 million, compared to its combined book value, which exceeded $300 million.

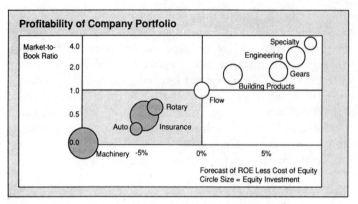

Figure 5-3. By overinvesting in its four unprofitable businesses, a company's value gap was identified to be $120 million, or 40 percent of the company's market value.

The most unprofitable business, machinery, was actually worth a neg ative $12 million—or, rather, the present value of its planned cash flow was minus $12 million. Surprisingly, this negative value was produced by an operating strategy designed to foster growth. The key element of the plan was a massive capital spending program designed to boost capacity and eliminate a competitive cost disadvantage. And although the program, if successful, would have significantly enhanced the unit's return on investment (ROI) from 8 percent to 12 percent, the long-term positive impact on value was more than offset by the near-term negative cash flow.

Based on a thorough assessment of market economics and profitability relative to competitors, we concluded that changing strategy at each of the four businesses (to emphasize profitability rather than merely growth) would cause their combined market values to be increased by at least $150 million within two years. As we explained to management, the current value gap caused by overinvesting in four unprofitable businesses was $120 million, or 40 percent of the company's market value. Of the four, the machinery business was subsequently sold in a leveraged buyout for book value and has since prospered.

Value Gap 2: Poor Balance Sheet Management

Poor balance sheet management is the second source of the value gap. It is caused by either underperforming assets or too little debt in the capital structure.

On the asset side of the balance sheet, two of the more prominent value drags are excess cash and underutilized real estate. The cash account can cause a value gap because of the low aftertax return that it earns. Redeploying excess cash by repurchasing shares, for example, generates a capital gain equal to the present value of the tax savings. Excess pension fund reserves are also a source of funds that can be worth more if returned to shareholders. So too, when corporate real estate is not being put to its highest and best uses, a business is also fostering its value gap. The capital tied up in undeveloped land, vacant office space, underutilized plants, or unprofitable retail outlets nearly always earns a return well below the cost of capital. To the extent that it can be redeployed into profitable businesses or, again, used to buy stock, a substantial capital gain will occur.

On the liability side, value can be created for equity holders by increasing financial leverage—up to a point. This, of course, is one of the sources of value that leveraged buyouts have utilized to recapture purchase-price premiums. The source of the value creation is the tax saving resulting from the deductibility of interest. As a rough rule of thumb, each dollar of new debt should increase the firm's equity value by 20 to 25 cents until the firm's financial risk becomes excessive. At this point, the benefits from further borrowing are offset by the restrictions placed on the firm that limit its capital availability and increase the probability that the interest expense will not be tax-deductible. This point, however, is significantly beyond the current leverage position of most U.S. companies.

The magnitude of the opportunity to increase returns through improved balance sheet management will, of course, depend on the amount of nonproductive assets on the company's books, and on its capacity to borrow. In the case of Gulf Oil, we estimated that redeployment of more than $1 billion of excess cash and full utilization of the company's debt capacity would have produced a 20 to 25 percent increase in the market value of Gulf's stock.

Value Gap 3: Excess Overhead

Excess overhead is the third source of the value gap, and its impact on value can be staggering. For example, the overhead at Beatrice Corp. was estimated at roughly $150 million annually, or 1.3 percent of its $12 billion in sales. By contrast, Esmark, at roughly $6 billion in sales, was spending only $25 million on overhead functions, less than 0.5 percent. If Beatrice could have managed down its overhead to $50 million, the resulting $100 million in pretax earnings would have created roughly

$1 billion of shareholder value. This represents nearly 30 percent of Beatrice's preacquisition market value, and 70 percent of the premium paid to acquire control of the company. This means that, going into the deal, Chairman Don Kelly could recover two-thirds of the acquisition premium if he could reduce the overhead at Beatrice to $50 million, with potential divestments, strategy changes, and the impact of leverage and taxes yet to be considered.

Restructuring to Close the Value Gap

Once a value gap has been identified, a restructuring program is undoubtedly the quickest way to close the gap. The act of restructuring, however, does not guarantee that value will be created for shareholders. In fact, an ill-conceived restructuring plan can actually widen the value gap.

Returning to the simple idea that restructuring can be divided into actions that generate and then redeploy large amounts of cash, we can now specify the criteria that determine whether a specific action will create or destroy value.

Sources of Cash

We shall begin on the sources-of-cash side.

Divestiture. Selling a business will create value only if the net divestment value exceeds its operating value. The operating value is the warranted or present value of the business unit's cash flow, as forecast in its strategic plan. It is the unit's contribution to the company's warranted value. The net divestment value is the present value of the aftertax proceeds from selling the business. Clearly, if the business has an operating value of $100 million today, divesting it will create value only if it can be sold for more than $100 million, after taxes, in today's dollars.

Asset Sales. The same criterion as for divesting businesses also applies to selling assets. The aftertax proceeds from the sale must exceed the value of the asset on an operating basis in order for the sale to create value. Thus, selling and leasing back a headquarters building at a fair market lease rate will generate cash but will not create value. However, selling an underutilized building and leasing back only half the space is likely to create value. The key to selling an asset profitably is finding someone else who can make better use of the asset than you can and who is willing to pay more than it is worth to you.

Increasing Debt. As stated earlier, borrowing tends to create value for shareholders, because interest is deductible for tax purposes while dividends are not. This effect occurs until the likelihood and cost of financial distress due to the leveraging of the balance sheet offsets the tax benefit. The criterion, then, is to borrow until the risk effect balances the tax benefit, a point or range that differs for each company. For a company that will not pay taxes for several years because of loss carryforwards, increasing debt will create significantly less value.

Cost Reduction. Reducing costs that have no adverse side effects will obviously create value—the overhead cuts at Beatrice being a good example. Many cost reductions, however, do have negative side effects. Cutting back in-house legal staff may actually cause legal costs to rise later on; reducing advertisement may cause revenue to fall; and so on. Clearly, for value to be created, a cost-benefit trade-off analysis must be done that accurately reflects the consequences of the cost reduction.

Uses of Cash

On the uses-of-cash side, restructuring actions to be evaluated include those discussed below.

Increased Investment in Existing Businesses. To the extent that existing businesses will be worth more if you invest more, this action will, by definition, create value. In many instances, though, the value of a business will *not* rise with additional investment, and may actually fall. The appropriate criterion, then, is to compare the warranted value of each business under its incumbent plan (without additional capital) with the value under a new plan reflecting a higher level of investment.

Acquisitions. The criterion for creating value with an acquisition is the mirror image of divesting: The acquisition must be worth more than you pay for it. Given that most companies must pay a control premium of roughly 40 percent, creating value is analogous to recapturing the control premium. Unfortunately, only 20 to 30 percent of all recent acquisitions have succeeded in recapturing the control premium and creating value for the acquirer. Successful acquisitions tend to be those in which the seller is somewhat undermanaged, in which there is synergy, usually on the cost side, or in which there is a large value gap to be exploited.

Share Repurchase and Dividends. Paying larger dividends does not, by itself, create value. The payment "locks in" the value created by other actions, such as distributing excess cash (eliminating double taxation), increasing financial leverage, or divesting a business. Repurchasing shares has the same characteristic of locking in a gain made elsewhere, with an important exception. If the company's warranted value, based on realistic strategic plans, exceeds its market price, repurchasing shares will create additional value. On the other hand, if the shares are overvalued, repurchasing shares will destroy value over time.

Repaying Debt.   Since increasing debt tends to create value for fully taxed firms, repaying debt will tend to destroy value, unless the current level of debt is excessive. For a tax-paying company with a Baa credit rating or better, repaying debt will partially offset any gains made by other restructuring options.

Moral of the Story

We can now see more clearly why Atlantic Richfield's restructuring created so much value for shareholders. On the sources-of-cash side, it is highly likely that the divestments were made at prices greater than their operating values. The reduction in capital spending scaled back an activity (exploration) that was viewed by the market as generating less than cost-of-capital returns. The company was a full taxpayer, so the additional borrowing produced tax benefits for shareholders. On the uses-of-cash side, Arco locked in the gains by increasing dividends and repurchasing shares.

Such is not always the case. Primerica Corp. completely restructured away from its core packaging business via divestments and acquisitions. Divestment gains were not large enough to offset the value losses in the acquisitions. The result was a forced sale in 1988 to Commercial Credit Co.

The moral of the story is: Like all else in business, restructuring creates value for shareholders only if it is done carefully and well.

PART 2

Restructuring Alternatives

6
Evaluating Strategic Alternatives

Andrew Capitman
Managing Director, Mergers and Acquisitions,
Bankers Trust Co.

Tina Winfield
Assistant Treasurer, Bankers Trust Co.

What are management's alternatives when confronted with a hostile takeover situation? In the effort to preserve its independence while at the same time maximizing shareholder value, management typically begins by seeking a "white knight" and/or evaluating its potential for executing a defensive recapitalization [leveraged buyout, leveraged recapitalization, leveraged employee stock option (ESOP) financing, or stock repurchase program]. Price is a key consideration, as statistics show that management's ability to control the outcome of these situations depends on its ability to outbid the hostile raider. In 1987 there were 31 contested public takeovers, 52 percent of which the hostile raider won by outbidding management and/or other interested parties. In 26 percent of these transactions, a white knight outbid the hostile raider, while in only 13 percent of the transactions, management succeeded in executing a defensive recapitalization by topping the hostile raider's final price.

These statistics illustrate that once a company is put into play as a result of a hostile bid, it is virtually certain to undergo a drastic change in terms of its capital structure, strategy, and, perhaps, management, notwithstanding any antitakeover measures that the company may have adopted. While management is not always able to thwart the raider's attempted takeover bid, it can be instrumental in raising the price ultimately paid for the company's shares through the introduction of other bids, including its own defensive recapitalization. The role of the financial adviser in these situations ranges from evaluating offers to identifying strategic white knight buyers to structuring and securing the financing for defensive recapitalizations.

When to Seek a Strategic Bidder

In the current U.S. market's contest for corporate control, third-party bids for a company, whether friendly or hostile, succeed when the price offered exceeds the amount that any other buyer is willing (or able) to pay. Acquirers with a strong strategic interest in a target, as well as a solid cash flow and balance sheet to enable them to secure financing, have the best opportunity of winning a bidding war. This is primarily because strategic buyers view the target in terms of its long-term impact on their own company's market positions, sales, and earnings. As a result, strategic buyers are sometimes willing to pay extremely high premiums.

Management typically seeks a suitable strategic buyer, or white knight, when its company is threatened by a hostile raider who has undervalued the firm and intends to break it up. It usually pursues this route when it is unable to meet the hostile raider's price by executing a defensive recapitalization. As the statistics cited at the beginning of this chapter illustrate, the target of a hostile attack is twice as likely to be acquired by a strategic buyer as it is to execute a defensive recapitalization. Several examples of strategic acquisitions are discussed below.

Rupert Murdoch's Acquisition of Harper & Row

Media baron Rupert Murdoch's successful acquisition of Harper & Row Publishers Inc., the 170-year-old book publisher, is illustrative of a strategic buyer coming to the rescue of a company being pursued by un-welcome suitors. Theodore L. Cross touched off the bidding war for Harper & Row by proposing a bid of $34 per share plus $40 million in debt, or approximately $190 million. Harcourt Brace Jovanovich Inc. stepped in with a bid of $50 per share, or $220 million. Murdoch, how-ever, concluded that the strategic value of the company would be much higher than these offers and proposed a bid of $65 per share, or ap-proximately $300 million.

Upon receiving its first two bids, Harper appointed a committee of its independent (nonmanagement) board of directors to review the offers. The committee deemed the offers too low and recommended that the company continue to operate independently, while seeking other op-tions. However, this argument was no longer valid in the face of Murdoch's offer, which brought shareholders a $40 premium over the price at which Harper's stock had traded one month earlier. In addition to being satisfied with the price, management believed that the oppor-tunity for both companies to expand as a result of the transaction was strong.

Kodak's Acquisition of Sterling Drug

The successful acquisition of Sterling Drug Inc. by Eastman Kodak Co. is another example of a company that actively sought and secured a white knight to rescue it from a hostile takeover attempt. On January 5, 1988, Sterling Drug, the maker of Bayer aspirin, Phillips Milk of Mag-nesia, and other pharmaceutical and household products, received a takeover bid of $72 per share or $4.2 billion from F. Hoffmann-La Roche & Co., the Swiss pharmaceutical giant. Sterling's management re-sponded that the offer and subsequent bids of $76 per share and $81 per share were grossly inadequate. In addition, management wanted to maintain its autonomy and keep its company intact, so that it could con-tinue to pursue its strategic goals.

Sterling immediately began holding discussions with other potential buyers. Eastman Kodak, the photographic and chemicals conglomerate, quickly swung into action with the full approval of its board of directors to take on the large amount of debt necessary to finance the transaction. For several years Kodak had been diversifying into the pharmaceutical industry, and Sterling was high on its list of potential targets. On January 22, 1988, Kodak offered Sterling $89.50 per share, or $5.1 bil-lion, forcing an end to Hoffmann-La Roche's hostile offer. Sterling fur-ther strengthened Kodak's position by giving it lockup rights in the form of an option to buy 10.5 million additional shares for $89.50 per share plus an option to buy its Sterling Glenbrook Laboratories business for $775 million in the event that a transaction was completed with another party.

Both parties viewed a Sterling/Kodak link as advantageous. From Kodak's perspective, it enabled the company to accelerate its entry into the $10 billion worldwide pharmaceutical industry and provided it with long-term sales and earnings potential. For Sterling, the transaction offered a friendly owner that promised to keep its operations intact. In addition, the transaction greatly enhanced both companies' research and development, marketing, and sales efforts.

When to Opt for a Defensive Recapitalization

In addition to considering friendly bids, management often explores the possibility of executing a defensive recapitalization. These structures, which include leveraged buyouts, leveraged recapitalizations, leveraged ESOP financings, and stock repurchases, frequently enable management and selected investors to beat the price a corporate raider would offer shareholders while keeping the existing management team in place to force the raider to raise its price. Either way, the ultimate objective of maximizing shareholder value is achieved.

Leveraged Buyouts

In 1979, Kohlberg Kravis Roberts & Co. (KKR) expanded the strategic alternatives available to senior management by engineering the first leveraged buyout (LBO) for a publicly traded company. These transactions, which enable shareholders to extract excess cash from a company by taking on thick layers of debt, have had wide appeal for numerous American corporations during the extended period of positive and moderately stable business and economic conditions that has marked the 1980s. Leveraged buyouts are characterized by their high debt levels and multitiered capital structures, the sometimes conflicting roles of participants, and the high transaction costs they usually require. Repayment schedules for these transactions are linked to the company's cash flow and/or asset values, both capital and human.

The stock market crash of October 19, 1987, did not significantly slow LBO activity. In general, the prices for takeovers have declined less than the overall market, and demand for these transactions has remained strong. However, debt-to-equity ratios of typical leveraged transactions have shifted to a slightly more conservative level, although the evidence suggests that continued economic confidence might see a return to more aggressive prices. More moderate price tags may result in an increased number of LBOs among middle-market companies.

The "crash of 1987" made the viability of exit strategies to lenders and investors less clear-cut. Asset sales, while still an important means of reducing debt, face a more selective and somewhat less buoyant market than in the pre-October 19 period. The incidence of initial public offerings (IPOs) of recently privatized companies has also slowed substantially. In addition, bridge financing, which before the crash facilitated many of the large LBOs by temporarily funding the subordinated debt requirement until permanent investors could be identified, has become increasingly difficult to obtain as investment bankers have backed away for a time from the high risks that these financings carry in the face of an uncertain market.

Generally speaking, companies that are good candidates for LBOs generate strong and predictable cash flows, operate in predictable businesses, possess undervalued assets, and have in place a strong management team. They typically have leading market positions, are not "high-tech" businesses, require limited capital investments (perhaps because they have recently completed a round of capital expenditures), and employ strong manufacturing efficiencies. In addition to these operational criteria, financiers look for low debt-to-equity ratios, historic profitability, and limited contingent liabilities to determine a company's ability to support the heavy debt requirements inherent in an LBO.

How to Determine Debt Capacity

Determining the appropriate purchase price of an LBO is critical, since the higher the purchase price, the more debt the company will have to assume. The purchase price is usually linked to multiples of operating earnings or cash flow. This includes both earnings before interest and taxes (EBIT), which assumes that depreciation will be fully reinvested in the form of capital expenditures, and earnings before interest, taxes, and depreciation (EBITD), which assumes that depreciation will not be fully reinvested, especially in the first few years after a buyout, and can therefore be used to improve the company's cash flow.

Immediately following October 19, purchase prices as a multiple of EBIT or EBITD declined from approximately 10 times EBIT and 8 times EBITD to 7–9 times EBIT and 5–6 times EBITD. As was mentioned earlier, the prices for LBOs and takeovers remained stronger than market prices. Debt-to-equity ratios also decreased from roughly 10:1 to about 8:1 or less, while interest coverage ratios (operating income divided by interest expense) for total debt increased. Prior to October 19, this ratio typically came to 1.2:1, meaning that operating income in some cases barely covered interest expense. Today, LBO financiers are seeking better operating and coverage ratios, to ensure that operating income safely covers interest expense. More specifically, senior debt financiers seek coverage of more than 1.5:1, and subordinated debt financiers seek ratios of at least 1.2:1 on cash interest.

The subordinated debt market has proved highly innovative in developing debt instruments to assist companies in meeting their interest and principal payments when they have leveraged beyond their maximum senior debt capacity. These include zero-coupon bonds, under which interest is accrued but not paid until maturity, and payment-in-kind (PIK) bonds, which enable companies to service their debt by issuing additional bonds. The interest on these securities is referred to as "paper interest" and is not figured into the interest coverage ratio, since interest payments are made in additional securities rather than cash.

Components of Funding

Senior Debt

Large financial institutions are the primary lenders of senior debt to leveraged buyouts. These loans have priority over junior obligations and equity in the event of liquidation. Providers of the equity on leveraged transactions usually want to maximize bank financing, since it is significantly less expensive than subordinated debt or equity.

Bank lenders are attracted to LBOs because they can generally charge a higher interest rate spread over their cost of funds on a buyout loan than they can on a conventional loan. To an increasing degree, banks are seeking broader roles in LBOs, including investing equity through bank affiliates, arranging or placing subordinated debt, offering interest-rate management techniques (swaps, caps, etc.), and providing advisory services.

Bank lenders usually project the payback schedules for LBOs to be approximately 33 percent over three years, 50 percent over five years, and 100 percent over seven to eight years. This can be a useful guideline in setting the amount of senior financing. Notably, many companies that have successfully executed an LBO have repaid their debt in advance of these projections. Sometimes senior debt financing may include a permanent working capital portion secured by receivables and/or inventory on a formula basis. Other assets, such as real estate, may likewise serve as a financing base.

In addition, there are numerous nonbank institutions that provide units or combinations of senior, subordinated, and equity financing.

These include asset-based lenders such as General Electric Capital Corp. (GECC) and Heller Financial Inc., as well as insurance companies such as Prudential Insurance Co. of America. These institutions often seek to participate in more than one level of financing. For example, GECC may commit to both the senior and subordinated debt on a middle-market transaction as well as provide a portion of the equity. This may result in a lower cost of borrowings, since the company is receiving the majority, if not all, of the funds necessary to finance the transaction from the same source.

Subordinated Debt

Subordinated debt or high-yield securities are used to fill the financing gap between the transaction's total funding requirements and the amount to which the senior lender is willing to commit, plus, in the case of leveraged buyouts, the base equity contributed to the transaction or, in the case of leveraged recapitalizations, left in the business. Subordinated debt is junior to senior obligations to the extent provided in the applicable subordination provisions and can generally be repaid only after senior obligations have been satisfied. However, the numerous layers of senior and subordinated debt associated with these transactions complicate this issue. One role of the financial adviser in these situations is to ensure that investors and management fully understand the marketability, terms, and conditions of each layer of debt.

High-yield securities generally mature in 8 to 15 years. The price of high-yield securities associated with leveraged transactions is typically 500 to 700 basis points (5 to 7 percent) above the price of U.S. Treasury bonds of comparable term. They trade, to a large extent, on their "name value" and particular credit characteristics, as well as on the general level of their interest rates. Shortly after October 19, high-yield securities faced very uncertain trading conditions; however, it is generally thought that the market for these securities has survived the storm and is doing well.

Subordinated debt, which may be structured as straight debt, convertible debt, or units of debt and equity, can be either issued in the public high-yield market or placed privately with institutional investors. The size of the issue is the single most important determinant of whether the subordinated debt will be sold in the public or private market. Most issuers prefer the public market to the private market because public securities carry lower yields and longer maturities, contain fewer covenants, and usually do not require an "equity kicker," all as a function of their greater liquidity. Smaller issues are most frequently placed privately with institutional investors, generally with more restrictive terms.

Drexel Burnham Lambert is credited with developing the public high-yield market and was in recent years responsible for more than 50 percent of all public issues. However, Morgan Stanley, First Boston, and Merrill Lynch have also made significant inroads in developing a distribution network. At this writing, the market remains enthusiastic for many public offerings.

Since October 19, seller financing, in which the seller gets most of its payment in cash but also takes back subordinated debt or preferred stock, has become more common. These seller-involved financings almost always carry a lower interest rate and include equity participation in the new company. Seller financing is not a new concept. In the 1960s, prior to the existence of the high-yield market, innovative financiers helped a number of troubled, privately held companies raise funds based on a company's cash flow as well as its assets. Generally, the buyers of these companies received seller financing in connection with these transactions, which were known as "bootstrapping" deals.

Preferred Stock

Recently, several LBO transactions have included preferred stock in the financing package to public shareholders. As a substitute for subordinated debt, preferred stock is typically used to improve the leveraged company's debt-to-equity ratio, since the preferred stock is included as equity and takes the place of debt. However, unlike interest on debt securities, dividends are not tax-deductible to the issuing company. This is not a problem in the first few years after a buyout, since taxable income after interest payments is often negligible if not nonexistent. Moreover, by using exchangeable preferred stock, the company can have the option to exchange the preferred stock later for high-yield debt securities. This exchange feature enables the company to take advantage of interest deductions in future years when the company begins to generate taxable income.

The preferred stock also can be structured to allow the company to issue additional shares of stock in lieu of cash dividends. Acting like a zero-coupon bond, such a security delays cash payments until the company's financial position improves. Since the likelihood of eventual repayment is less and because the preferred shareholder must pay tax (cash) on the value of the stock dividend (noncash), a higher return is typically demanded.

Equity

The equity in an LBO is usually provided by one of the large LBO funds or venture capital funds. The funds are generally investment partnerships, comprised of institutional and other investors as limited partners and LBO funds as general partners, which control investment decisions and manage the portfolio. It is estimated that in 1988 these firms, which include KKR, Forstmann Little & Co., Morgan Stanley & Co., and Prudential-Bache Capital Funding, have targeted at least $25 billion for leveraged buyout investments. Moreover, the leverage typically used in these deals enables this investment pool of funds to make acquisitions totaling approximately $200 to $250 billion. Table 6-1 illustrates the capital structure of six LBO transactions. Two of these LBOs are profiled below.

The Classic LBO: American Standard Inc.

The leveraged buyout of American Standard Inc. in 1988 is a classic example of an LBO. This transaction was made in response to a hostile takeover bid of $56 per share, or $1.8 billion, from Black & Decker Corp., another large American conglomerate. Although American Standard was a worldwide market leader in each of its product lines (air conditioners, building products, and transportation), its stock price was undervalued, making it a prime candidate for a takeover. The company considered a recapitalization before seeking a "white knight" to rescue it from Black & Decker, which had raised its offer to $77 per share, or $2.48 billion. Prior to the offer, American Standard's stock had been trading at approximately $37 per share. Kelso & Co., a New York-based leveraged buyout firm, won the company, with an offer of $78 per share, or $2.5 billion.

The transaction was the first major multinational LBO, further expanding the possibilities for these types of transactions. The company has operations in 35 countries and generates more than 60 percent of its operating profit overseas. The borrowings under the credit facility were provided in the United States, West Germany, Canada, Great Britain, and the Netherlands. The senior debt structure minimized the company's exposure to high tax and high interest-rate environments. Funds were provided by a syndicate of 21 banks, which had the option of funding their loans either in local currency or in U.S. dollars through a swap. More than $1.5 billion of currency and interest-rate swaps were required for this transaction.

The Breakup Deal: Beatrice Foods

The $7 billion leveraged buyout of Beatrice Foods Co. by KKR in 1986 was one of the largest and most successful LBOs ever completed (see

Table 6-1. Capital Structures of Selected Leveraged Buyouts
(Percentage of Total Capital)

Date completed	Company	Equity	Preferred stock	Subordinated debt	Senior debt*	Other†
4/86	Beatrice Foods Co.	6.40%	0 %	29.60%	64.00%	0 %
7/87	Borg-Warner Corp.	2.20	2.20	23.90	71.70	0
3/88	American Standard Inc.	7.92	2.38	26.12	63.58	0
4/87	Supermarkets General Corp.	6.15	0	13.85	80.00	0
2/88	Seaman Furniture Co. Inc.	12.73	0	0	87.27	0
4/85	Pannill Knitting Co. Inc.	5.98	4.10	20.49	63.53	5.9
	Average	6.90%	1.45%	18.99%	71.68%	0.98%

*Includes senior financing, senior notes, and existing debt.
†Includes cash and marketable securities.

Table 6-1). Beatrice, the quintessential brand-name product conglomerate, was structured as a "breakup deal," a transaction in which management sells off parts of a company to pay down debt and reduce the heavy interest burden on the company. The transaction marked the beginning of a trend in buyouts of this size characterized by the quick divestiture of undervalued assets to strategic buyers in order to realize the true market value of its businesses. In conglomerates like Beatrice, the sum of the parts proves to be greater than the market value of the entire company as a unit.

Upon completion of the LBO, the new management of this international food and consumer products company began selling off businesses to reduce its debt. By year-end 1986, the company had divested Avis, Coca Cola bottlers, and its dairy, cold storage, and printing businesses. By early 1987, the company had sold its bottled water and Beatrice International businesses. It then split its remaining businesses into two separate entities: Beatrice, which held mainly food products, and E-II, which held consumer products. Later that year, the management of E-II and certain investors took it public, retaining an equity interest in the company, which they subsequently sold to American Brands for a significant profit. In 1988, Beatrice sold Tropicana. As a result of these transactions, the company was able to retire the majority of its bank debt. The final challenge facing Beatrice investors and management is to find buyers for its remaining operations, which include Swift Meats, Hunt-Wesson Foods, and a cheese business.

Tax Considerations

The Tax Reform Act of 1986 eliminated some of the tax provisions favorable to leveraged buyouts, making such transactions more costly to investors. The most important of these changes was the repeal of the *general utilities* doctrine, pursuant to which, under prior law, a corporation generally did not recognize gain or loss on distribution of its assets in complete liquidation, or on sales of property following the adoption of a plan of liquidation that was completed within 12 months, except for recapture of depreciation and certain other items. Similarly, if an acquiring corporation elected (under Section 338 of the Internal Revenue Code) to treat a stock purchase as an asset purchase (to step up the basis of the acquired company's assets), no gain or loss would be recognized by the acquired corporation other than recapture amounts.

By reason of the 1986 act, a corporation now will generally recognize gain or loss when it distributes property to its shareholders in complete liquidation or sells or exchanges property following the adoption of a plan of liquidation. The amount of gain or loss recognized is determined as if the property were sold at fair market value. Moreover, if an acquiring corporation makes a Section 338 election, the deemed sale of assets will be fully taxable to the acquired corporation. The act also eliminated any capital gain differential, making all corporate income subject to tax at a 34 percent rate.

The use of a technique involving the creation of "mirror subsidiaries" as a means to avoid the impact of the repeal of the *general utilities* provision to an acquiring corporation on the disposition of unwanted assets was eliminated by the Tax Reform Act of 1987.

The result of the foregoing changes is to increase significantly the tax cost to an acquirer of obtaining a step-up in basis in assets or to dispose of unwanted assets. As a result, transactions like that of Beatrice are now less practical. Instead, companies that have acquired new businesses may well try to manage them more efficiently rather than break them up. A premium thus is placed on operating management and on enhancing values and improving earnings.

Unlikely Candidates for an LBO

Not all companies are good prospects for an LBO. Companies in high-tech or unpredictable industries are poor candidates, as are companies that do not have stable, recession-resistant cash flows or solid secondary forms of repayment. The bankruptcy filing in July 1988 of Revco Inc., a 2000-store drug chain, is considered indicative of the problems that result from overly optimistic sales and earnings projections, poor communication among senior management, and an ineffective asset sales program.

In some instances, financial buyers cannot compete with strategic buyers on price. The ultimately successful acquisition of the JWT Group Inc., parent of J. Walter Thompson, the New York-based advertising agency, by WPP Group PLC, a London-based advertising agency, in June 1987 is illustrative of this point. JWT attempted to thwart WPP's initial takeover proposal of $45 per share, as well as its revised offer of $50.50 per share, by encouraging friendlier buyers to make competitive bids for the company in addition to attempting to execute a leveraged buyout in conjunction with Riordan, Freeman, Spogli, a Los Angeles-based leveraged buyout firm. In response to the high level of interest shown by other potential acquirers, WPP raised its price to $55.50 per share, or $566 million, agreed to retain management, and abandoned its plans to hire back previously ousted managers. The improved terms resulted in JWT agreeing to the transaction. Notably, two months prior to WPP's initial bid, JWT's stock price was trading at approximately

$29, underscoring the high premiums that these transactions can bring shareholders.

One concern with many LBOs is the potential conflict of interest between management and shareholders over price. LBOs offer management the opportunity to acquire a company whose value it has to that point sought to enhance. Critics claim that once management is in the position to buy its company, it may use its detailed knowledge of the company to undervalue it. Advocates argue that the market will align price with value, as in the JWT Group transaction. (See Chapter 12 for a further discussion of LBOs.)

Leveraged Recapitalizations

In 1985, the management and majority shareholders of Multimedia Inc. pioneered the leveraged recapitalization as an alternative to the straightforward public leveraged buyout. In a leveraged recapitalization, public shareholders exchange their stock for a substantial payment of cash (and in some cases debt), as well as shares, commonly referred to as "stubs," in the recapitalized company. The aggregate cash (and/or debt) portion of the exchange, along with the valued price of the new share, usually matches the price a third party or hostile raider would pay. Management usually does not exchange its shares (or exercise any of its share options) for cash, but opts to acquire tax-free additional shares equal to the value (cash and debt) paid to the public shareholders. The net result is a public company with an LBO-type capital structure and management that controls a good deal of the company's equity. Table 6-2 illustrates the capital structures of these transactions. One of these deals is discussed below.

Holiday Corp. Recapitalization

Holiday Corp., the world's largest hospitality company, initiated a recapitalization program after real estate developer Donald Trump acquired a 4.8 percent interest in the company. Several factors made Holiday an excellent candidate for leveraging, including undervalued real estate businesses, industry leadership positions, strong brand-name recognition in both its hotel and its gaming businesses, and a stable, recession-resistant cash flow from its franchising operations and casinos.

A recapitalization proved to be the most effective way for Holiday to achieve its goal of increasing shareholder wealth through the payment

Table 6-2. Capital Structures of Selected Leveraged Recapitalizations and ESOPs
(Percentage of Total Capital)

Completed date	Company	Equity	Preferred stock	Subordinated debt	Senior debt*	Other†
11/86	Holiday Corp.	0%	0 %	20.83%	79.17%	0 %
9/87	Hospital Corporation of America	0	17.61	24.96	57.43	0
4/86	FMC Corp.	0	0	31.11	64.71	4.18
7/86	Colt Industries Inc.	0	0	33.80	55.30	10.90
10/85	Multimedia Inc.	0	0	41.92	58.08	0
6/88	Shoneys Inc.	0	0	0	97.44	2.56
	Average	0%	2.93%	25.44%	68.69%	2.94%

*Includes senior financing, senior notes, and existing debt.
†Includes cash and marketable securities.

of a $65 cash dividend. Shareholders retained 90 percent of their equity interest, while management was granted a new 10 percent interest by means of a restricted stock plan. A leveraged recapitalization greatly increases a company's debt-to-equity ratio and generally is comparable to the leverage found in an LBO even though the company remains public. In Holiday, total debt jumped from 67 percent to 146 percent of previous total capitalization, resulting in negative equity of approximately 46 percent.

Holiday's stock price has fared extremely well. Since the close of this transaction, the "stub" equity, which opened at $17 per share, has risen to $26 per share and was as high as $37 before October 19. Table 6-3 illustrates the change in stock prices of five companies' pre- and post-leveraged recapitalizations.

A leveraged recapitalization can be a very effective means of dealing with a corporate raider, since (1) it establishes a high floor price with which a corporate raider must compete; (2) shareholders may opt for a leveraged recapitalization even though an outside bid offers a higher immediate total value, because they are willing to wait for the unrealized value of their shares to grow; (3) it eliminates the conflict-of-interest problem between management and shareholders that is typical in a leveraged buyout situation; and (4) following a recapitalization, a company can adopt justifiable charter amendments and share repurchase plans to protect itself from a hostile takeover given the small size of market capitalization compared to the total debt in the transaction.

Shareholders participating in a leveraged recapitalization will be subject to tax to the extent they receive cash or debentures or notes in exchange for their shares. The transaction is not taxable to the company. If the receipt of such cash or debentures or notes is pro rata to all shareholders, it will be characterized as a dividend to the extent of the company's earnings and profits, thereby favoring corporate shareholders eligible for the dividend-received deduction over individual shareholders. In order for the recapitalization to result in capital gains treatment for public shareholders, their equity interest must be reduced— for example, by the issuance of new equity to management or other members of a buyer group. If capital gains treatment results, the gain is measured by the excess of the cash and the value of notes and new stock, if any, over the tax basis of the old stock that was exchanged. Individual shareholders who would like to remain invested in a recapitalized company and assure capital gains treatment can sell their stock in the open market prior to the distribution date and reinvest the aftertax proceeds in the stock.

Table 6-3. Leveraged Recapitalizations: Stock Price Changes

Date	Company	Stock price		Dividend paid	Postdividend	Stock price	
		Preannouncement range	Predividend			9/30/87	7/26/88
7/86	Colt Industries Inc.	$70	$96⅛	$85 + 1 new common	$11	$14¼	*
4/86	FMC Corp.	90¾	99	$80 + 1 new common	19¼	54½	$35¼
11/86	Holiday Corp.	70½	82¼	$65	17⅛	33	25¾
10/85	Multimedia Inc.	60½	58½	$39.90 cash + $29.73 debentures	19½	69¾	72½
6/88	Shoneys Inc.	20	27¼	$16 cash + $4 sub. deb.	11½	NA	11½

*Not trading.

When to Pursue a Partial Restructuring

Employee Stock Ownership Plans

In 1956, Louis Kelso pioneered the *employee stock ownership plan* (ESOP) leveraged buyout to enable employees to acquire a small California newspaper chain from its retiring owner. Thirty years later, the leveraged ESOP remains a very real alternative for companies contemplating a leveraged buyout.

In 1987, Hospital Corporation of America (HCA), the largest healthcare company in the United States, opted for an ESOP when it was faced with the challenge of continuing to grow and remain profitable in a highly regulated, increasingly competitive environment. The concept involved the sale of 104 acute-care hospitals and related facilities (approximately 60 percent of HCA's exposure to this segment) to a newly formed company, HealthTrust Inc.–The Hospital Company. This company was purchased by an ESOP and certain senior members of HCA management for $2.1 billion. The purchase resulted in pension savings of $28 million, tax savings of $20 million, and interest savings of $10 million. Significantly, HealthTrust has paid down $125 million more of its debt than was required, without any asset sales.

The advantages of ESOP financing are applicable to corporate restructurings in every industry. First, ESOPs are virtually the only tax-advantaged structure left in the American tax code. Second, ESOPs increase employees' commitment to their companies, since these structures result in their becoming significant shareholders and having an opportunity to share in its profits.

An ESOP is distinguishable from a profit-sharing or other qualified retirement plan in that it may borrow from the company, its shareholders, or third parties the funds necessary to purchase employer securities, even when the lender requires a company guarantee. Such borrowings are prohibited to all other employee benefit plans. Many of the benefits of establishing an ESOP result from this unique borrowing ability. Under provisions of the Deficit Reduction Act of 1984, banks, insurance companies, and other qualified corporate lenders may exclude from income 50 percent of the interest received on such a loan. As a result, loans to ESOPs have generally been extended at favorable interest rates. In addition, subject to certain limitations, contributions by a company to an ESOP to pay the principal and interest on an ESOP loan are deductible by the company, as are certain cash dividends on employer securities held by an ESOP that are paid out to plan participants or used to repay an ESOP loan.

Using the proceeds of an exempt loan, the leveraged ESOP will purchase either newly issued stock from the company or outstanding stock from current shareholders. Therefore, ESOPs can be used for:

- Making an acquisition or financing internal growth
- Defending against possible takeover attempts in the future
- Taking a public corporation private
- Selling a wholly owned subsidiary
- Reducing the proportion of company stock held by the general public
- Increasing employees' stake in the company, thereby improving their productivity

(For a fuller discussion of ESOPs, see Chapter 13.)

Stock Repurchases

Stock repurchases are usually a more modest method of restructuring compared to a leveraged recapitalization. Through repurchases of common stock, a firm can alter its capital structure, increase its debt-to-equity ratio, gain the benefits of higher leverage, and send a strong message to the stock market.

A repurchase is a signal that managers, who presumably possess an insider's knowledge of a firm, are convinced that their firm's stock is worth more than its current price. Their conviction is seen as strong enough to lead them to pay a premium for the stock despite the risk of dilution if they are wrong. The net result is upward pressure on the price of a firm's equity.

A repurchase is defensive for three reasons. First, if executed properly it will boost a stock's price/earnings (P/E) ratio. Second, it eliminates or reduces the layer of shareholders most likely to tender to a raider. Third, it quickly adjusts a company's leverage ratios, thereby eliminating excess debt capacity.

A stock repurchase need not occur merely for defensive purposes. Repurchases have merits for ongoing concerns. Repurchases can quickly change a company's capitalization and raise the value of its equity.

Repurchases can be executed using either of two methods: tender offers or open-market transactions. In a partial tender offer, a firm offers to purchase its stock for a specified price, usually at a premium over market. The offer remains in effect for a specified time period, typically three to four weeks. Historically, defensive tender offers have been for 15 percent of a company's shares, at a 25 percent premium over prevailing market prices, producing a 13 percent permanent gain in price per share. Open-market purchases generally involve smaller quantities of stock than tender offers. They are executed through brokers at normal commission rates. No premium is paid. As such, open-market purchases are less powerful than tender offers.

However, open-market purchases still offer significant benefits. They tell of management's confidence in their company. They eliminate the least loyal layer of equityholders. They boost the demand for the company's shares and raise the price per share. They provide a use for excess cash. They are taxed as capital gains, an advantage over dividends. And they need not severely upset a company's financial flexibility, since they are normally phased in over a period of several years. (See Chapter 14 for more on the strategies and tactics of share repurchases.)

Choice of Adviser

Corporate America's acceptance of a highly leveraged balance sheet is underscored by the large number of corporations that have either acquired a strategic target or executed a recapitalization by taking on large amounts of debt. The financial world is equally supportive, with a host of financiers and investors eager to finance these transactions. However, the rules of the game are changing. Improved operating margins depend more on management's strategic decision making than on its ability to unload nonessential assets, since many companies have already streamlined their operations. In addition, increased competition among financiers and investors to participate in these transactions is resulting in a decrease in the high fees and expected returns associated with these transactions. The ability of these transactions to withstand a recessionary period will be their final test, since most have occurred during a strong upturn in the economy.

More than ever, one of management's most important decisions when faced with a hostile takeover situation is the choice of its financial adviser. An experienced financial adviser can quickly assist management in evaluating its alternatives and pursuing the appropriate course of action to maximize shareholder value. It can advise management on its financing alternatives and be instrumental in arranging financing. It can put management in contact with appropriate strategic bidders and negotiate a successful transaction. In short, the selection of a financial adviser is critical to a management that must realize the best possible price for its shareholders.

7

Determining the Value of Restructuring Alternatives

Judson P. Reis

*Executive Vice President, Managing Director of
Investment Banking, Kleinwort Benson Inc.*

Robert Bruner

*Associate Professor of Business Administration,
University of Virginia*

One of the greatest challenges in analyzing restructuring plans is to determine their effects on investors. This is because most restructurings consist of a *bundle* of financial changes whose effects can intertwine in complicated ways, clouding the effect on value. Because of the large and profound changes that restructurings impose on firms, managers need a way to decompose these effects and analyze the proposals straightforwardly.

In this chapter, we advance a framework for putting a value on restructuring alternatives, for identifying the sources of that value, and for determining how that new value will be allocated among stakeholders in the firm. In addressing this, we will also show that the valuation framework is applicable to a wide range of possible actions, and that the relevant set of "investors" includes not only stockholders, but bondholders as well. Finally, we acknowledge the limitations of a narrow attention to value and widen our focus to related issues such as flexibility, incentives, and clienteles.

A Proper Benchmark

Managers and their analysts may be called upon to evaluate a wide range of restructuring transactions: acquisitions, divestitures, spin-offs, share repurchases, exchange offers, leveraged buyouts, leveraged cashouts, and employee stock ownership plans (ESOPs). Typically a restructuring *program*, intended to occur over a period of years, may include a number of these transactions. The sheer complexity of restructurings can cloud straightforward thinking.

To begin with, what should be the proper benchmark for evaluating restructuring proposals? Modern professional practice suggests that the potential change in the market value of common stock, including distributions made to stockholders, is the ultimate basis of analysis. But even this is inappropriate if applied simplistically. For instance, all too often shareholders of the target of a leveraged buyout offer simply compare the tender offer price with the price at which they purchased the stock or the price that prevailed before the buyout offer was announced.

Such a comparison is myopic. Shareholders of a public company can synthesize many of the features of a leveraged buyout *on their own*, without actually having to give up control of the company—in fact, a leveraged recapitalization is a synthetic leveraged buyout for public shareholders. From this perspective, the relevant question is not whether a proposed restructuring creates value, but rather whether it creates *more* value than the next best alternative. There are several recent examples of successful leveraged recapitalizations, including FMC Corp., Holiday Corp., Owens-Corning Fiberglas Corp., Colt Industries Inc., and Union Carbide Corp.

The implication of this standard of evaluation is that an extremely important early step in any analysis of restructuring proposals is to identify a set of feasible alternatives as a basis for comparison of the target proposal. If anything, excellence in business stems from choices among alternatives rather than simple, yes–no decisions. Defining alternatives and then having to compare them is an excellent discipline on the breadth and completeness of analysis. It can reveal hidden assumptions and the real determinants of value creation in a proposal.

Unraveling Restructurings: The Drivers of Value

With a potentially wide range of tactics to choose from, senior managers need to know what effects on value to look for, and how individual effects can combine to produce a net change in stock price. We can think of restructurings as having an impact in one or more of the areas discussed below.

Changes in Assets and Operations

Asset or operational redeployments call on the skills of general managers straightforwardly. Such redeployments may range from work force changes and wage renegotiations at one end to the purchase or sale of property and plant, divisions, or subsidiaries at the other. Repositioning a product in a market would also fall in this category, as would significantly restructuring the reporting relationships within a division or group. To a large extent, this kind of restructuring is an ongoing process at many companies. In recent years, prominent internal restructurings have been completed at Procter & Gamble Co., Citicorp, and Hewlett-Packard Co.

These kinds of restructurings affect stock price through several avenues:

- *Increases in operating efficiency,* as evidenced by wider margins and higher asset utilization
- *Exploitation of synergies* inherent in the horizontal, vertical, or matrixed combination of teams and divisions within a company
- *Changes in asset risk* stemming from better management of assets or more efficient diversification of activities

Changes in efficiencies and synergies would directly affect the cash flows of the firm, while changes in asset risk would affect the rate of return that investors would require; i.e., lower asset risk would require a lower market rate of return, and therefore earnings or cash flow would be capitalized at higher multiples.

Changes in Financing

Many restructuring plans propose major changes in the right-hand side of the firm's balance sheet, including changes in:

- The mix of debt, preferred stock, and common stock
- The maturity structure of debt
- The basis of debt (i.e., fixed or floating rate)
- The currency of liabilities
- The use of exotic financial instruments
- The investor clientele or owners of the firm's securities

Material changes in these ways are relatively infrequent events at most firms and may seem somewhat arcane to the senior manager. Nevertheless, these kinds of changes can create substantial changes in a firm's value. Most of the public leveraged recapitalizations noted above involved a combination of these changes and resulted in significant increases in value to stockholders.

Financial changes can affect investor values in three ways. First, through the *exploitation of tax shields,* a firm's tax expense is reduced, and the cash flow made available for payment to all investors (i.e., stockholders and bondholders) is increased. As we will show in an example below, this annual tax savings can actually be valued and contributes directly to the value of common stock. Second, financial changes can affect investor values through *changes in risk.* For instance, we know that the total risk profile of the firm into which investors buy consists of business or operating risk, and financial risk. As the firm increases its financial leverage, its financial risk must rise, and thus the investors' required rate of return must rise. Third, financial changes can cause *wealth transfers between bondholders and stockholders.* For instance, in recent years fixed-income investors have become more vocal about the deterioration in the market value of their securities as firms restructure—the wealth they lose does not just disappear but rather accrues to the benefit of the equityholders.

Unlocking Hidden Value

At one level or another, almost all restructurings seek to exploit value that is latent in a firm. Asset redeployments exploit this value by rearranging operations and assets. Financial restructurings generally exploit unused financial capacity. At issue is whether investors and managers see the value hidden in the firm. If not, then it will pay an outsider to purchase control of the company and implement the restructuring for his or her own account.

In essence the exploitation of hidden values assumes the existence of a *market inefficiency.* By virtue of keen competition, consistent market inefficiencies will be difficult to find. Yet recent restructurings are stunning examples of the exploitation of such inefficiencies. For example, Metromedia was taken private by its chairman, John Kluge, for $750 million, and then broken up for $3.2 billion. Beatrice Foods was taken private for $5.6 billion; though the restructuring is still in progress, it appears that investors will earn a substantial premium on their investment. In these and other cases, it appears that large diversified corporations trade at a discount from their true asset value; this value may be known internally but not acted upon by the firm's managers; or more likely it may be unknown until an entrepreneur takes control of the company and tests the market. Either way, investors gain by exploiting the misvaluation of assets in the market.

Changes in Stakeholder Contracts

The benefits of any of the foregoing categories often elude investors unless they can draw into the restructuring important players on whom the actual success of the restructuring depends. The means for doing this is to adjust the incentives for managers, employees, bondholders, and even communities to think more as if they were investors in the firm. Too often, this is interpreted as merely sharing in the gains from restructuring; but that can be only part of any new contract, for all the stakeholders must be prepared to share in the downside as well.

Some examples of how the risks and rewards of restructuring have been shared will illustrate how the "contracts" among stakeholders can be revised.

- *Managers.* In most leveraged buyouts, managers are sold substantial equity positions in the company, often at preferred prices or terms. At the same time, LBO promoters may require the managers to commit substantially all of their financial resources to the purchase of the stock. This means that the returns to managers often exceed the returns to the financial backers of the LBO, and that the managers face financial ruin if the LBO fails.

- *Employees.* Many restructurings today feature an ESOP through which the line workers participate in the equity of the firm.

- *Bondholders.* Most large, leverage-changing transactions today involve the renegotiation of credit agreements between lenders and borrowers. In essence, this renegotiation is a recontracting process. Increasingly, lenders in LBOs are requesting equity participations through warrants or purchase of shares of common stock.

- *Communities.* Communities can be asked to commit to the success of a restructuring through the provision of tax breaks and industrial revenue bonds. In turnaround restructurings, local governments and community groups might participate more actively in the raising of capital—as was the case in the highly publicized buyout of the Weirton Division from National Steel in 1980.

In effect these "recontractings" determine how the value created in the restructuring will be distributed among the stakeholders of the firm. Ultimately this influences the market value of equity held by the public through any economic dilution imposed by these recontractings.

To summarize so far, we have suggested that the effects on value in restructurings may be categorized into four areas: asset redeployments, financial changes, exploitation of market inefficiency, and recontracting among stakeholders. Within each category, we have identified particular effects on cash flows, required rates of return, and claims to value.

A Framework for Analyzing Effects on Value

All the effects we have enumerated so far can be analyzed independently and then knitted together into an aggregate stock price effect using the discounted cash flow framework. The reason for looking at the various effects independently is that it addresses the problem with which we opened—i.e., the tangling interaction of restructuring effects and transactions.

Our approach is based on the idea that the present value of two cash flow streams combined is equal to the *sum* of the present values of the individual streams. This is exactly true where the discount rates for the two individual streams are equal. Even if the discount rates for the two individual streams are not equal, the idea still makes strong economic sense. To see that this is true, think of what would happen if you could buy a *portfolio* of the two individual streams for less than you could buy the combined stream: You would buy the portfolio and sell short the combined stream. This buying-selling action by you and other arbitrageurs would take place until the present values of the two investment alternatives became equal.

The important implication of this idea is that we can value firms by their component parts and estimate changes in value by summing the changes in the components. This amounts to viewing the firm from the standpoint of a *market-value balance sheet*. The market value of the entire firm is simply the sum of the market values of its assets. The market value of the firm's equity is equal to the market value of assets less the market value of debt. (This kind of market value accounting uses many of the same identities as book value accounting.) In other words, this is a bottom-to-top valuation approach, where we begin with a careful understanding of the values of the components of the firm and then sum them to a value for the entire firm.

In practice many financial engineers, LBO promoters, and corporate raiders operate in precisely this way. The task of finding hidden value in a firm is almost impossible without this technique. And since, as we have argued above, the search for hidden value is at the core of the restructuring movement, this valuation framework is the most appropriate for analyzing restructuring proposals.

The Market-Value Balance Sheet

The market-value balance sheet valuation approach can be pursued in the following manner. First, as a foundation for any comparisons of alternatives, it is useful to develop pro-forma book-value balance sheets. This helps keep straight the various changes that a restructuring will impose on the firm and clarifies some of the reporting implications of each alternative.

Developing a market-value balance sheet is mainly a process of aggregating the values of smaller components. This can be done in several ways. The following is one way of organizing the effort.

1. *Net working capital.* The first, and perhaps easiest, component of a market-value balance sheet to estimate is net working capital, the difference between current assets and current liabilities. These items are cash or near-cash, so it is reasonable to assume that the market value of net working capital is equal to book value. Obviously where one suspects significant amounts of bad receivables, obsolete or undervalued inventory, etc., an adjustment is in order.

2. *Long-term assets.* This category covers anything that is not a current asset, and represents the point in our analysis that differs most sharply from the accrual accounting approach. Here we seek to place a value not only on *physical assets,* such as plant, equipment, and real estate, but also on *intangible assets* such as patents, brand names, trademarks, specialized know-how, unusual market power, and options for future growth. The presence of an intangible asset is indicated mainly through a greater cash flow from a plant or product line, though it may be that there exist recent bid prices for the specific intangible assets against which to test any cash flow-based values.

Certainly the acquisition interest in branded consumer-products businesses provides several very good examples of the market value of intangible assets. One also needs to look for "hidden" assets that might not appear on a conventional balance sheet, such as below-market leases that can be sold or pension fund surpluses that can be realized.

3. *Debt tax shields.* As we discussed above, debt financing almost always increases the free cash flow of the firm. This is because governments subsidize some portion of interest expense by allowing firms to deduct it from taxable income. A tax shield is tax expense saved because of the deductibility of interest expense. This expense savings is analogous to the cost savings from installing a new machine and can be valued in the same manner using the discounted cash-flow technique. Thus, an asset must be listed on the market-value balance sheet, equal to the present value of the debt tax shield. An example of how this shield can be estimated and valued is presented in the following section.

4. *Market value of assets.* This is simply the sum of the preceding three categories.

5. *Debt.* Turning to the right-hand side of the market-value balance sheet, we must list the market value of the debt obligations of the firm less any debt deducted in step 1 above. Valuing debt is a straightforward problem in forecasting cash flows and discounting them. However, care must be taken to use market yield to maturity on obligations of similar risk (rather than the original coupon rate of the debt).

6. *Equity.* Recalling the economic identity that the value of assets must equal the value of capital, the value of the firm's equity can be computed as a "plug" figure, or the difference between the market value of assets and the market value of debt.

Having derived the market value of all equity, it is necessary to calculate a per-share value by dividing by the new number of shares outstanding, assuming no preferred stock, convertible securities, or warrants. (Each of these other types of securities must also be included in creating a market-value balance sheet, but they have been ignored herein for the sake of simplicity.)

The result of this analysis is a pro-forma share price associated with each restructuring alternative that can be compared. Gains or losses in share price can be contrasted with changes in the value of debt to determine the presence, if any, of wealth transfers between stockholders and creditors. The benefits of changing assets or operations, of improving operating incentives, and of unlocking hidden value would appear in the cash flows underlying asset valuations, whether these be short-term (i.e., selling the asset for its true economic worth) or the long-term cash stream generated through continued ownership. In short, the market-value balance sheet framework embraces the main sources of value in restructurings and is highly adaptable to special situations.

An Example: Union Carbide Corp.

Union Carbide (UCC) was a leading producer of petrochemicals, plastics, industrial gases, specialty chemicals, and carbon products. In addition, it had several attractive consumer products businesses. In December 1984, water was introduced into a methyl isocyanate holding tank and caused the tragic accident in Bhopal, India. UCC's stock, which had been trading in the middle to upper $40s, plunged to the low $30s shortly after the accident occurred. During January 1985, the Bass brothers acquired 5.4 percent of UCC's outstanding shares. This was followed on August 14, 1985, by an announcement by GAF Corp. that it, too, had acquired a 5 percent stake.

On August 29, 1985, UCC's board adopted a comprehensive restructuring plan, which included (1) the repurchase in the open market of up to 10 million shares (about 14 percent); (2) divestiture of nonstrategic businesses; and (3) the reversion of $500 million of excess pension assets.

Subsequent to the restructuring announcement, GAF increased its holding to 9.9 percent of UCC. Then, on December 10, 1985, GAF announced a tender offer of $68 per share in cash. In order to finance the acquisition, GAF outlined a plan to sell $4 billion of UCC's assets following assumption of control. The UCC board replied that the GAF offer was grossly inadequate and unfair.

In response to GAF's attack, the board of directors announced a second company restructuring plan on December 15, 1985. This second plan consisted of five steps. First, it involved an exchange offer for 38.8 million of UCC's common shares, representing 56 percent of the total outstanding, for a per-share package of $20 cash and debt securities worth about $65. Second, certain assets were to be sold (specifically, UCC's consumer products division), and the capital gain over book value was to be paid to shareholders. Rights to this special dividend were to be distributed to shareholders and would be listed for trading on the New York Stock Exchange. Third, shares would be split 3 for 1 upon completion of the exchange offer. Fourth, the regular annual dividend would be increased by 32 percent. As the fifth step, the company adopted a shareholder rights plan, which required that if the company were taken over, all shareholders would receive at least $85 per share in any business combination.

As of mid-December, the relevant questions for Union Carbide's management and directors were: (1) What value would the December 15 proposal create for UCC's stockholders? (2) Would this new proposal be superior to the August proposal? (3) Would this plan dominate the $68-per-share cash tender offer recently commenced by GAF Corp.? The valuation framework sheds light on these questions.

Analysis Of Union Carbide's Restructuring Plans

Table 7-1 presents an analysis of the August and December restructuring plans, deriving expected share prices and comparing those plans to the ex ante share price as well as the share price that actually resulted. The notes in the table detail the assumptions underlying the calculations.

The analysis draws on the accounting identities described in the preceding selection—except that the balance sheet is estimated in market value terms. Some of the assumptions are that (1) the market value of net working capital is assumed to equal book value; (2) the market value of net fixed assets is estimated by solving for it in prerestructuring balance sheets; (3) the present value of debt tax shields is estimated by discounting at the cost debt the annual tax savings resulting from the deductibility of interest expense. With the value of assets determined, the value of equity is determined in a straightforward fashion by subtracting the market value of debt from the market value of equity. For the purpose of this analysis, it was assumed that the market and book values of debt were equal.

In order to compare the August and December proposals directly, it is necessary to hold constant certain assumptions such as the value of net working capital and fixed assets. As a result, the analyses in columns A, B, and C use estimated market values as of September 30, 1985. Column D analyzes the December 1985 proposal using financial information for December 31, 1985—this should conform reasonably to the perspective of UCC's directors at the time the revised restructuring proposal was advanced. Column E presents the actual outcome up to September 8, 1988.

To compare the value-creation potential of the August and December restructuring plans, look at columns B and C in the table, where the results of the two plans are compared using consistent assumptions. The

Table 7-1. Determining the Value of Restructuring Alternatives
Union Carbide Corp.

	Alternative 1: Aug. 1985 proposal	Alternative 2: Dec. 1985 proposal
Terms of proposal	Repurchase 10 million shares. Divest unspecified assets.[a] Revert $500 million in excess pension assets.[b]	Exchange for 38.8 million shares: $20.00 per share in cash $25.00 per share in 15% senior debentures $20.00 per share in 13.25% senior debentures $20.00 per share in 14.25% senior debentures Sell consumer products division and distribute any gain over book value directly to shareholders via a special dividend.[c] Distribute rights to the special dividend and list these for trading on the NYSE. Raise the regular dividend from $3.40 per share to $4.50 per share. Split the remaining shares outstanding 3:1.

[a]Assets sales proposed under alternative 1 are not reflected in the analysis here since the volume of assets to be sold was not announced and since there was no explicit plan to return the sale proceeds to shareholders.
[b]Researchers are divided on whether stock prices already impound gains from the reversion of excess pension assets. We assume that these gains were not previously impounded.
[c] In this analysis the effect of the asset sale and distribution is reflected in line 20, "Right to special dividend."

Table 7-1. Determining the Value of Restructuring Alternatives (*Continued*)
Union Carbide Corp.

Line	A Before restructuring (Sept. 1985 data)[d]	B Alternative 1 (after repurchase, before asset sale) (Sept. 1985 data)[e]	C Alternative 2 (after exchange, before asset sale) (Sept. 1985 data)[f]	D Alternative 2 (after exchange, before asset sale) (Dec. 1985 data)	E Current results (after exchange, after asset sale) (through Sept. 1988)[g]
	Book-Value Balance Sheets (Figures in Millions)				
1 Net working capital	$3166	$2986	$3166	$2865	$2998
2 Net fixed assets	5244	5244	5244	5264	2180
3 Assets	8410	8230	8410	8129	5178
4 Debt	4391	4391	7135	7135	3163
5 Equity	4019	3839	1275	994	2015
6 Total capital	8410	8230	8410	8129	5178
	Market-Value Balance Sheets (Figures in Millions)				
7 Net working capital	$3166[h]	2986[i]	3166[j]	2865	2870
8 Net fixed assets	1861[k]	1861[k]	1861	3796	2696
Present value of debt					
9 Tax shields	964[l]	964	2093	2093	1975[m]
10 Market value of assets	5991	5811	7120	8754	6641
11 Debt	2835[n]	2835	6239	6239	3363[l]
12 Equity	3156[o]	2976[p]	881[p]	2515	3278[q]
13 Total capital	5991	5811	7120	8754	6641
14 Number of shares (millions)	74.476	64.049	107.028[r]	107.028[r]	145.714[s]
15 Price per share	42.38[t]	46.46	8.23	23.5[u]	22.50[v]

[d]This case is based on the balance sheet dated Sept. 30, 1985.

[e]This case adjusts the balance sheet dated Sept. 30, 1985, and does not include effects of asset sales because of the uncertain volume of those sales and the likelihood that all proceeds would be retained by the company.

[f]This case adjusts the balance sheet dated Sept. 30, 1985, and simulates the results expected by UCC's board after the exchange, but before the asset sale. The divestiture was not effected until June/July 1986.

[g]This reflects share transactions up to Sept. 8, 1988, including the 3:1 stock split and a sale of 30 million shares on Dec. 30, 1986.

[h]The market value of net working capital is assumed to be equal to the difference between current assets (book value) and nondebt current liabilities (also book value).

[i]Original net working capital less shares repurchased for $680 million (@$68), plus an increase in cash of $500 million from the reversion of excess pension assets.

[j]Assumes that new debt borrowed just equals the dollar value of shares repurchased.

[k]The market value of net fixed assets is determined by solving for it in the "Before restructuring" case.

[l]The present value of debt tax shields was estimated by multiplying the marginal tax rate for 1985, 0.48, by the amount of interest-bearing debt.

[m]On Dec. 5, 1986, UCC tendered for all the outstanding debt securities issued in the restructuring, thus reducing the amount of debt outstanding.

[n]Interest-bearing debt.

[o]74.476 million shares at $42.375 per share.

[p]A plug figure.

[q]The market value of 145 million shares at the closing stock price of $22.50.

[r]74.4 million shares, less the 38.8 million shares repurchased, and adjusting for the 3:1 split.

[s]The fully diluted number of common shares as of Sept. 8, 1988.

[t]Closing share price on June 13, 1985, two months before GAF filed its Form 13-d.

[u]The presplit closing stock price on Dec. 16, 1985, was $70.50.

[v]Closing stock price, Sept. 8, 1988.

Table 7-1. Determining the Value of Restructuring Alternatives *(Continued)*
Union Carbide Corp.

Line	A — Before restructuring (Sept. 1985 data)[d]	B — Alternative 1 (after repurchase, before asset sale) (Sept. 1985 data)[e]	C — Alternative 2 (after exchange, before asset sale) (Sept. 1985 data)[f]	D — Alternative 2 (after exchange, before asset sale) (Dec. 1985 data)	E — Current results (after exchange, after asset sale) (through Sept. 1988)[g]
			Shareholder Wealth Analysis (per Share)		
16 Value per share	$42.38	$46.46	$ 8.23	$ 23.50	$ 22.50
17 Number of shares	1	1	3	3	3
18 Pre-split equivalent value	$42.38	$46.46	$24.69	$ 70.50	$ 67.49
Per pre-split share:					
19 Value of equity	$42.38	$46.46	$10.87[w]	$ 31.02[w]	$ 29.69[w]
20 Right to special dividend	0	0	39.63[x]	39.63[x]	33.22[y]
21 Value of debt securities	0	0	36.48[w]	36.40[w]	45.09[w]
22 Cash payment	0	0	11.20[w]	11.20[w]	11.20[w]
23 Total value per old share	$42.38	$46.46	$98.10	$118.25	$119.20

Shareholder Wealth Analysis (Aggregate)

24 Value of equity	$3156	$2976	$ 881	$2515	$3278
25 Right to special dividend	0	0	1414	1001	1185
26 Value of debt securities	0	0	2522	2522	3087
27 Cash payment	0	680	776	776	776
28 Total value	$3156	$3656	$5593	$6814	$8326

[w]In analyzing the exchange offer, we assumed that 56% of each "old" share was exchanged for the package of $20.00 in cash and $65.00 in debt securities, while 44% was retained in the remaining shares outstanding.

[x]On the first day of trading, Mar. 4, 1986, the special dividend rights closed at a price of $39.625.

[y]The actual distribution paid out per right was $33.22.

[z]The actual market value of the debt securities had risen from $65 to $80.52.

bottom panel of the table shows that the December restructuring proposal yields $98.10 per old (presplit) share. This outcome dominates the ex ante stock price of $42.375, the August proposal ($46.46), and GAF's offer of $68. Indeed, it appears that the directors were correct in rejecting GAF's offer.

The simple comparison of columns B and C ignores the significant runup in UCC's stock price in the September-December period, as shown in Table 7-2. This table suggests that some of this increase is due to a 10 percent gain in the entire stock market. Yet clearly other factors are at work. Compare the resulting wealth per share (line 23, Table 7-1) for the December restructuring plan using the September and December financial data (columns C and D). In December the second restructuring was associated with $118 in shareholder wealth, as opposed to $98 in September. The gain of almost $20 is consistent with a belief by investors that UCC management would *actually* return significantly higher levels of cash to investors—through interest, principal, and dividend payments—than was in prospect before the restructuring.

Table 7-2. Union Carbide Corp. Stock Price Movement during Restructuring Period

Date	Union Carbide common stock	S&P 500 index
July 1, 1985	$45.875	192.43
July 15	48.375	192.72
July 30	51.25	189.93
Aug. 15	52.00	187.41
Aug. 30	57.25	188.63
Sept. 16	53.625	182.88
Sept. 30	54.875	182.08
Oct. 15	56.25	186.08
Oct. 30	59.375	190.07
Nov. 15	59.875	198.11
Nov. 29	63.625	202.17
Dec. 16	70.50	212.02
Dec. 30	70.50	210.68
Jan. 15, 1986	74.625	208.20
Jan. 30	81.50	209.33
Feb. 14	86.875	219.76
Feb. 28	96.00	226.92
Mar. 14	19.375*	236.55
Mar. 27	22.125	238.97
Apr. 15	22.375	237.73
Apr. 30	24.25	235.92
May 15	23.125	234.43
May 30	23.75	247.35

*Shares traded ex-dividend for the extraordinary payout.

The actual outcome is presented in column E of Table 7-1. As of early September 1988, it appears that the value actually delivered to shareholders was $119.20, close to the estimated value of the restructuring based on our analysis (column D, $118.25). The gain in value of about $77 per old share ($119.20 − $42.375) is attributable to three sources, as follows:

- The exploitation of unused debt capacity and tax shields
- The redeployment of assets to higher-valued uses (i.e., the sale of assets at a large gain)
- The commitment to return cash to shareholders

The August restructuring proposal and GAF's strategy intended to exploit some of these effects; yet what distinguished the December proposal was the aggressive return of value directly to shareholders—in the form of cash, notes, increased dividends, and priority rights to asset sale gains.

This analysis raises some caveats as well. Whereas the focus of this chapter has been determining financial value, senior managers must also consider other possible effects from restructuring, such as changes in financial flexibility, changes in managerial and employee incentives, and changes in the ownership clientele of the firm. For instance, the restructuring as executed by Union Carbide would restrict the firm's ability to finance an attractive expansion opportunity—directly through a constraint on the ability to raise new debt capital, or indirectly through debt covenants. Some financial slack is useful as long as there is reasonable probability of its use. Similarly, the pressures of servicing high levels of debt can heighten incentives for some tasks, and dampen others, such as profitable and prudent risk taking. And finally, restructurings that involve changes in the number of shares outstanding might alter the ownership profile of the firm, changing the balance of control and board composition.

Key Questions

Restructurings are complicated events, but they need not be impossible to value. In this chapter, we presented a framework for analyzing restructurings, which essentially decomposes a firm into its components for purposes of analyzing the benefits of restructuring. The framework entails constructing a market-value balance sheet for the firm—specifically including the benefits of debt tax shields—and, from that, deriving the resulting share price. The proper analysis would include comparing the share price from any contemplated restructuring to the share price resulting from the next best restructuring alternative: generally, the share price associated with the "do nothing" alternative is a poor benchmark for decision making.

This approach highlights a number of key questions for a senior manager to ask in evaluating restructuring proposals:

1. Will it create value? What is the source of the new value?
2. How is the value to be allocated among all the players?
3. Is this the right time? What are the costs or benefits from delaying?
4. How consistent is the restructuring with currently evolving (*a*) industry conditions, (*b*) competitive position of the firm, and (*c*) financial strategy of the firm?
5. How will the restructuring change the voting control of the firm? Is such a change necessary? How much of the restructuring can be accomplished purely internally?

Answers to questions like these provide senior managers with the basic elements for evaluating restructuring proposals and anticipating the determinants of ultimate success or failure.

8

Anticipating Market Reaction to Major Corporate Changes

Donald W. Mitchell

Managing Director, Mitchell and Company

Tough business decisions have become harder to make in recent years as the risks associated with incurring Wall Street's displeasure have become greater—the stock may drop, corporate raiders may be attracted, the company may be sold at an inadequate price, and many people may lose their jobs in the new owner's pursuit of short-term gains. Two reactions have predominated: Take no risks, or anticipate carefully the market's reaction as alternatives are considered. The conservative approach of taking no risks has itself become a problem for company managements when the investment community perceives there to be excellent opportunities on which to act.

Executive surveys have shown that there is usually an inadequate knowledge level about likely market reactions prior to deciding either to pursue or not to pursue a change in the corporate direction. This explains the frequency of adverse results; but it does not suggest that managements should only pursue things that Wall Street will like. Better decisions and implementation will be made, however, if the investor's point of view is well understood in advance.

Why are the majority of executives misled about important value questions? The most frequent reason is the presumption that the answer is already known. After all, few public companies fail to have frequent opportunities to speak with the investment community every day. In addition, almost all companies own expensive software that purports to forecast future stock price. Further, investment bankers are usually happy to provide advice when asked. There is, however, a hidden problem for management in that these sources are better equipped to deal with business as usual than they are with major changes. Successful use of information from these sources in ordinary times about ordinary events masks the latent potential of major errors associated with restructuring and other large adjustments.

A second source of confusion is the limited availability of information about how major changes affect shareholder value. This confusion is made worse because each company's stock price responds differently to identical actions. Most companies are totally unaware of their relative price elasticities with alternative changes.

The third major source of misunderstanding is assuming that internal standards apply identically to the financial markets. For example, a company may avoid discontinuing a losing business because of the losses that will be reported. Frequently, investors will cheer such an action because it means the end of an unpromising situation. As this point suggests, the two sets of standards do not perfectly coincide.

The obvious answer for the concerned executive considering alternatives is to create special methods designed to deal with major corporate changes. Before addressing how to do that, it is worthwhile to describe the kind of changes we should consider with special methods.

The vast majority of corporate decisions will elicit only minor reactions from the investment community. From our research, we have compiled a brief list of some actions that are very likely to have a substantial, immediate, and long-term impact on stock price:

- Acquisitions costing more than 15 percent of your own market value

- Discontinuances of low-return or money-losing operations accounting for more than 10 percent of corporate assets

- Divesting businesses that are more than 15 percent of corporate profits or assets

- Dividend cuts or payout increases

- Increasing the rate of capital investment 25 percent beyond recent levels

- Issuing new shares
- Recapitalization
- Retiring shares equaling at least 8 to 15 percent of those outstanding with cash or other financial instruments
- Taking high-value subsidiaries public when the market value of the subsidiary will be at least 25 percent of the parent's value
- Write-offs of whole business areas equal to 10 percent of corporate equity
- Smaller amounts of these kinds of actions done in the same year to create a similar-sized, cumulative impact on the company

Quantum Chemical Corp. is a useful example. Over the last several years, the former National Distillers and Chemical Corp. has taken the following actions as part of a strategic restructuring that had shareholder value implications worth considering in advance:

- Divestitures of metals and insurance businesses (1984)
- Acquisitions of two liquid petroleum businesses (1985–1986)
- Chemical company acquisitions, and divestitures of spirits and wines businesses (1986)
- Share repurchase (1987)
- Increased rate of capital expansion (beginning in 1988)
- Major recapitalization, including payment of special dividend of $50 per share, plus planned divestiture of oleochemical operations and company ESOP stock purchase (1989)

During this period, Quantum Chemical went from being a conglomerate to a highly concentrated company that is now the nation's leading polyethylene producer and propane retailer. This company has been more active than most, but more than half of all restructuring companies will face a value-significant decision at least every six months over a three- to four-year time period. In Quantum's case, each action seems to have contributed to shareholder value. Most restructuring companies do not do so well.

At Mitchell and Company, we have pursued this question of decision effectiveness within our own client base, and have discerned two primary reasons for differences in value-improvement success, both of which relate to management practices. First, infrequent implementors of successful major actions had very incomplete data sets with which to work, looked at issues in isolation from other steps, had a lower com-

Table 8-1. Percentage Change in Clients' Stock Price Adjusted for S&P 500 Following an Announced, Recommended, Above-Minimum-Scale Restructuring Change

Approach	One year	Two years	Three years
Broad value improvement	+56.6%	+89.2%	+179.7%
An issue at a time	+12.2%	+29.8%	+42.5%
Ratio of value gains for broad value improvement versus an issue-at-a-time program	4.6 ×	3.0 ×	4.2 ×

mitment from top management to stock price growth, and knew less about value improvement, yet perceived themselves as very knowledgeable about how to achieve value growth. The second difference showed up between those who looked at the question of value improvement broadly versus those who considered one issue at a time for its value impact.

As shown in Table 8-1, a primary observable difference between the broad and the issue-at-a-time groups is that the former generated far larger stock price gains from the average action than did the latter. This demonstrates the primary benefit of the broad approach—focusing management attention on the best alternatives.

One final point is worth mentioning: Few people who advise on shareholder value provide information about how their advice has worked. Be wary when that is the case. Perhaps they are better at selling advice than at anticipating market reactions.

Overview of Techniques for Investigating Shareholder Value Improvement

Four techniques have proved most useful in creating accurate price anticipation: fundamental analysis; case histories; demand measurement surveys; and company-specific models. What is unusual about these techniques is that reliable results require a congruence of confirming answers from all four sources. This points to the technique error that creates so many anticipation mistakes: Evidence is not thoroughly cross-checked with alternative sources. A good analogy can be made to the process of identifying the characteristics of a living dinosaur from scientific tests on fossilized remains. No single piece of evidence can be relied upon to tell the whole story.

Fundamental Analysis

Fundamental analysis is, of course, the area of greatest familiarity and comfort to corporate decision makers. Our research shows that it is a good starting point for developing an agenda of possible actions to pursue. Senior management's comfort with a direction is greatly strengthened by seeing that the change leaves them with a better company.

One word of caution is in order: Don't be a technique chauvinist (someone who looks at a question in only a few ways). Most methods are narrow in the extreme and can be quite misleading. A good example is discounted cash flow measurement and its variations. In many circumstances, the assumptions one has to make are sufficiently uncertain as to overwhelm the differences among alternatives.

Another warning: Don't get caught optimizing a narrow view of the future. Choosing options that permit prosperity, compared to the alternatives, under a wide range of circumstances is a much more realistic approach.

Interpretations of these analyses have also proved misleading to a number of companies. I frequently meet executives from natural resource and real estate-rich companies who show me elaborate analyses of how valuable their companies are. In almost every case, the assets later proved to be either unsalable, were sold at a large loss, or had no impact on stock market value until sold at a large gain. An example of the last was Dillingham's Ala Mauna shopping center in Honolulu, which was worth as an asset more than double the parent's stock price for many years, but only in announcing its planned sale did the stock price eventually rise to reflect this well-known value.

The source of this confusion is assuming that value in one form translates automatically into stock price increases. Value has many different forms. Here are some of the more important ones:

- Public stock price in whole
- Public stock price in pieces
- Private sale value
- Restructured value in pieces
- Asset value
- Leveraged buyout price

- ESOP LBO price
- Merger value with a parallel competitor
- Liquidation value

Rarely will these values be identical in any two forms, and still more rarely will increases in one value form rapidly expand stock price. As a result, increases in nonstock values can simply be an invitation to hostile takeover bids. Many formerly independent corporations learned this lesson the hard way after superb fundamental programs to improve the nonstock values of their operations.

Many people contest this point, feeling that all these forms are identical, but the evidence of how quickly companies can be broken up at a profit after paying a large premium for the stock is all around us. This phenomenon is well supported by our research, which shows that the stock price value of a company is usually one of its lowest value forms. This troubling circumstance is especially likely to occur if the company in question has made few major changes to enhance share price value.

One final word of caution: If an action does not support a fundamental direction the company wants to take, don't pursue the action solely to help stock price. Such ill-based steps almost always backfire eventually, if not immediately. Fundamental analysis is a good way to smoke out some of these discrepancies.

Case Histories

Looking at the similar experiences of comparable others has a second, more valuable application beyond the benefit of cross-verification. This analysis can also provide a sense of the odds concerning success and failure, patterns of more successful practices, and an indication of the degree of impact likely to follow. We have found that this sort of evidence is usually effective in allowing executives to feel more confident about their conclusions.

Despite the obvious benefits, many companies have trouble pursuing this analysis accurately. The two most frequent problems are a lack of relevance in the selected examples and an inadequate measurement of how many of the price and operating changes were a consequence of the action or actions under consideration.

The former problem is compounded by the tendency of academics, investment bankers, and casual analysts in general to look indiscriminately at every case that ever occurred without properly segmenting effective examples and their characteristics. Since most actions produce mixed results at best, on average, this approach often inaccurately encourages a wrong conclusion.

Factors that are often important in developing accurate comparability include size, relative transaction value, profitability, economic environment, stock market level and trend, and various operational nuances. The latter problem of normalizing out the effects of other factors is fairly difficult to do well. We have often seen quite attractive, and unattractive, actions described as the opposite because of analytical errors. You are probably better off having a specialist organization do this case history work for you, if it is at all difficult to analyze.

What you learn from case histories is always unexpected. For example, a client of ours looked at the question of unrelated acquisitions for companies like itself. The other options seemed limited, and the company was interested in determining whether success could be reasonably expected following any approach to this difficult task. Here are some of the surprising answers concerning attractive purchase target screening criteria:

- Cost-control processes had to be similar.
- Marketing needed to be relatively unimportant.
- The business should be unusually stable, and not fast-growing.
- Ideal candidate business would have been resold two or more times in five years, and starved for capital by its new owners.
- The headquarters needed to be near the client headquarters.

We have developed an elaborate data base that looks at the operational and value changes that have occurred in more than 6000 companies since 1945. Case history development can be slow and painful. Certainly, companies wanting to do these analyses in a few days in response to a takeover threat will frequently find themselves unable to do this step on their own in time.

Demand Measurement Surveys

Historical analyses and models based on history have a huge drawback—failing to take into account new influences that were not present historically can lead to tremendous misdirections. For example, the extrapolation of a straight line in the middle of a road is a straight line—forever. Come to a turn in the road, however, and that extrapolation will leave your car in the ditch. In fact, our research shows that 100 percent of all unsuccessful value improvement programs and actions were conducted without the benefit of demand measurement surveys. Such surveys play a useful role in this situation by providing that needed contemporary reality check. The analogy here is best drawn to the test market of a new product before it is made broadly available, with the difference being that the task is to measure how the supply and demand for the company's shares will be affected in the near and longer terms by a given course of action.

Our firm has found that three sets of respondents are especially important: influential sell-side analysts; decision makers at institutions and large holders who own the stock now; and decision makers at large institutions who own similar stocks but no shares of the company in question. Accurate results require large numbers of responses and representation of a high percentage of the current and potential buying power. Although difficult, the survey methodologies are now sufficiently developed that the work can be completed in a week when fast response is needed (such as in the early stages of a hostile takeover).

Much as electoral pollsters use experience to improve their forecasts, we have learned a great deal about how to predict stock price results from demand measurement survey answers. The basic methodology is quite simple: Current responses are calibrated to past responses and price-change results in the prior few months or weeks of a similar market environment. Calibration of estimated longer-term results does, of course, depend on what happened in prior years. A key contemporary calibration is to test the strength of responses compared to those for similar companies and respondents' general preferences. This approach has the further benefit of reducing bias by making it unclear who the sponsor of the survey is. Fewer than 10 percent of those interviewed will usually be able to identify the true sponsor in response to a question on that point; even then there is no certainty.

Demand measurement surveys are confused by some with the plethora of investor relations surveys done by polling and public relations firms. Those surveys are designed primarily to improve communications with investors and have limited use in measuring demand for the stock following an announcement of a major change.

The benefits of a program involving several steps over an isolated action can be easily demonstrated in these demand measurement surveys. Stock purchase demand can usually be more than doubled over the response to any one action by putting that action into a desirable combination with one or two other actions. An interesting example of the value of the demand measurement surveys is to compare how the management of a company responds to such a survey compared to the investment community. There is usually little correlation between the two.

The investment community responses will closely match the case history indications. This is further evidence that many managements systematically underestimate their potential to benefit from major changes of the sort discussed in this chapter.

The current trend to intensively measure the varieties of discounted cash flow value of businesses has done little to help this tendency except in identifying divestiture candidates. An example of problems created by this one-dimensional valuation work is that a management mistakenly believes that its breakup value on a cash flow basis and stock price are similar. The consequence is usually to be satisfied with that situation and look no further. The same company may, on the other hand, have large untapped value potential to expand by competitor acquisitions followed by taking the combined units public. Investors, at the same time, may be very upset that little is being done to expand value. In fact, a real vulnerability that many companies have is the low esteem the investment community has for their management's value-improvement abilities. This is especially likely to be true when no major value-improvement actions have occurred in the last five years.

One large company was examining the option to make six major changes through such a survey, and learned that although investors liked the changes in a certain order, these investors also believed the company would never do anything but increase dividends. Before the program was announced, a hostile bid occurred, emphasizing three of the possible changes; and the results of the survey were critically important in dealing with this very negative perception. (The hostile bid was defeated.)

Company-Specific Models

An effective mathematical model for stock value improvement, decision-making purposes needs to take into account the fundamental analyses, case histories, demand measurement survey, and the company's historical stock sensitivities. Using these inputs, accurate models of how the company's stock will respond can be built. Let us emphasize that very few companies use this technique. Almost all rely on off-the-shelf software that is not written to reflect individual patterns of market sensitivity.

Company-specific models will invariably show that at least two major actions are now attractive. These are usually unperceived by management. We have seen cases in which as many as nine major actions were shown by the models to be currently attractive. Usually, a number of actions will not become useful until circumstances change—such as the

Table 8-2. Case Model Output of Value Improvement Opportunities:
Market Capitalization Comparisons
(In Billions of Dollars)

	1988	1989
Base case	$4.78	$5.54
Repurchase 10% at $18.33 in 18 months	5.29	6.53
Repurchase 15% at $19.33 in 24 months	4.88	6.28
10% high-value subsidiary IPO, cash into parent	6.66	7.27
10% high-value subsidiary IPO, cash into subsidiary	7.27	7.60
Repurchase 15% at $19.33 in 24 months plus 10% subsidiary IPO, cash into subsidiary	6.68 to 7.67	7.57 to 8.44

completion of earlier actions, a higher or lower stock market, or
changed economic conditions.

A brief summary of a model output is shown in Table 8-2 on a dis-
guised basis. The base case simply represents the "business-as-planned"
case for one economic and market scenario. Notice how combining repurchase and taking a high-value subsidiary public are likely to provide
a higher market capitalization than either one alone. The expected
longer-term results were still higher than those shown here, but are
omitted for the purpose of brevity.

Before leaving the techniques section, let us reiterate the importance
of using all four techniques properly and only pursuing directions that
are supported by each of the four.

Some Special Problems

Each contemplated step presents special problems of market anticipation. We will address some of the more important classes of issues in
evaluating alternatives.

Share Repurchase

Analyses of share repurchases tend to be dominated by earnings-per-
share and liquidity considerations. While useful, these are not sufficient
for anticipating the stock market reaction.

The success of share repurchases tends to be heavily influenced by
what percent you repurchase, what major actions you later take, and
how strong your underlying business performance is after the repur-

chase. Unfortunately, share repurchases are heavily used to manage earnings per share (EPS) when earnings are weak and no further actions are planned.

The most frequent misunderstanding about share repurchase is that you must use cash. There are highly successful instances where new securities were exchanged instead for the common stock. Inexpensive money-market preferred stock is perhaps the most intriguing alternative under the right market circumstances.

The second most frequent misunderstanding is that the benefits are directly proportionate and limited to the percentage repurchased. Thus, the popular belief is that a 10 percent repurchase will raise share price by 10 percent—using the stock-split analysis methodology. In fact, successful repurchases can lead to much better results compared to the market. Witness the increases (stock price change relative to the S&P 500 from announcement date) experienced by certain of our clients following the announcement of this action when recommended in above-scale amounts:

Year 1	Year 2	Year 3	Year 4	Year 5
46.8%	73.7%	154.3%	243.9%	402.4%

A powerful recent example is the repurchase of more than 90 million shares by Ford at a time when profits, cash flow, and market share were surging. The repurchase has retired more than 16 percent of outstanding shares while market capitalization has gone from about $9 billion to more than $25 billion (as of summer 1988). The share repurchases are planned to continue.

Divestitures and Discontinuances

As suggested earlier, divestitures and discontinuances are underappreciated by corporate managements. The results are strongly positive in certain circumstances, and benefits continue to accrue for many years to come.

Perhaps the classic example of this phenomenon was the discontinuance of Lockheed's L-1011 program on December 7, 1981. The write-off amounted to $400 million (unusually large for those days), and Lockheed's equity fell by more than two-thirds as a result. Over the period from one month before the announcement to two-and-a-half years later, Lockheed's stock grew 207 percent compared to the S&P 500's growth of 34 percent. On the first full trading day, the stock climbed by

19 percent. Of course, Lockheed continued to operate that business because of commitments to customers, but as a discontinued operation.

The situations to avoid are write-offs of less than total operations and too frequently disposing of weak operations. Most companies act as though these divestitures and discontinuances always hurt stock price in the near and longer terms, and would rather just avoid these problem areas.

Acquisitions

Most people are surprised to learn that properly done acquisitions are the most effective form of major action for value improvement. Here are our clients' results following recommended, large acquisitions, again adjusted for the S&P 500:

Year 1	Year 2	Year 3	Year 4	Year 5
27.1%	165.6%	285.4%	396.2%	527.6%

Of special concern is the delay in the stock market's reaction to successful acquisitions. Even in the best cases, the price increases may not begin to be significant for 18 months. This means that, immediately following a large acquisition, a company's discount-to-breakup value normally increases. If the purchase is a successful one, the consequence is likely to be negative for avoiding takeover. In fact, that is a primary reason why Norton Simon Inc.'s acquisition program made it so attractive to Esmark, why Beatrice later sought and acquired Esmark, and why Esmark management later bought Beatrice.

The normal problem is exacerbated when the acquisition causes a company to trade in a lower stock-price valuation group. There are more than 400 such groups, and the downward adjustments from changed business mix await the unwary. This happened to Du Pont when the company bought Conoco, costing Du Pont shareholders an additional $5 billion above the $8 billion paid for Conoco even before oil prices dropped. The same occurred to American Express when the company bought Fireman's Fund.

Leveraged Buyouts

One of the major recent changes in value is the price that a business or company will bring if purchased in leveraged buyout form. The reasons for this include a willingness of lenders to accept lower cash flow and earnings coverage of interest costs, reduced interest rates in recent years, and greater willingness of investors to add equity capital for attractive situations.

This trend has surprised many managers who do not realize what their company is valued at in the LBO market. The example of Bell & Howell shows why this can be the case. Bell & Howell shares traded at under $10 a share in 1981 when a restructuring began that was to turn the company into an attractive publishing company following a lackluster record as a business equipment manufacturer. By mid-1986, the share price had climbed to almost $50 per share. The company went private in early 1988 at $64 per share, although 1987 earnings were only about a third higher than 1981. Yet the company sold for seven times the 1981 price.

If you are like the managements of many companies, your idea of what price you would sell for in an LBO is way out of date. Have an outside professional quietly update this for you.

Partial Public Offerings

Another frequently missed opportunity is to take the shares of a highly valued subsidiary public. Our research has shown that more than 60 percent of all major public companies have this opportunity, but few of them have pursued this route even as far as a thorough study.

A particularly attractive application of this approach was the public offering of American Television & Communications Inc. (ATC) stock by Time Inc. in August 1986. Earlier, Time had purchased the cable television operations of Westinghouse at a high price, reflecting the market price for such transactions in 1986. The new ATC combined Time's old ATC unit plus Westinghouse's operations. By taking the combined units public, Time raised more than $300 million to help pay for the acquisition premium. A year later, we calculate that Time's market value was also about $300 million higher than it would have been without the offering.

Such partial public offerings (PPO) of high-value subsidiaries have been an excellent way to expand stock price quickly, but the longer-term benefits do not grow as rapidly. The following is the experience of clients following recommended PPOs relative to the S&P 500:

Year 1	Year 2	Year 3	Year 4	Year 5
50.6%	78.0%	162.7%	169.7%	243.1%

Our proprietary data base of such high-value subsidiary offerings has shown one other interesting benefit: the tendency of these units to subsequently gain significant market share and profit margin. Interviews with key executives at these newly public units suggest that greater perceived access to capital resources, investment community pressure to perform, higher motivation, and setting higher objectives all played a role in this success.

Recapitalization

When the subject of recapitalization is raised, one company many inevitably think of is FMC Corp. This company also makes an interesting example of the difficulties in anticipating stock market reaction to a novel program. In the throes of takeover resistance efforts, FMC repurchased about 70 percent of its outstanding shares and later increased that amount to more than 75 percent.

What is the score to date? In late 1985, before the takeover frenzy, FMC's market capitalization was $1.75 billion and debt was $300 million, for a cost to acquire of $2.05 billion before paying an acquisition premium. In mid-1988, FMC's market capitalization was $1.3 billion with debt at the $1.2 billion level, for a cost to acquire of $2.5 billion before the takeover premium is paid. This is an increase in total cost of about 20 to 25 percent while the popular market indexes are up about 50 to 55 percent during the same time period. Including the cash paid out to repurchase the stock, FMC's shareholders are, however, still way ahead, having seen their position in cash and stock almost quadruple during the same time period.

FMC certainly met its objective of not being taken over. One has to wonder, however, how well recapitalization programs will measure for avoiding future takeovers. The primary problem with any program as extreme as recapitalization is that it greatly restricts the company from pursuing other value-enhancing actions until the debt is significantly reduced, several years hence. Such an action also bets strongly on one view of the future (an optimistic one), which may not come to pass. One hopes that the result will not be to become more vulnerable to takeover specialists in the future because of the long-term consequences of recapitalization.

Internal Reorganization

A favorite management belief in some companies is that cutting staff overhead, reorganizing the corporate management structure, and announcing a new management philosophy will drive ahead shareholder value by heralding a new era in profit growth.

These companies are drawn by a people-oriented focus that in many circumstances is probably commendable. The stock market reaction is inevitably, however, a big yawn. People often view these changes in companies having problems as no more than shuffling the deck chairs on the *Titanic*. The results, if positive, will be rewarded only after a considerable time delay. IBM Corp. is the leading current user of this approach, with stock price little changed from mid-1983 to mid-1988 while earnings were about flat.

Matching Actions Together to Solve Problems—Dividend Cut Example

Conventional wisdom is that a dividend cut is a big no-no for all but troubled companies. Optimists will claim that stock price will rebound, however, after six months to a year.

Must a company experience predictable declines? The 1988 dividend cut by Avon Products Inc. provides an interesting example of how the historical pattern can be broken in a positive way. After many years of promising never to cut its dividend, continuing earnings problems made that action a necessity. Avon realized that not everyone held the stock for its high dividend yield. If those who did could be satisfied, the selling of Avon stock should be minimal on the news. As a result, Avon created a temporary preferred stock paying the same dividend as the Avon common had been paying. Any shareholder could swap his or her shares for the new preferred up to 25 percent of the total shares outstanding. This allowed an immediate dividend cut for 75 percent of the common shares, three years to sell out for those who wanted the dividend yield, and an eventual total dividend reduction.

How did the stock react? After one slightly down day (not everyone reads such announcements carefully), the stock climbed to a premium over where it had been and stayed there in the immediate aftermath. The exchange offer was only 3 percent oversubscribed. In this day of "invent your own paper," it is almost always possible to avoid negative stock situations if well-managed counterefforts are pursued.

Timing and Planning

A frequent problem that companies have with major changes involving more than one step is that they misorder the steps in terms of value maximization. This is normally a result of "I'll spend the money after I have the cash" thinking. For example, if a large unit is to be sold, the funds are often used for share repurchase following the sale. The result is that the stock will probably be repurchased at a higher price than would have occurred if the order was reversed. The option to do this, of course, exists only when public disclosure of the future sale need not be made at the time of the repurchase.

A related problem is one of pairing announcements of something positive for stock price with something negative. The Avon example describes the potential for this approach. This problem is especially acute with regard to large acquisitions, particularly if they are perceived negatively (rightly or wrongly).

The demand measurement survey is an especially powerful tool for this problem of overcoming negative reactions because individuals can describe the circumstances under which their concerns would be overcome. From this work, it becomes clear that almost any negative situation short of involuntary bankruptcy can be overcome. Company-specific models are also powerful tools, because they can pick up minor subtleties in ordering what might otherwise be missed.

The greatest planning problem is that executives are not willing to look far enough ahead in considering the ramifications of what they are considering. If share repurchases are working well for me, should an LBO follow at some point? If my new acquisitions prosper, how should I balance my risk exposure?

Takeover Risk

You wake up one morning to read that a raider has taken a position in your shares, plans to buy more, and may decide to make an offer for the whole company. A quick call to your lawyer confirms that there are no antitrust barriers to his actions and that everything else has been done legally. Your investment banker further confirms that the raider is always present at the Drexel Burnham gatherings, and that junk bond financing at a 60 percent premium to last night's closing stock price should be no problem. What do you do now?

One option that many companies are now pursuing is announcing several actions to improve the company's strength and share price before the stock purchasing by the raider goes much further. This is not, however, always done well. On the other hand, it must be done quickly. Many companies report that they received remarkably awful advice following the start of the raid about how to avoid the takeover through announced changes.

A better solution is to have your stock-price improvement planning in a state of readiness such that you know accurately your discount-to-breakup value, and what your three most attractive alternatives are for immediate share gain. Unbelievably, fewer than 5 percent of all companies that have pursued antitakeover actions such as staggered boards, poison pills, and special shareholder rights have addressed these two means of preparation. That is comparable to an army keeping its guns in good repair while not purchasing any ammunition.

Stage of High Predictability

Evaluating how major changes in a company can help or hurt share price has reached a stage of high predictability following the use of the four techniques described in this chapter to cross-check each other. However, company managements generally have not taken this opportunity as seriously as they do their budgets and strategic plans.

Since these techniques evolved largely outside of universities and the investment banks, the normal channels for spreading these methods have proved undependable. Because of the large potential to expand wealth and jobs in our society, one hopes that this situation will change. Certainly, the unwelcome attentions of corporate raiders will provide an incentive for all but the most troubled companies to become more aware of the value in this type of restructuring planning.

9

Preserving or Enhancing Corporate Control in a Restructuring

John A. Marzulli, Jr.
Partner, Shearman & Sterling

Ralph A. Walter
Associate, Shearman & Sterling

The occurrence of a corporate restructuring may or may not have an impact on corporate control. A relatively simple restructuring—for example, one involving merely the payment of a dividend pro rata to all shareholders—would not change the control relationship between the corporation and its shareholders that existed prior to the restructuring. More complex restructurings may affect corporate control in one of two ways:

- First, the restructuring may result in a change in the ownership patterns of the corporation's voting securities as they existed prior to the restructuring. This may occur by increasing the percentage of such voting securities owned or controlled by management, or by placing a block of voting stock in the hands of a so-called white squire or friendly raider, frequently as a part of the financing for the restructuring.

- Second, although the restructuring may preserve existing stock ownership patterns, shareholders or the board of directors may adopt antitakeover devices in connection with the restructuring that are designed to preserve corporate independence.

There are many rationales for including, as part of a restructuring, provisions that are either designed to or have the effect of protecting the corporation from unsolicited takeover proposals. Typically, a restructuring involves incurring substantial additional debt to finance the payment of large sums of money to shareholders. This significantly reduces the market value of the "stub equity," thereby making the company relatively less expensive for an acquirer to purchase. At the same time, the increased debt burden on the company significantly reduces the board's flexibility in responding to an unsolicited takeover proposal. There is also frequently perceived to be a need to more closely align the interests of management with the interests of shareholders and to provide management with additional incentives to operate a highly leveraged company. The latter need is typically addressed by increasing management's outright ownership interest in the company or by increasing the equity-based component of management's overall compensation scheme.

It is also sometimes financially advantageous to change preexisting ownership patterns for reasons other than corporate control—for example, to ensure capital gain treatment rather than dividend treatment on a stock repurchase. Even in a tax environment where dividend income and capital gain are taxed at identical rates, there is an advantage to capital gain treatment. Cash distributions characterized as proceeds from the sale of a capital asset are taxable only to the extent that there is a gain in excess of a shareholder's basis. Cash distributions characterized as a dividend are taxed as ordinary income to the extent of a company's tax earnings and profits; if the dividend exceeds such tax earnings and profits, the excess is treated as a return of capital to the extent of a shareholder's basis in his or her shares and, thereafter, as capital gain. Capital gain treatment generally is accorded to noncontrolling shareholders whose ownership interest in the company is reduced as a result of a distribution or repurchase recapitalization transaction.

Another reason to change the preexisting ownership pattern is to take advantage of the additional borrowing capacity provided by the use of a leveraged employee stock ownership plan (ESOP) to increase the employees' equity-based participation in the success of the company.

Inasmuch as there are many reference materials available covering antitakeover devices (which may be adopted at any time in the absence of a restructuring), this chapter focuses primarily on the ways in which a restructuring may affect the control relationship between the restructured company and its stockholders.

Methods of Altering Historical Stock Ownership Patterns

Increasing Management's Ownership Interest

Regardless of the form of the restructuring, the method chosen for increasing management's relative ownership interest in the company depends in large part on whether or not management, prior to the restructuring, has a significant equity interest in the company. In the situation where management does own significant equity, it is frequently possible to increase management's equity as a percent of the total outstanding equity without issuing any additional shares to management. This may be accomplished either through an issuer self-tender or exchange offer in which management does not tender its shares, or through an issuer stock repurchase program.

  In the situation where management does not possess a significant equity stake in the company prior to the restructuring, it generally will be necessary as a part of the restructuring to issue additional equity to management. On the assumption that management does not have the financial resources to purchase a substantial equity stake outright, this will usually be accomplished through the issuance of stock or options to management through either existing or newly adopted equity-based compensation plans. Management can be issued restricted stock (which, unlike stock subject to option, votes immediately upon issuance, notwithstanding any restrictions on transfer), or options. A similar result can be obtained through a merger recap or reclassification where management shares or options are converted solely into stock or options of the recapitalized company but do not participate in any nonequity payments otherwise made to public shareholders.

Increasing Management's Voting Interest

If management cannot increase its own equity stake in the restructured company, the next best course of action may be to place shares in the hands of persons who are associated with the company and, perhaps, influenced by management. In the past, voting securities held by an

ESOP have been viewed as being, in effect, management shares. This is so for two reasons: First, the power to vote unallocated shares often has been accorded to the ESOP trustees, who have frequently been members of management; second, although the power to vote vested shares is passed through to the plan participants, employees typically remain loyal to management, especially if the raider is perceived to be a "bust-up" artist.

Because ESOPs usually serve a beneficial business purpose, in contrast to purely antitakeover devices such as "poison pills" (shareholder rights plans), courts have upheld the issuance of a significant percentage of equity to ESOPs that were subject, directly or indirectly, to some degree of management control, so long as the plans were adopted after long and careful consideration by the board.

As a result of increasing judicial scrutiny of the alleged entrenchment purpose behind the adoption of ESOPs that were established following a challenge to corporate control, many recent defensive ESOPs have provided for an independent trustee and for confidential pass-through voting of allocated ESOP shares, with unallocated shares voting in the same proportion as the allocated shares. In addition, under the Employment Retirement Income Security Act, 29 U.S.C., Sections 1101-1114 (1985), which governs the fiduciary obligation of ESOP trustees, such trustees are legally bound to act in the best interest of all ESOP beneficiaries (not just the present participants) and may be legally bound to tender ESOP shares subject to their discretionary powers if such action is in the beneficiaries' best interests. Nevertheless, because of employee loyalty, raiders generally continue to view ESOP shares as being, in effect, management shares.

Increasing the Voting Interest of a White Squire

If voting securities cannot be placed with management or with employees generally through an ESOP, a substantial voting block sometimes can be placed in the (relatively) friendly hands of a white squire. Often this is justified by the white squire's providing a significant portion of the financing needed to effect the restructuring. As a substantial investor, the white squire frequently is able to negotiate certain protections for its investment which, assuming the white squire continues to be friendly, help insulate the company from unsolicited bids. In the rather unusual situation of a hostile tender for control of Newmont Mining Corporation, by paying an extraordinary dividend to shareholders, Newmont actually provided its white squire, Consolidated Gold Fields PLC (already a substantial 33 percent shareholder) with the funds needed for Consolidated Gold Fields to "sweep the street" (buy Newmont shares on the open market) and increase its stake to 49 percent.

The use of a white squire can have consequences quite undesirable from management's point of view. As is apparent to anyone who has followed the continuing saga of Chris-Craft Industries Inc.'s 17.5 percent investment in Warner Communications Inc., the grant to a minority investor of significant board representation may backfire. Chris-Craft has publicly opposed the terms of Warner Communications' management compensation and, according to management, has attacked management policies in order to extort the company to buy back its minority stake for an excessive profit.

A Change in Ownership Patterns Should Not Constitute a Change in Control

When Is a Recapitalization a Change in Control?

It is important to note that when speaking of a change in ownership patterns as a part of a corporate restructuring, we are speaking of something less than a "change in control." While a corporate restructuring generally is not considered to be a change in control triggering the board's fiduciary duty to auction the company and obtain the highest available price, as was discovered by American Standard Inc. during its ultimately successful efforts to fend off the Black & Decker Corp., a change in control that masquerades as a restructuring nevertheless will be treated by the courts as a sale of the company.

The question of when a change in ownership patterns resulting from a restructuring becomes a change in control has now been judicially determined in a number of contexts. As with all decisions in this area, peculiar facts produce peculiar results, and legal advisers will not always be able to advise absolutely that a particular restructuring does not involve a change in control. At the two extremes, it seems clear that a restructuring that does not alter historical ownership patterns (even if the adoption of antitakeover devices are part of the restructuring) will not be deemed a change in control, while a restructuring that clearly leaves a management group with more than 50 percent of the voting equity of the restructured entity will be deemed a change in control. Between those two extremes lies uncertainty.

Three recent decisions at this writing, *Newmont Mining, American*

Standard, and *Macmillan,* have examined whether changes of historical ownership patterns constitute a change in control. All three cases involved defensive restructurings that significantly altered preexisting ownership patterns and were adopted in response to unsolicited takeover proposals. *American Standard* and *Macmillan* involved situations in which management was the beneficiary of the increased equity participation, and *Newmont* involved an increased equity stake by a third-party white squire.

In *Ivanhoe Partners v. Newmont Mining Corp.,* Newmont faced a hostile partial tender offer from Ivanhoe. Ivanhoe had purchased a sufficient number of Newmont shares to allow Consolidated Gold Fields PLC, Newmont's largest shareholder, to terminate its long-standing standstill agreement with Newmont, pursuant to which Gold Fields had been prohibited from owning more than one-third of Newmont's shares or electing more than one-third of its directors. Newmont subsequently negotiated a new standstill with Gold Fields, which allowed Gold Fields to increase its stake to 49.5 percent in Newmont through open-market purchases, but which limited Gold Fields' representation on Newmont's board to 40 percent of the directors. Newmont then issued a dividend of $33 per share to all shareholders, which provided Gold Fields with the financing necessary to conduct open-market purchases that increased its equity position in Newmont to 49.7 percent. The Delaware Supreme Court held that no sale of control had occurred because the standstill agreement guaranteed Newmont's continued independence and because Gold Fields had purchased its stock from private sellers and not from the company.

In *The Black & Decker Corp. v. American Standard Inc.,* following a hostile tender offer by Black & Decker, American Standard proposed a reorganization recapitalization involving the payment of a cash and debenture dividend to shareholders, and the sale of stock to both management (in exchange for outstanding options) and to the company ESOP (for cash). The recapitalized company would be owned 24 percent by management and 35 percent by the ESOP. The board also amended certain benefit plans so that the company's $80 million pension surplus would have been unavailable (except for reinvestment) upon a "change in control," but specifically excluded the recapitalization plan from the definition of change of control, thereby precluding bidders other than management or the ESOP from utilizing the surplus.

Rejecting management claims that the recapitalization plan merely represented an effort to keep American Standard independent, the Delaware Federal District Court found that the plan constituted an offer by the board to gain control. The court held that the lowering of the public's stake from 92.6 percent to 45 percent, after the exercise of all management stock options, would constitute a change in control amounting to a sale of the company. The court also found that by sweetening its recapitalization after Black & Decker had increased its offer, American Standard implicitly recognized that the company had reached the auction stage. Accordingly, the court held that the board's attempt to lock up the pension surplus violated the board's obligation to conduct a neutral auction for the company under the principles set forth in *Revlon Inc. v. MacAndrews & Forbes Holdings Inc.* ("*Revlon*").

Finally, the case of *Robert M. Bass Group Inc. v. Edward P. Evans* involved a spin-off and dividend recapitalization worth $65 per share that was proposed by Macmillan Inc. in the face of a tender offer by the Bass Group worth $73 per share. The recapitalization proposed to split Macmillan into two entities: Information was to be spun off to shareholders; and Publishing was to be highly leveraged and was to provide shareholders with a cash dividend, a debenture, and stub equity. A management group that held a 4 percent equity position in Macmillan proposed to forego the cash and debenture aspect of the dividend, and exchange options and restricted shares recently granted to management (together with the value of the cash and debentures dividend foregone) for 39 percent of the spun-off entity's equity. In addition, the Macmillan ESOP was to purchase 26 percent of Macmillan's stub equity using company-provided debt. The board's financial advisers viewed the management offer as adequate in the face of the higher offer, despite its lower value, based on the assumption that the recapitalization did not effect a "change in control."

Noting that management's 39 percent stake in Information gave it effective control of 50 percent of the Information shares that were likely, based on historical patterns, to be present and voting at any given meeting of shareholders, the Delaware Chancery Court held that a sale of effective control would occur under the recapitalization. By failing to consider that a control premium was due for management's stake, the recapitalization was held to be clearly inferior to the competing, higher bid and thus constituted an unreasonable response to the tender offer. The exclusion of a shareholder vote on whether to accept the economically inferior management proposal exacerbated the recapitalization's unreasonableness.

As the *American Standard* and *Macmillan* decisions illustrate, the implementation of a defensive recapitalization in response to a perceived threat to the company that provides for the issuance to management and/or an ESOP of an equity stake in the company sufficient to constitute "effective control" may be deemed to be a "sale of the corporation." Whether a given restructuring that is proposed in the context of a contest for control entails a sale of control and triggers the board's obligation to auction the company will depend on the facts and circumstance of each case.

In making such a determination, courts have looked to whether the percentage of shares acquired would as a "practical certainty" guarantee the power to choose a majority of the directors in due course, in light of the existence of other organized blocks of stock sufficient to outvote the block in question or other circumstances making it likely that enough shareholders would band together to keep the acquired block from obtaining control. In such circumstances, courts have recognized that substantial minority interests ranging from 20 percent to 40 percent often provide the holder with working control, especially where the balance of the shares are widely held.

Effect of Change in Control Determination

Once a sale of control may be deemed to have occurred, the principles set forth in *Revlon* become applicable. These principles require the board to assume the role of a neutral auctioneer charged with obtaining the best price for the stockholders of the company. Under *Revlon,* the board will be obligated to accept the best offer for the company and may "tilt the playing field" and favor one bidder over another only after a full auction and if the bid favored is clearly more favorable under the circumstances.

As discussed elsewhere in this book, a board of directors is not obligated to negotiate with tender offerers for the sale of a company, or to accept an undesirable offer, even if the offer provides for a substantial premium over the then-prevailing market price. Indeed, a board has a fiduciary duty to oppose tender offers that are contrary to the best interests of the company and its shareholders. This duty is circumscribed by the requirement that the response to the threat to the corporation must be "reasonable."

In contrast to a recapitalization adopted primarily in response to a takeover threat, courts have shown great deference to the vigorous defense of recapitalization plans that are already under way at the time a bid is announced. Accordingly, courts have upheld ongoing recapitalizations having significant antitakeover effects that effectively precluded the offerer from going forward with its bid, and which offered a present value to shareholders that was less than the amount offered by the competing bidder, as in the case of the Henley Group Inc.'s failing bid for Sante Fe Southern Pacific Corp.

Although defensive measures adopted to defend an ongoing recapitalization plan will be subject to the more strict "reasonable response" standard, the original adoption of the plan will generally be scrutinized under the "ordinary business judgment" rule, that is, whether the plan serves a legitimate business purpose and does not have a clear purpose and effect of entrenching management. However, an ongoing recapitalization that effects a transfer of effective control amounting to a "sale of the company" may not be entitled to scrutiny under the ordinary business judgment rule, but may be scrutinized under the more strict standard of *Revlon,* if *Revlon* auction principles are deemed to have been triggered by the competing bid.

Mechanics for Changing Ownership Patterns

With this background, we can examine how ownership patterns can be affected by various forms of restructuring. At the outset, it should be noted that if additional shares are to be issued or equity-based compensation plans are to be adopted in connection with a restructuring, a shareholder vote may be required or advisable even if the form of the restructuring is not such as would otherwise require a shareholder vote under applicable state corporate law. Stock exchange rules may require shareholder approval prior to the issuance of new stock. Or, if the existing equity-based compensation plans of the company do not already permit the substitution of new common stock benefits for the existing common stock benefits, or it appears that other material changes will have to be made to the existing plans, the company may wish to obtain the benefits of the safe harbor for executive officers of the company who will be participating in the plans under Rule 16b-3 promulgated under the Securities Exchange Act of 1934, as amended (the "1934 act").

1. *Merger recapitalization.* In a recapitalization structured as a merger, a shell corporation is merged with and into the company, with the company as the surviving corporation. In the merger, outstanding shares of common stock held by the public are converted into shares of new common stock of the surviving corporation (the so-called stub equity), plus cash, and/or debt securities. Management and employee stock ownership plans receive only shares of the stub equity in exchange for their shares of the company's stock, and generally any nonequity payments to management are also invested in new company shares of equal value. The law of the state of the company's incorporation and the company's charter will determine the shareholder approval requirements that apply to the merger recapitalization; most mergers will require some degree of shareholder approval.

For publicly traded companies, the securities into which the common stock will be converted pursuant to the merger must be registered with the Securities and Exchange Commission (SEC) under the Securities Act of 1933, as amended (the "1933 act")—absent availability of the exemption from registration afforded to securities issued pursuant to an issuer exchange offer by Rule 3(a)(9) under the 1933 act. Also, the proxy/prospectus for the shareholders meeting must comply with the proxy rules promulgated pursuant to the 1934 act. Preparation, filing, and review of the registration statement and proxy/prospectus by the SEC will typically require 60 to 90 days.

Although the shareholder approval requirement may make it more difficult to effect the transaction, a merger recapitalization approved by shareholders presents the most favorable opportunity for increasing the equity stake of management vis-à-vis the public and is most likely to be upheld by the courts. It is also common to request shareholder approval of additional antitakeover charter provisions, such as the implementation of a staggered board, the adoption of supermajority voting requirements with respect to business combinations, and the removal of directors without cause, or the authorization of "blank check" preferred stock for use in a poison pill. Usually, these additional items are submitted to shareholders together with the recapitalization plan as a single proposal, with the dividend serving as the "carrot" for obtaining approval of the antitakeover proposals.

2. Reclassification recapitalization. In a recapitalization involving a reclassification of currently existing stock by charter amendment, public stockholders of the recapitalized company typically will receive some combination of cash, debt securities, and stub equity in the recapitalized company. Management and employee stock ownership plans, on the other hand, usually forego the nonequity portion of the reclassification distribution and receive only equity in the recapitalized company, and increase their proportionate voting power vis-à-vis the public. Reclassifications generally require shareholder approval of the charter amendment under the law of the state of incorporation. In contrast to the merger structure, under Delaware law, shareholders are not entitled to appraisal rights in a reclassification. The 1933 act registration and 1934 act proxy requirements applicable to a merger recapitalization also apply to a reclassification.

Until recently, the issuance, pursuant to a reclassification recapitalization, of "supervoting" stock having voting rights greater than the per-share voting rights of existing common stock, but containing transfer restrictions requiring the stock to be converted into lower voting stock if sold, was a popular method of increasing the ownership position of insiders and long-term holders. The issuance of such supervoting stock by companies traded on a national exchange or quoted on the National Association of Securities Dealers Automatic Quotation System is now prohibited under Rule 19c-4 of the 1934 act, which prohibits the issuance of stock having the effect of nullifying, restricting, or disparately reducing the per-share voting rights of existing common stock shareholders of the company.

3. *Dividend recapitalization.* A dividend recapitalization typically is less useful for increasing the proportionate voting power of management because the dividend must be distributed equally to all stockholders (although the cash portion of a dividend may be reinvested by management in additional company shares). Most dividend recapitalizations are accompanied by the issuance of stock to a company ESOP, and options or restricted stock to management in order to have the desired effect. A special one-time cash dividend may be used to increase the voting power of a white squire, as in *Newmont,* where the dividend proceeds were used to acquire additional shares of the company's stock in a street sweep.

Shareholder approval of a dividend generally is not required. If the applicable state law does not permit payment of the dividend desired—for example, if payment of the dividend would impair capital in violation of the law of the company's state of incorporation—a merger recapitalization requiring shareholder approval may be necessary. Cash payments in a merger are not considered dividends subject to the capital impairment limitations applicable under state law. The issuance of supervoting stock pursuant to a stock dividend, like the issuance of supervoting stock pursuant to a reclassification, is prohibited under Rule 19c-4.

4. *Stock repurchase, tender, or exchange offer recapitalization.* An issuer self-tender for a fixed number of shares of common stock, whether for cash or securities of the company, will increase the relative ownership position of management vis-à-vis the public if management agrees not to tender its shares into the offer. An issuer may also repurchase a significant number of its securities through an open-market purchase program subject to appropriate legal safeguards so that the purchases are not deemed to be a tender offer under Section 14d of the 1934 act. Usually, even though no competing bid has surfaced, the exchange offer is likely to offer a substantial premium in order to induce shareholders to tender. Therefore, if management chooses not to tender in order

to increase their equity interest vis-à-vis the public, management may be at a financial disadvantage.

As has been noted, a self-tender or repurchase program is an effective technique for increasing management's ownership if management already has a significant ownership interest in the company, but is less useful if management does not have a significant equity stake prior to the tender offer. In a situation where management does not have a significant equity stake, it is important in connection with the restructuring to arrange for the issuance of additional equity to management. This device generally does not require shareholder approval but, in the case of an issuer tender or exchange offer, will be subject to the timing obligations imposed by the 1934 act, which requires among other things that a tender offer remain open for a minimum of 20 business days. Since the adoption of the "all-holders" rule under Section 13e-4 of the 1934 act, a company may no longer exclude certain stockholders (such as a hostile bidder) from a self-tender or exchange offer, and the consideration paid to any security holder pursuant to the tender offer must be the highest consideration paid to any other security holder.

5. *Spin-offs, split-ups, dispositions.*   A spin-off of a subsidiary or division and distribution of stock in the new entity to stockholders typically does not afford management an opportunity to increase its proportionate equity ownership because the distribution is made pro rata to all shareholders. However, if the spin-off is accompanied by a nonequity dividend, management may elect, with board approval, to forego the nonequity component of the dividend and exchange the value of their holdings for shares in the spun-off entity, as was proposed by the management of Macmillan. Management's equity position may be proportionately increased by giving it a larger stake in the spun-off entity than is offered to public shareholders. As a dividend, this structure ordinarily would not require shareholder approval. However, courts have held that such transactions, if proposed in response to a competing bid (as in the *Macmillan* case), may not be "crammed down" on shareholders and preclude shareholders from considering an economically equivalent (or superior) offer.

Under Delaware law, shareholder approval may be required if the spun-off operations are deemed to constitute "all or substantially all" of the company's assets under Section 271 of the Delaware General Corporation law *and* the spin-off constitutes a "sale" or "exchange" of assets of the company for purposes of Section 271. Although no cases have addressed the latter issue directly, prudence suggests that the company obtain shareholder approval if the spin-off involves all or substantially all of the company's assets. No shareholder approval of a spin-off is required under the rules of the New York or American Stock Exchange.

Generally, the shares of a company's subsidiary being spun off to the company's shareholders in a distribution do not have to be registered under the 1933 act, provided that (1) recipients are provided with an information statement (if no shareholder approval is sought), in either case complying with the proxy requirements of the 1934 act; (2) the spin-off shares are registered under the 1934 act prior to the distribution; and (3) certain other conditions are met. A spin-off will be tax-free to the shareholders of a parent company, provided that certain highly technical requirements under Section 355 of the Internal Revenue Code are met.

6. *White squire transactions.* A transaction with a white squire may be variously structured as a short-term capital infusion or as a long-term strategic investment. The former structure is frequently used to enable the company to undertake another form of restructuring, such as the self-tender effected by Gelco Corp. (financed by Merrill Lynch's equity purchase) or the dividend paid by Harcourt Brace Jovanovich (financed by First Boston, which demanded a significant equity stake to monitor its investment).

In the case of Gelco Corp., the equity issued to the white squire (constituting approximately 51 percent of the voting power of the company when added to existing management shares) was sufficient to constitute effective control. However, such shares were viewed as being a substitute for bridge financing: The shares paid a high fixed dividend, were redeemable at the company's option, and were free from voting restrictions. Accordingly, the sale to Merrill Lynch was not deemed to constitute a shift in control of the company.

By contrast, long-term defensive white squire transactions, such as Consolidated Gold Fields' investment in Newmont Mining, often have the primary purpose of enabling the white squire to obtain a long-term equity stake sufficient to deter unsolicited bids. The "neutrality" of the white squire may be assured to a significant degree by a standstill agreement. In the Newmont case, the standstill agreement provided for white squire board representation proportionate to the board's nominees (with the remaining directors being independent) and for transfer restrictions on the white squire's stock, which limited resales to third parties who agreed to abide by the standstill terms.

Although upheld under the facts present in Newmont, such devices may be subject to attack as furthering managerial entrenchment, and must be carefully drafted to pass judicial scrutiny. Because of the potential entrenchment issues presented by such transactions, white squire standstill agreements generally should not be viewed as a guarantee for increasing management's voting power.

Additional Antitakeover Devices

As has been noted, a highly leveraged company is an easier target for hostile acquirers. Management may wish to couple the incurrence of additional debt with the adoption of antitakeover devices that will increase the possibility that shareholders will realize the longer-term benefits of the restructuring. A shareholder vote will be required to adopt certain antitakeover devices, such as charter amendments providing for a staggered board, supermajority voting, or fair-price requirements for extraordinary corporate transactions, "blank check" preferred stock, or restrictions on action by written consent (which, under Delaware law, must be in the charter). By increasing the vote required to approve mergers—for example, from a majority to two-thirds or more—an effective veto of unsolicited acquisition proposals can be placed in the hands of management without giving management complete control.

It is well settled that shareholders have no fiduciary duties to their fellow shareholders to tender stock into a tender offer or to vote in favor of a merger just because a good price is offered. In addition, tying the value paid to shareholders to approval of the antitakeover devices will give shareholders the incentive needed to give their approval. Other defensive measures may be adopted by the board alone, without shareholder approval, such as a poison pill, a bylaw amendment restricting shareholders' ability to call special meetings, or a selective stock repurchase program.

Securing Independence

Corporate restructurings are designed to enhance shareholder values. As such, they protect against unsolicited takeovers by reducing or eliminating the premium over market that a potential acquirer can afford to pay. The mere fact that the restructured company may be less attractive financially to potential acquirers does not mean that the restructuring itself cannot be a useful vehicle for securing continued independence by increasing the percentage of a company's voting securities subject to the control either of management or of a white squire or ESOP friendly to management.

The percentage of ownership interest granted in the restructuring and the extent to which the voting power represented by such interest is deemed to be subject to management's control are crucial factors in any judicial determination of the validity of the restructuring. The grant of an ownership interest that constitutes effective control may well be deemed to be a "sale of control" under *Revlon*. If so, in the event that another bidder surfaces, the board's duty to auction the company under *Revlon* may be triggered, and may thwart the board's ability to defend the company's independence, let alone the restructuring.

The timing of the adoption of the restructuring in relation to the challenge to corporate control will significantly affect the ability of the restructuring to withstand judicial scrutiny. Restructurings adopted well in advance of a challenge to control are less likely to be viewed as being motivated by management entrenchment. Even if the restructuring clearly has antitakeover effects, so long as it was adopted prior to the control challenge, it is more likely to be reviewed under the ordinary business judgment rule rather than the heightened scrutiny of the "reasonable response" test.

Finally, the decision of whether or not to seek shareholder approval of the restructuring is an important one that must be weighed against the additional time and risk presented in seeking such approval. Shareholder approval not only provides an opportunity to adopt additional antitakeover defenses that may protect the restructuring, but also, if shareholders approve the transaction, offers significant protection against the restructuring being overturned by the courts.

10

Creating Value through the Unbundling of Corporate Assets

Barbara Moakler Byrne

Managing Director,
Shearson Lehman Hutton Inc.

More and more, the unbundling of corporate assets is proving to be a particularly effective way of enhancing shareholder value. Like any powerful tool, however, it has to be applied with care, or it can backfire on its user. Unbundling often radically alters a company's structure, finances, and operations. The decision on whether to pursue this strategy should not, therefore, be governed simply by its anticipated effect on share price. It must be tailored to the specific characteristics of the assets under consideration and integrally related to a well-defined corporate restructuring strategy. Only when management has a comprehensive view of what the unbundling will accomplish can it choose intelligently the unbundling method that best serves its objectives.

Nevertheless, the issue of asset valuation does lie at the core of all unbundling decisions. In the recent spate of corporate unbundling, managers have obviously been responding to the investment community's growing inclination to focus more narrowly on return on equity and shareholder value as measures of company performance. Reacting against the vogue for corporate diversification in the 1970s, investors are now more impressed with corporate strategies that build upon a company's core business. More specifically, they have become convinced that companies will be more competitive if they let go of assets that are undervalued (or, more precisely, are perceived to be undervalued) in a corporation's market capitalization—or even worse, assets that are dragging down the valuation of the corporation itself. By unbundling, management can at the same time sharpen its operating focus on the business lines in which the company is strongest and thereby enhance shareholder value. What is more, the unbundling improves the company's ability to ward off hostile takeover bids.

Unbundling decisions properly start, then, with a determination that certain corporate assets are undervalued. Such assets usually have one or more of the following characteristics:

- *Small size.* Assets that contribute such a small part of the parent company's earnings that their valuation is subsumed by that of the parent, yet whose operations are comparable to publicly traded companies that are trading at higher earnings multiples than the parent's.

- *Hidden strengths.* Assets that are carried off balance sheet, have fully depreciated book value, or generate limited income, yet have substantial value because of their strategic worth or cash flow-generating capability.

- *Inappropriate valuation.* Specific assets are normally valued on a basis that is uniquely appropriate for them—either financial (which can in turn be based on earnings, cash flow, or capital multiple), operating, or risk-adjusted. If the financial markets apply a valuation method to the parent that is not appropriate for the subsidiary, the subsidiary's full value may not be realized within the parent's market capitalization.

- *Inappropriate ownership structure.* Assets, particularly those with a strong, consistent cash flow, that would be valued higher in the market if they were under a different corporate structure (or a smaller one).

- *Inefficient management incentives.* Assets or subsidiaries, particularly those with an entrepreneurial corporate culture, that are experiencing rapid growth within a mature parent company and that would perform better under a separate, clearly focused management with an incentive-based compensation system.

- *Potential synergies.* Assets that would realize greater value by being sold to another entity with which they have operating, financial, or tax synergies. This is particularly true for assets with associated tax-loss carryforwards that are not being fully utilized by the parent company.

There are also instances in which the corporate asset causes the *parent* company to be undervalued. This typically occurs when the subsidiary is in a declining or depressed industry whose operations investors perceive as a drain on the earnings or management of the parent company. Or the subsidiary may be involved in a business with a different, and usually more adverse, regulatory or risk environment than the parent company's.

Unbundling Options

Once management determines that an asset is undervalued (or is causing the parent company to be undervalued), it should then review the unbundling options available, seeking the one that addresses most effectively the cause of the undervaluation and that best conforms to the company's tax and operational profile.

The most basic unbundling decision revolves around the issue of continuing control: Will management wish to retain some form of interest in the assets or subsidiary? If it will, then a partial spin-off, minority sale, or joint venture is called for. If not, then the answer is a divestiture—through spin-off, a swap of assets or operations for stock or assets, or an outright sale, either to a corporate purchaser or to employees by means of a leveraged buyout and/or employee stock ownership plan (ESOP). (See Table 10-1.)

Various kinds of spin-off devices can be used to accomplish either a partial or a complete unbundling. While the financial press refers to spin-offs generically, they actually fall into three different categories:

Table 10-1. Unbundling Options

To retain an interest	No continuing interest
Initial public offering	Initial public offering
Master limited partnership	Shareholder distribution
Shareholder distribution (including alphabet stock)	Swap of corporate assets with a third party or swap of assets for stock
Sale of minority interest	Sale to a third party or to present management through a leveraged buyout
Joint venture	

initial public offerings (IPOs), master limited partnerships (MLPs), and shareholder distributions. Each may in turn be structured in several ways to meet management objectives.

Initial Public Offering

In an IPO the parent company sells shares of a subsidiary to the public. There can be any variation of primary and secondary shares and of subsidiary and intercompany debt to maximize cash proceeds and to minimize the tax consequences of the sale to the parent. The parent can continue to receive cash from the subsidiary through dividends or payments of ongoing contractual or intercompany obligations. Similarly, the parent may retain varying degrees of interest in the spun-off company. With at least an 80 percent interest, it can tax-consolidate the subsidiary; with greater than a 50 percent interest, it can continue to financially consolidate and control the subsidiary. At lower ownership levels, the parent carries its interest in the subsidiary on an equity basis. However, it may still be able to control the subsidiary through disproportionate voting rights or supermajority provisions.

An IPO of primary shares in a subsidiary creates a higher-valued acquisition currency in the form of publicly traded equity that was undervalued in the parent's market capitalization. It generates added market liquidity, reduces acquisition-related dilution, and can be used as a financing vehicle for the parent or for the subsidiary. This device was used in the 1986 IPO of Chemical Waste Management Inc., a subsidiary of Waste Management Inc. Raising $326 million through dividends and the repayment of intercompany obligations, the parent also increased its equity because the market value of the subsidiary exceeded its carrying value on its books. In the $510 million IPO in 1988 of 13 percent of Burlington Resources Inc., a natural resource company, by its parent, Burlington Northern Inc., a railroad and resource conglomerate, net proceeds were contributed to the subsidiary to fund future growth. Such an offering of a U.S. subsidiary can also be an attractive way for a foreign company to gain access to U.S. public markets while retaining full control. Von Roll Ltd., a Swiss steel producer, did this in 1987 in its $37 million IPO of its U.S. subsidiary, New Jersey Steel Corp.

A secondary-share IPO is an alternative to a third-party sale. It permits the parent to restructure the subsidiary and position it in the public markets to promote successful operations, continuity of management, and investor visibility. In 1986, USX Corp. sold its chemical subsidiary, Aristech Chemical Inc., for $320 million in this manner.

An IPO's potential disadvantages of an unbundling vehicle will depend on how it is structured. When the parent company retains an interest in the subsidiary, the offering can be an expensive way to raise parent equity, especially if the subsidiary has projected high earnings growth and good cash flow-generating characteristics. Such an IPO also restricts the parent's access to the subsidiary's cash flow, which the parent can tap only through dividends or payments of on-going contractual or intercompany obligations. An IPO in which the parent does not retain an interest usually costs more to execute than a third-party sale.

Moreover, IPO spin-offs that are not carefully structured usually fail to create value. Care must be taken to ensure that by differentiating earning streams the IPO does not encourage parent shareholders to sell the parent and buy the subsidiary, thereby impairing the parent's market value. In addition, the IPO must be of sufficient size, with broad enough distribution, to ensure adequate market liquidity. Most important, the parent must avoid creating the perception that it is stripping the subsidiary of current cash proceeds, future financial flexibility, and upside potential.

An IPO generally is most appropriate when a subsidiary is undervalued due to its:

- Small size relative to its parent, and operations that, if separately traded, would bring a higher price-to-earnings multiple than the parent's.
- Limited contribution to the income of the parent.
- Improper valuation within the parent company because of the different nature of its assets, or capital, business, or financial needs .

Master Limited Partnership

A parent company may contribute undervalued assets to a master limited partnership, then sell or distribute limited partnership units to its shareholders or the public. The Revenue Act of 1987 limited the type of undervalued assets that can be contributed to an MLP: They must now be, generally, real estate or natural resource operations. (Before, any asset or operation with consistent cash flow was eligible for restructuring into an MLP.) The parent, as the MLP's general partner, always retains control of the underlying assets, regardless of how few limited partnership units it owns. The general partner can also retain some of the upside potential in the underlying assets through incentive fees, promoted interests, and advantageous splits in distributions.

An MLP allows assets to be sold at a multiple of distributable cash flow rather than net income, and allows the company sponsoring the MLP to exercise management control while effectively moving the assets off balance sheet and transferring ownership risks to investors. MLPs typically maximize cash proceeds with publicly or privately placed debt, as in Penn Central Corp.'s 1986 MLP spin-off of Buckeye Partners Ltd., a products pipeline. Penn Central was able to maintain control over the pipeline while receiving more cash proceeds than would have been obtained through a third-party sale.

MLPs do have disadvantages as a spin-off vehicle, including sensitivity to interest-rate changes, since they trade on a cash basis, and the high level of cash distributions required, which could hamper operations in a company with sustained and substantial capital needs. In addition, an MLP sponsor may need to support the MLP to boost investor confidence by subordinating the return on its own retained limited partnership units to ensure a minimum guaranteed return for the public holders.

An MLP generally is most appropriate when the underlying assets generate high predictable cash flow and possess some or all of the following characteristics:

- Stable operations that are relatively insensitive to cyclical swings

- High basis held by the parent corporation, to minimize tax on sale

- Moderate capital expenditure requirements (or capital expenditures that can be financed externally), which can maximize cash available for distribution

- Ability to take tax deductions in order to shelter distributable cash flow

Distribution of a Corporate Business to Shareholders

A parent company can distribute shares of a wholly owned subsidiary to its existing shareholders. Generally, such a distribution is structured to be tax-free, with no gain or loss recognized by either the parent company or the shareholders.

Certain conditions must be met for a tax-free distribution: Parent shareholders must have a material continuing interest in the distributed subsidiary; there must be a valid business purpose for the transaction; the subsidiary must be at least 80 percent owned by the parent; at least 80 percent of all stock must be distributed; both parent and subsidiary must have actively conducted their respective lines of business for the five years preceding the distribution; and control of the subsidiary must not have been acquired in a taxable transaction in the five years immediately preceding the distribution.

A pro-rata tax-free distribution is the most popular form, accounting for more than 90 percent of all shareholder distributions in the past 12 years. (A pro-rata distribution is the technical definition of a spin-off.) Other possible forms are a "split-off" (giving each shareholder the option to exchange parent company shares for the subsidiary's), or a "split-up" (a pro-rata distribution of subsidiary shares to parent company shareholders executed when the parent company is liquidating).

An alternative form of distribution to shareholders is "alphabet stock," a separately traded class of parent company common stock whose value is tied to a specific subsidiary. Alphabet stock allows the parent to retain control of a subsidiary regardless of the amount of shares it distributes. The parent always consolidates the earnings of the special subsidiary, reporting earnings for each class of shares. Alphabet stock usually is issued through an exchange offer or a dividend to shareholders. It has been used only twice—by General Motors Corp. in its acquisitions of Electronic Data Systems Corp. and Hughes Aircraft Co.—to create a higher-valued acquisition currency by capitalizing businesses that have clearly distinguishable streams of earnings and that would trade on a freestanding basis at a higher price-to-earnings multiple than the parent's.

A shareholder distribution allows investors to value the parent and the subsidiary as separate entities and permits shareholders to participate in any improvement in the distributed company's performance, avoiding the perception that the parent company sold the subsidiary at the low point of a cycle. It also transfers the assets and liabilities of the subsidiary at their book value, with no gain or loss by the parent. Consequently, unless the assets involved in the spin-off have lost value and a write-off is required prior to the distribution, a parent can divest a subsidiary with a higher book than market value without incurring a loss.

This was demonstrated in the distribution effected in 1983 by Time Inc., which was battered by recession and the high capital expenditures required by its Temple-Inland Inc. forestry business. A tax-free distribution enabled the parent company to avoid a capital loss in the disposition of Temple-Inland and provided Time more efficient access to capital markets. Shareholders benefited from a change in the business cycle and its positive impact on Temple-Inland's value.

Although a shareholder distribution raises less cash than other disposition alternatives, it can enhance the performance of both entities and reduce parent company debt by leveraging the subsidiary. Shareholder liquidity can be increased by allowing shareholders to maintain their position in the parent company, with the possibility of selling shares in the spun-off entity in the future. This is particularly useful in meeting the disparate needs of second- and third-generation members of a family controlling a publicly owned company. For family-controlled Rollins Inc., two tax-free shareholder distributions in 1984 captured independent market values for the company's energy services and communication subsidiaries and simultaneously increased shareholder value and market liquidity.

A shareholder distribution may also be appropriate for a parent company that wants to divest a subsidiary for strategic reasons, but finds that the sale of the subsidiary would not maximize shareholder value because of the substantial amount of taxes the sale would produce. Typically, such spin-offs involve natural resource properties with a potential for substantial associated depreciation recapture liability. The proposed 1988 tax-free distribution of 100 percent of Sun Exploration & Production Inc. from Sun Inc., and the spin-off of the remaining 87 percent of Burlington Resources from Burlington Northern, are prominent examples of this type of transaction.

Shareholder distributions have certain disadvantages. No immediate cash is raised, the parent's business shrinks, and it loses control of the subsidiary. The device requires substantial lead time and management effort to ensure tax-free status. If such status is not granted by the Internal Revenue Service, the distribution is taxable to shareholders as an ordinary dividend and to the parent company as a capital gain or loss.

A shareholder distribution generally is most appropriate for:

- A company that has a large insider (family or management) ownership block that is interested in obtaining greater liquidity without losing control of company operations, and that has an undervalued subsidiary with a clearly distinguishable earnings stream that would trade at a higher price-to-earnings multiple than its parents

- A company undervalued due to a subsidiary in a declining or depressed industry, whose operations investors perceive as a drain on the earnings or the management of the parent company

- A company for whom a taxable sale of a subsidiary would trigger substantial tax liabilities

Other Options for Partial or Complete Unbundlings

In addition to the three spin-off devices outlined above, there are other options uniquely suited for either partial or complete unbundlings. Partial unbundlings may be accomplished through a joint venture or a direct sale of a minority interest in the subsidiary or parent company. (A third option, not covered here, is the use of sale-leaseback transactions to realize certain asset values, particularly those involving real estate.)

Joint Venture

Joint ventures allow subsidiaries to be used as currency in forming a partnership that increases the scope and size of the subsidiary's operation. Although a joint venture is not a divestiture, it gives the parent the opportunity to deconsolidate an underperforming asset that is a drain on the parent, while maintaining an interest in the company. In 1986, for example, GTE Corp. and United Telecommunications Inc. each contributed their long-distance telephone units to a joint venture they named U.S. Sprint Communications Co. As a result, both subsidiaries were able to realize economies of scale, and both parents were able to deconsolidate money-losing subsidiaries.

A joint venture can also create a strategic alliance that provides the subsidiary with access to critical markets, technology, or distribution channels that can significantly enhance the subsidiary's market competitiveness, profits, and value. For Intel Corp., a major semiconductor firm, a 1988 joint venture with Siemens AG, the West German computer company, provided entry to computer manufacturing. Siemens in turn gained access to U.S. markets in which it had no established channels of distribution.

While they are the least radical form of unbundling, joint ventures still entail certain trade-offs. The parent has to share management control of the subsidiary, has its asset base reduced due to deconsolidation if its ownership interest falls below 50 percent, and has the subsidiary tax deconsolidated if its ownership interest falls below 80 percent.

Direct Sale of Minority Interest in Subsidiary or Parent Company

In a sale of a minority interest, a company sells an equity interest in itself or a subsidiary to a third party. The sale can be structured in several ways, but generally involves less than 20 percent of a subsidiary in order to be able to continue to tax consolidate the subsidiary. Minority-interest purchasers contribute capital to a company in return for access to management, technology, information, or new or more secure markets. Minority-interest sellers achieve a strategic alliance in new markets and capital to help position themselves to capture market share in those markets. In addition, from a defense standpoint, such minority investors generally are management-friendly should a hostile takeover attempt emerge.

Management should be aware that, to realize the synergistic benefits from the sale of a minority interest, a substantial amount of the parent's and the investor's management time and effort is generally required. Management should also take into account the potential future liability of the implied "put" of the minority interest back to the parent company should the investor choose to sell its ownership interest.

Sales of minority interests are generally most appropriate for:

- A company in a capital-intensive business where a strategic alliance will help to gain a firm foothold in untapped expanding markets

- A company in a capital-intensive and cyclical industry or with high working capital needs, and which distributes large amounts of a single type of vendor's products, where a strategic alliance can create value by securing low-cost and stable channels of distribution for the minority-interest purchaser and a steady, competitively priced and financed vendor relationship

The most recent examples of the former type of transaction have occurred in the securities industry. Several "bulge-bracket" firms, such as Shearson Lehman Hutton Inc. and Goldman, Sachs & Co., have sold minority equity interests to Japanese financial institutions in order to gain additional capital, promote mutual education about each other's way of doing business, and gain access to distribution capabilities in one of the world's largest and most insular financial markets.

The use of minority interests in the form of vendor financing has been demonstrated most recently in leveraged buyouts. In the 1987 LBO of Hertz Corp., Ford Motor Co. acted as the principal equity participant; a year later it sold 20 percent of Hertz's equity to Volvo North America Corp. for $100 million cash plus a supply arrangement to increase the use of Volvo cars by Hertz. In another example of this technique, Masco Corp., a building materials supplier, agreed in 1988 to purchase LBO debt and preferred equity of Payless Cashways Inc., a do-it-yourself home-improvement retailer, in exchange for a multiyear supply contract and a preferred equity position.

If management wishes to effect a complete unbundling, it has two other options: a swap of corporate assets, and direct sale to a third party.

Swap of Corporate Assets

In an asset swap, corporate assets can be exchanged for those assets of another company that are similar in type, perform the same function, or are used in the same line of business, so that no gain or loss is recognized on the transfer of assets except for cash and other nonrelated property exchanged. Tax-free swaps can also involve the exchange of equity for assets, regardless of whether the companies involved are in the same line of business.

The most advanced use of this mechanism was the 1980 sale by Esmark Inc. to Mobil Corp. of the Transocean exploration unit of its Vickers Energy Corp., through a swap. Mobil tendered for 54 percent of Esmark's shares at a price totaling its bid for Transocean and swapped the shares with Esmark for the shares of Transocean. The tax-free transaction enabled Esmark effectively to repurchase its stock with the tax-free proceeds from its disposition of Transocean.

Asset swaps involving similar operations can strengthen a company's competitive position and create value through the economies of scale achieved by the use of an established distribution system. Such economies were obtained by Borden Inc. and Unilever's Thomas J. Lipton Inc. subsidiary, which in 1987 swapped assets and operations in product lines that could be distributed more advantageously through the other company's established market channels. Borden swapped its powdered soft-drink business for Lipton's Pennsylvania Dutch Egg Noodle business plus cash, making Borden the largest pasta marketer in the United States and strengthening Lipton's position in powdered drink mixes.

Similar asset swaps carry certain potential drawbacks. To the extent that nonsimilar assets, cash, or a net reduction of liabilities are transferred, a taxable gain is recognized in the swap. The major disadvantage of a tax-free swap of equity for assets, as in the Mobil-Vickers transaction discussed above, is that a transitory ownership of stock cast a cloud of doubt over the tax-free status of the transaction. In fact, the tax-free nature of that transaction was challenged by the IRS because of the temporary nature of Mobil's shareholder position. In January 1988, the tax court ruled in favor of Esmark; the decision may be appealed. Consequently, at this writing there is some uncertainty as to whether this technique is currently viable. Alternative modified swap structures have been devised that partially achieve the objectives of the Esmark transaction. These typically involve the creation of a time lag between the purchase of shares and the asset swap, as in CalMat Co.'s 1988 divestiture of its cement business to Onoda, a Japanese cement company.

Swaps of corporate assets are generally most appropriate for:

- Companies that intend to use the proceeds of an asset disposition to acquire similar productive assets or similar businesses to reposition the asset base

- Companies that intend to shrink their asset and equity base and for whom the tax-free exchange of assets is an effective way to repurchase stock

Direct Sale to Third Party

The most direct and most common form of complete unbundling is a sale to a third party, in an arm's-length transaction with a corporate buyer or LBO purchaser. A direct sale can be accomplished quickly and generates cash proceeds. In fact, it usually generates more cash for the parent company than any alternative, since the purchaser frequently has operating or financial synergies with the subsidiary being sold and thus can achieve values not inherent in the operations. Generally, however, it is the least flexible of all unbundling options in allowing the parent to continue in a core business. A sale also does not create an acquisition currency, and is fully taxable. In a leveraged buyout of the subsidiary, particularly where a leveraged ESOP is involved, management and employees of the subsidiary participate as equity investors in the subsidiary, which will be run as an independent entity. Because the company is not merged into an existing company's operations, disruptions to employees and communities can be minimized.

A direct sale of a subsidiary or asset is generally most appropriate for:

- A subsidiary or operation that has high strategic synergies for a potential group of third-party purchasers

- A subsidiary or operation with a strong market share, mundane and diversified products in a noncyclical industry, stable cash flow, and a rich asset or collateral base where capital expenditure requirements are relatively low and where the assets could sustain a high level of debt

Unbundling and a Company's Financial and Strategic Objectives

Finally, in planning an unbundling strategy, management must decide how the unbundling will promote the overall financial and strategic objectives of the corporation. It will need to determine how important it is for the company to:

- Continue in certain businesses for core strategic reasons (and beyond that, whether to continue to tax consolidate or financially consolidate the subsidiary)
- Generate the maximum amount of cash
- Create an acquisition currency
- Promote the core business by using the asset as a swap vehicle
- Allocate parent company debt to the undervalued subsidiary or assets
- Structure a transaction that is tax-free

Table 10-2 summarizes the effectiveness of each unbundling option in meeting these goals.

The choice of unbundling method will also need to be geared to the financial and operating characteristics of the target assets themselves, including their tax and book basis, earnings and cash flow, growth potential, and debts or liabilities. Management should compare the asset's

Table 10-2. Unbundling Options and Corporate Goals

Corporate Goals	Retain Interest					No Continuing Interest			
	IPO	MLP	Shareholder Distribution	Sale of Min. Int.	Joint Venture	IPO	Shareholder Distribution	Swap	Sale
Continue in Certain Businesses	High	Moderate	High	High	Moderate	Low	Low	Moderate	Low
General Maximum Cash	High	High	Low	Moderate	Low	High	Low	Low	High
Create an Acquisition Currency	High	Moderate	High	Low	Moderate	Low	Low	High	Low
Promote Core Business	Low	Low	Low	Low	Moderate	Low	Low	High	Low
Allocate Parent Debt	High	High	High	Low	Low	High	High	Low	Moderate
Structure Tax-Free Transaction	Moderate	Moderate	Moderate	Low	High	Low	High	High	Low

Effectiveness: ● High   ◑ Moderate   ○ Low

current rate of return with the parent company's potential use of the proceeds to be obtained from the unbundling.

The Unbundling Strategy of Burlington Northern

Once management has a clear sense of its corporate restructuring priorities, the characteristics of the undervalued assets, and the effectiveness of the various unbundling methods in realizing those priorities and addressing those characteristics, it can begin the final process of choosing a specific unbundling option. The spin-off of Burlington Resources by Burlington Northern illustrates how a proactive approach to corporate restructuring can effectively employ unbundling devices.

In early 1988 Burlington Northern assessed its operations to determine whether a restructuring could enhance shareholder value. It had two diverse lines of businesses: railroad transportation and natural resources. The natural resource base consisted of land containing timber, coal, and other minerals that was granted to the railroad in the late nineteenth century by the federal government. Other natural resource operations—principally Meridian Oil and Gas, an exploration and production company, and El Paso Natural Gas Co., a gas transportation company—were acquired by Burlington Northern in the early 1980s to expand this resource base.

Burlington Northern determined that the natural resource assets, typically valued in the financial markets on a cash flow or assets basis, were not being fully valued in the market capitalization of Burlington Northern, which traded as a railroad on a multiple-of-earnings basis. Other railroad transportation companies with comparably rich asset bases, most notably Santa Fe Southern Pacific Corp., had similar disparities in the valuation methodologies applied to them. Their experience demonstrated that if management did not realize hidden asset values for shareholders through a management-initiated restructuring, a hostile takeover might be attempted to displace management and strip assets from the company.

Burlington Northern's management decided that an uncoupling of the resource and transportation business would most effectively enhance shareholder value and provide each business, particularly the resource company, with more efficient access to the capital markets. To permit this, management in early 1988 negotiated to be released from covenants in the company's 100-year-maturity debt instruments, dating from the 1890s, which required that funds from the development or sale of resource properties received in the government land grants be reinvested in the railroad. The company's principal objectives were to maintain the investment-grade rating of the railroad's debt and to provide the natural resource company with a strong capital structure so it could grow through acquisition as well as development. Consequently, management believed a complete separation of the two businesses was required. It also wanted to avoid a taxable sale of the natural resource company because of the substantial depreciation recapture taxes associated with the natural resource assets.

It finally decided on a two-step transaction. All the company's natural resource assets and associated liabilities were combined into one subsidiary, named Burlington Resources. The parent dedicated an additional $300 million to the resource entity as a contribution of capital. However, the parent's debt maintained its investment-grade rating. Burlington Northern then executed a $510 million primary-share IPO of 13 percent of Burlington Resources, the net proceeds of which were to be used to fund the growth of the resource base. The second step, announced simultaneously with the IPO, was the parent's intention to distribute the remaining 87 percent of Burlington Resources' shares to Burlington Northern's shareholders, subject to the receipt of a favorable tax ruling from the IRS. The distribution took take place in late 1988, after it had owned the El Paso Pipeline Co., acquired in 1983, for five years, the waiting period prescribed by tax law.

This two-tiered transaction allowed Burlington Northern's shareholders to benefit from the separate and tax-free positioning of the parent company as a leading railroad with an investment-quality capital structure, and of the natural resource company as a leading U.S. independent oil and gas producer and gas transportation company with a strong capitalization and a rich timber, mineral, and land asset base.

The unbundling strategy devised by Burlington Northern points the way for other companies. Undervalued assets were revealed by a careful examination of the asset base. Management then designed an unbundling plan that would most effectively capture those assets' "hidden" value, yet at the same time promote the ongoing progress of both parent and subsidiary. This comprehensive approach to unbundling will nearly always bring the greatest rewards, for it is the kind that most impresses those who will ultimately be its judge—the investment community.

11

Restructuring for Corporate Change: The Planned Divestiture Program

Peter J. Clark
Managing Director,
Maplestar Consulting Group

Divestitures were once the black sheep of corporate restructuring in the United States: necessary but reluctantly applied remedies for a host of performance ills ranging from unwise acquisitions to underachieving divisions and subsidiaries. Today, the negative image persists in some management circles. This is in spite of the fact that considerations underlying corporate divestitures have increased in complexity, along with a growth in the sophistication of the restructuring instruments used for separating one business unit from another.

Emphasis in this chapter is on the development of a corporate divestiture strategy in response to requirements of the competitive marketplace. The specific instruments of divestiture are only peripherally covered in this chapter; the mechanics of business unit sales, joint ventures, and spin-offs have been extensively covered in the current acquisition literature, and are not emphasized here.

The Divestiture Impulse: Increasing Complexity

Why would a chief executive officer (CEO) divest a key division, subsidiary, or joint venture interest? Most outside observers will jump to the conclusion that the business is a loser, or that current management cannot turn around the subsidiary or division. A sense of deflation is unavoidable: Americans tend to be expansionist by nature, and divestment suggests retreat to managers raised to think of growth as inherently good.

The negative image is supported by precedent. Conglomerateurs of the 1960s and early 1970s such as James Ling of LTV Corp. collected business units like so many bottle caps, only to face forced sale later as cash flow failed to cover acquisition interest payments. RCA Corp. and Xerox Corp. both jettisoned their mainframe computer units in the face of IBM Corp.'s dominance of large systems. ITT Corp. purchased Levitt Homebuilders, then sold the business back to its original owners upon discovering that management's expertise lay elsewhere.

Yet other divestitures defy quick categorization. New circumstances have complicated the reasons for selling, spinning off, or otherwise divesting a division or subsidiary. *Deregulation* has provided momentum for highly publicized divestitures in the surface and air transportation and telecommunications industries. The breakup of AT&T is a prime example of the latter. Changes in the structure of surface transportation regulation contributed to Greyhound Corp.'s spin-off of its bus operations to a former employee.

The acquisition boom of the 1980s contributed to an offsetting development of divestitures as a takeover defense. Management of a company "in play" may today decide to use a "scorched earth" divestiture to slow down raiders by removing desirable business units and transferring them to another firm. The raider presumably relents, as one of the attractions of the target has been removed.

Divestitures and New Corporate Strategies

Another type of divestment action that falls outside the "troubled business" category is the corporate restructuring divestiture. Over a period of time, management of the parent organization redefines and recalibrates its business unit portfolio, presumably in pursuit of a new corporate strategy that will be readily understood by employees, customers, and outside providers of capital. Examples include the following:

- ITT and Gulf and Western Inc., under CEOs Rand Araskog and Martin Davis, respectively, increased their firms' shareholder value and stock prices through corporate streamlining programs.

- Chairman and CEO Don Webber of Contel Corp. reports a desire to return to basic telecommunications upon taking on his new role. Under Webber's predecessor, Charles Wohlstetter, Contel invested in a broad range of technology concerns.

A concern of some executives is that the losses resulting from such repositioning will damage the divesting company's image in the marketplace and complicate efforts to raise capital. On the contrary, Wall Street may reward repositioning with a higher market value, since the new company is leaner, better focused, and better positioned to respond to challenges in the competitive marketplace.

A repositioning divestiture is possible only when senior management views its business operations as component parts in an overall corporate design. No business unit can be labeled "untouchable." Consider the following comments made to *The Wall Street Journal* by Wilson H. Taylor, president and CEO of CIGNA Corp.: "I am not committed to any business, product, organizational structure or approach" that does not increase shareholder value...."You can't run a big modern corporation and [allow] anything [to be] a sacred cow."

The Planned Divestiture Program Comes of Age

These deliberate divestitures differ from the forced sales of past decades in several ways. First, the ad hoc forced sale is likely to be handled by the chief financial officer, a senior strategy officer, or another corporate manager—but rarely, if ever, by the chief executive officer. The chief executive may insist on acting as the leader of the strategic repositioning divestiture program. Second, today's planned divestiture tends to be proactive by intent and design, whereas a single business unit sale is often propelled by external events. Third, the overall planned divestiture program may actually include near-term alliances, licensing arrangements, and even small acquisitions to position the unit for future divestment.

Forced divestitures of years past were typically implemented at operating levels of the firm, accompanied by a cryptic message from the chief to "fix it or get rid of it." The divestiture was seen as a problem itself, not the solution to a problem. Senior management wished to concentrate on expansion opportunities and elected to delegate responsibility for divestiture cleanup to others.

Enter the corporate workout specialist, the counterpart to a bank's senior loan workout officer. In many organizations, a single individual or group is assigned responsibility for correcting problem investments and operations. These lucky souls often were the same individuals assigned responsibility for implementing divestitures. At a hydronics company in the Midwest, the senior planning officer with an operations background is the man on the spot. At other firms, the chief financial officer is likely to be the designated divester, in part due to his or her ongoing relationships with auditors and outside providers of funds.

Strategic Underpinnings of the Corporate Divestiture Program

Ideally, the CEO will elect to manage the divestiture program that helps reposition the company. Selection of financial intermediaries and instruments is adapted to the requirements of each deal. No one divestiture predominates. Together, the combination of sales, joint ventures, and spin-offs points the corporation in a new direction for the future.

But which direction? A poorly conceptualized or poorly implemented divestiture program is worse than none at all. Except in the case of divestitures forced by hemorrhaging losses (which require immediate action), each separate action must be structured to be consistent with the corporation's future strategic objectives.

Both acquisitions and divestitures are often justified by management on the basis of strategic "fit," or the lack of same. The vagueness of the word lends itself to almost limitless interpretation. And the meaning of the phrase sometimes changes with changing circumstances. At the time of acquisition, the purchase of a specialty steel mill by a manufacturer of cold-rolled steel is welcomed as a good fit with the company's other market niches. The acquired business flounders as competitors redouble their efforts. Management now states that the fit of the ill-fated acquisition was poor and announces a return to emphasis on the basic business.

Divestitures and Customer Segmentation

Is the management issue, then, fit or execution? Probe beneath the public relations verbiage and the consultant's diagrams and one may find a strategy built on what management wants to do, rather than what customers desire, as seen in these three examples:

- Hays T. Watkins helped create CSX Corp. through the merger of the Chessie System Railroad with Seaboard System Railroad in 1980. The new company was envisioned by management as a future "one-stop" intermodal transporter, allowing customers to ship products across land or sea. Watkins acquired Sea-Land Corp., the giant container shipping company, and an oil company with a barge subsidiary. The CEO also picked up some admittedly nontransportation units, including Greenbrier Hotel and a fiber-optics venture. A 1987 ad asked: "Is This Any Way to Run a Railroad?" In March 1987, the oil and gas production unit was sold for $612 million. In the company's 1987 annual report, Chairman Watkins indicated that some of the acquired units might be shed, and, indeed, in 1988 CSX initiated divestitures of its Rockresorts properties and its natural gas pipeline unit, Texas Gas Transmission Corp.

- A telecommunications company viewed by customers as a local exchange carrier proclaims itself one day to be a systems integrator, expert at developing complex voice, data, and image systems into high-performance, high-capacity corporate networks. The problem is that neither the company's products nor its people are perceived by key customers as being equal to the alternatives offered by other system integrators. Probable result: a business unit that is a candidate for future divestiture or termination.

- Management at a consumer lending company sought an upscale image by acquiring other financial services. Unfortunately, there was little or no linkage between current customers, primarily blue-collar workers, and the medium-size business accounts that made up most of the customer base of the newly acquired leasing operations. The result: a forced divestiture several years later, attributed to a "poor fit."

The key analysis activity with regard to the issue of fit is customer segmentation. Products and technology adoption statistics can be manipulated to justify management goals. But customers' *own* sense of market segmentation—how they view the company and the competitiveness of products and services—is (or should be) a critical element in acquisition and divestiture strategy.

Considerable lip service is paid to the importance of the customers' sense of market positionings, but often managements' perceptions prevail. Some corporations *are* able to change their customer image and thus their market franchise: Ford, NCR, and Apple Computer are recent examples. More often, however, the boundary of a business unit fit is the perception of the firms' customers, suppliers, and employees.

A comprehensive program of divestiture planning contains two key parts. First, considerations of strategic fit are combined with statistical measures to help identify the units that should be nominated as divestiture candidates. Second, a flexible program is developed to guide the divestiture implementation with the intent of maximizing the present value of sales proceeds.

Identifying the Divestiture Target Candidate: Operating versus Financial Valuation

The issue of strategic fit has been raised. But even if the unit fits, timing may call for a sale under certain conditions, such as when market value is visibly more than the unit's intrinsic worth as perceived by management.

But who determines value? Ask a corporate financial analyst what a business is worth, and the answer will likely be based on the internally generated cash flow of the company, net of capital additions. Pose the value question to an investment banker, and the response will probably be market value—i.e., stock price times the number of shares outstanding, adjusted for the prevailing acquisition premium for comparable securities.

The business unit's calculated "value" may differ by 30 to 40 percent depending on the approach used and specific value assumptions. Which of the two value approaches is correct? The answer: both. The expected practice is for advocates of each approach to adapt their analyses to validate their methodology.

The corporate analyst "solves" for the cash flow valuation of the business unit backwards, beginning with external market value, thus ensuring that projected corporate cash flows result in an identical valuation as market value. The investment banker may employ one of the raider statistical valuation tools in use today; some of these approaches utilize cash flow calculations for five years, with future value after that point based on market price-to-earnings multiples. This future value portion of the calculation formula may equal 60 to 70 percent of the total value of the business under evaluation. The calculation rationale is thus essentially circular: Market value is "justified" by market value.

Both valuation approaches are needed. The cash flow method addresses the question, "What is it worth?" while the financial-market reference point responds, "What will an outside party probably pay?" Address only the first issue but not the second, and managers of the divestiture program lack an understanding of market value. If, however, purchase price is the only consideration, acquiring management may be hard-pressed to justify the requested acquisition premium. Accordingly, the strongest argument can be made for calculating the business unit's value on *both* bases. If this is accomplished, the resulting difference, or "gap," can be utilized to help identify appropriate divestiture candidates that have not already been specified as a result of "fit" analysis.

Situation 1: Value Gap with Greater Financial Value

Consider the following situation. A data processing services concern develops a new operations software business, which management believes relates closely to the firm's other systems and services. However, the growing company will require considerable research capital in the coming years. Because of this, operations-based valuation (based on cash flow less required future capital) may be considerably less than the prospective future market value. Management faces a tough decision: either take the money now by selling all or part of the business today, or develop the cash-hungry unit internally but risk starving other operations.

Situation 2: Value Gap with Greater Operations Value

Another example is a gap in which financial value is less than operations value. In a breakup analysis, management may find that the combined worth of units appears to be more than the value assigned by the market for the units together, under parent company management. Reasons may include a lack of confidence in parent company management, or the fact that external investors view the units as being significantly different, thus justifying a severe discount.

Situation 3: Declining Financial Value in Absolute Terms

In a third situation, the financial value of the unit being analyzed declines each time that value is calculated. Even if this decrease occurs in concert with other market changes, parent company management faces a stark reality: either sell the unit now or risk possibly watching the unit decline to virtually no value at a later date.

The gap between operations and financial valuation of the company's separate business units (SBUs) should ideally be calculated on a recurring basis to avoid missteps caused by analysis at a single point in time. Accordingly, management may wish to establish an annual value review of all SBUs of the corporation in order to monitor apparent value changes.

The Implementation Issue: Liquidate, Position, or Develop

Once a business unit has been identified for possible divestiture by the operations/financial valuation gap methodology, the process has just begun. Divestiture implementation must be adapted to the characteristics of the unit under examination and to marketplace conditions in order to maximize sale proceeds.

Some units' values are maximized by immediately proceeding to auction and inviting a wide range of financial and synergistic corporate buyers to participate in the bidding. This typically works best for a unit that is believed to have broad purchase appeal and that does not have specialized proprietary technology or operating characteristics. If the industry falls into a "vanity" category with high personal appeal (airlines and entertainment companies sometimes fall into this category), prospects for a maximum bid improve.

Also, immediate sale following the decision to divest may work best for deteriorating business units. The race is on to salvage some remaining value out of a deteriorating situation. The business unit is often liquidated under such circumstances, rather than sold intact.

A transitional period between the divestiture decision and the transaction may make sense if the business unit is burdened with chronic market or operations problems or if the business is limited to a narrowly defined market niche, which may be unfamiliar to outside bidders. An outside buyer will not know whether the apparent problems are correctable or not; but management of the selling organization has lived with the unit's challenges and their ramifications, and thus they may be better positioned to take initial steps toward a solution.

Cosmetic corrections by the selling company, such as renaming, assignment to a different corporate group, or minor balance sheet revisions, are not real problem-solving actions and may not be worth management's efforts. Outside bidders often reason that they could make these same corrections themselves. Worse, unanticipated changes could add future costs and complexity if the "solutions" later had to be redone.

Making Predivestment Changes

Material predivestment changes, however, can help to increase sales proceeds if questions about the intended divestee are resolved. Eliminating contingencies prior to sale is a positive move that may increase the price received for the unit. In 1988, several pharmaceutical company bidders pursued acquisition of A. H. Robbins Co. despite continuing questions about the potential exposure associated with outstanding Dalkon Shield litigation. If it had been possible to cap the exposure, it logically follows that additional prospective buyers would have been forthcoming, and future return and future risk could have been calculated more accurately. At another company, selling management significantly enhanced the purchase appeal of their intended divestee by concluding an assignable labor pact with the firm's three primary labor unions on particularly favorable terms prior to the intended closing date.

But some predivestiture actions may decrease value unless the selling company management is careful. As an example, a North American electronics company launched a major new research and development program in the weeks before an announced divestiture, reasoning that this would impress potential owners with the firm's proprietary technology. But the CEO's action actually reduced the number of potential suitors to a single major firm. The dramatic expenditure confirmed in some observers' minds what they feared the most: that the company was run by technocrats who were insensitive to marketplace shifts.

Beyond presale packaging, the potential divestee's customer and competitive circumstances may require a more active program of development before the company can be positioned for sale. Such a program may come to include new technology licensing arrangements, joint marketing initiatives, joint ventures, or even minor acquisitions. The goal is to apply an effective new business development strategy to units of the corporation in order to transform a business with limited appeal into a potential divestee with a built-in market of purchasers.

When Predivestiture Development Makes Sense

A logical question is, "If selling company management is going to spend the time and resources to improve the business, why divest it at all?"

This is an understandable issue; development prior to divestment makes sense only under certain circumstances, such as:

- *Chapter 11 declaration or a chronically uprofitable unit.* Until the business is rescued from its tailspin, potential bidders are virtually nonexistent. Emerge from bankruptcy and establish new financing, supplier, and customer arrangements, and the unit becomes marketable as an ongoing entity.

- *Division of another business unit.* The proposed divestee may not currently be a business, but merely a disaggregated collection of products and employees. The assets must be configured into a separate business unit with distinct customer accounts, products, and revenue flows.

- *Sliver market niches.* Some corporations have pursued the niche product development tactics of the 1970s until they are essentially a collection of frail sliver markets. Instead of being a protected, proprietary business franchise, the sliver may be highly *unstable* since virtually any major competitor can attack the unit's market position by sustaining losses for a temporary period of time. Unless an absolute technology market barrier to entry exists, the result can be severe erosion of market share.

To their dismay, some American machinery companies today find themselves in a competitively untenable position. The head of one machine tool company laments that his firm has reduced its market share in pursuit of high-profit market niches. The problem is that the market positions are too narrow to mount an effective defense when new competitors enter. Today, he says, "We can be attacked from above or below, and the protection of a proprietary market is not there."

The solution for the sliver dilemma may be: a new third-party product purchase to reduce product voids; technology barriers to entry; or improved advertising and promotion to increase customers' perception of important differences in quality and performance. Sometimes, all three approaches must be used in combination.

Time and Expense of Predevelopment

How much time and expense should management commit to develop the business prior to divestment? A divestiture program that takes more than nine months from the time of the divestment decision to the time of the transaction is probably not worth the effort. Presale development should be limited to a small number of opportunities; otherwise, divestment resolve may be weakened.

Organizational realities being what they are, a prolonged development program will result in additions to permanent staff, programs, and other embedded costs that may actually reduce the unit's attractiveness to outside buyers. The nature of the presale development situation may justify use of a designated internal task force for implementation, or an outside group dedicated to achieving specific improvement goals.

Targeting the Acquirer

The comprehensive divestiture program includes consideration of specific identification of the buyer or buyers believed to be best suited to generate a superior bid. Ideally, this involves a rigorous evaluation of prospective suitors on the basis of:

- Indicated cash or reserve financial resources available for completing an acquisition of the size contemplated.

- Apparent interest by the company in expanding into areas of the divestee based on public proclamations and private guidance to outside advisers.

- Cash flow fit with the divestee's operations: Is there a seasonal or countercyclical mesh of the two businesses?

- Overlapping customers, suppliers, or proprietary technology.

This "long list" of prospective buyers is not necessarily restricted to companies that have expressed an interest in the designated divestee in the past. The optimal price may be paid by a prospect other than companies currently expressing interest.

Leveraged Buyouts—The Pendulum Swings?

Will the early 1990s be a period of unprecedented divestiture activity? Restructured leveraged buyouts (LBOs) completed in the 1980s are a possible source of future divestiture volume.

Each major acquisition period in the postwar era has been followed by a corresponding divestiture swing as a decreasing pool of available target companies eventually becomes overbid. Overpriced companies eventually cannot support their huge acquisition debt levels, thus resulting in forced sales of at least part of the operation. Emergence of the "growth stock" conglomerates of the late 1960s was followed by an offsetting wave of sales and spin-offs in the 1970–1972 period as excesses of the boom were corrected. Similarly, the mid-1970s expansion was followed by retrenchment in 1979–1981.

The LBO has been the characteristic acquisition mechanism of the 1980s. Will the pendulum again swing back toward divestiture? The sheer volume of LBO deals suggests a robust volume of divestiture activity even if most LBOs succeed:

- As quality LBO targets become scarcer, acquisition justification relies increasingly on techniques such as deferred or excused payments, equity reclassification, and layer upon layer of junior subordinated debt and mezzanine financing to make the deal work.

- Push the limits of financing and deal-structuring creativity too far, and the transaction becomes a veritable house of cards. LBO packagers attempt to minimize equity; that leverage, in turn, increases susceptibility of the divested business to cyclical swings. Under extreme conditions, even a mild recession can alter customer cash flows sufficiently to force some sales if the unit is too levered to withstand marketplace changes.

- Even if the divestee/LBO has fixed debt, an economic downturn may virtually eliminate the deal's cash flow safety margin.

Any or all of these argue for development of a contingency divestiture plan to reduce the burden imposed by acquisition debt. Advance planning increases the probability of success; waiting until the need for a sale arises before planning the divestiture program may mean sale proceeds that are less than anticipated.

Integral Part of Strategy

The corporate divestiture program is no longer symbolic of management retrenchment. On the contrary, an active divestiture program should be an integral part of top management's strategy for maximizing shareholder value through effective business development. In an ongoing divestiture strategy, no single business unit is immune from consideration. Established methodologies exist for identifying prospective divestment targets, and specific strategies should be developed to optimize the return from each divestiture opportunity.

12

New Developments in Leveraged Buyouts

Carl Ferenbach
General Partner, Berkshire Partners

The leveraged buyout is a relatively new form of corporate organization. The modern era of leveraged buyouts began as an evolution from entrepreneurial bootstrapping to professional management during the late 1970s and has been broadly popularized during the mid-1980s. According to information developed by the journal *Mergers and Acquisitions,* for the four years ended in 1987, leveraged buyouts averaged between 8 to 10 percent of total merger and acquisition activity as counted by total dollars of transactions completed; and, according to the same source, about 20 percent of businesses divested during this period were leveraged buyouts. If we go back to 1979, about $700 million of LBOs—less than 2 percent of the market for corporate acquisitions—were completed.

In this chapter we will analyze the growth in the number of leveraged buyout transactions and the reasons for it; and, to show how the processes of acquisition and financing these transactions—what one might call "deal technology"—have evolved, we'll compare the leveraged buyout of Signode Corp., completed in August 1982, with a hypothetical similar transaction for Signode had it been accomplished in August 1988. Then we will offer some observations on the changing role of management in leveraged buyouts, and on investor liquidity. Finally, we will forecast the evolution of trends that are just now beginning to develop.

The Growth in LBOS

While there have been many developments in both the modern corporation and the international capital markets that have combined to foster the growth of leveraged buyouts, four events in the 1979–1980 time frame signaled the expansion to come more than any others:

- Paul Volcker, as chairman of the Federal Reserve Board, set in motion policies that resulted in the unleashing of huge amounts of capital. As a result of Volcker's policies, capital that had moved into land, gold, collectibles, and other inflation hedges became attracted to financial assets, leading ultimately to the massive growth of an entirely new range of financial instruments.

- In 1979, Kohlberg Kravis Roberts & Co. (KKR) completed the acquisition of Houdaille Industries for $350 million, by far the largest LBO completed to that time. The investment firm proved with this transaction that the LBO was a viable alternative form of acquisition for most corporations.

- Apple Computer went public, signifying the new role that the personal computer and other office products, which evolved from the revolution in electronics, would play in financial analysis. Without the personal computer and related software development, the most basic tool for analyzing future cash flows from a business would not have been available in a cost-effective way to the many financial entrepreneurs who have driven the growth in leveraged buyouts.

- Finally, the investment banking firm Drexel Burnham Lambert located its high-yield debt activity in Beverly Hills, California, and supported its expansion as a tool to compete for business—and ultimately for major acquisitions. Without the liquidity provided to the high-yield market by Drexel and others, capital would not have been available to fuel the growth in leveraged buyouts.

These four developments put the financial buyer on a level plane with the corporate buyer in the competition for prime corporate properties.

Of these, the growth in capital has had the most significant impact on the growth of leveraged buyouts. As noted earlier, during recent years

LBOs have averaged 8 to 10 percent of acquisitions completed. This expansion in the level of activity came during a period when the value of acquisitions completed per annum grew from a pre-1984 norm of less than $100 billion to amounts approaching and exceeding $200 billion. Prior to 1984, the so-called mezzanine or high-yield portion of acquisition debt for LBOs was privately placed. The availability of a public market vastly expanded the funds available while lowering their cost.

The development of the high-yield market has led in turn to three important developments that will affect leveraged buyout financing into the 1990s.

First, because risk capital has become readily available, the commercial banking system, which provides the senior debt financing for LBOs, has been compelled to organize itself to service this market and has done so in several ways:

- To provide financing and service, banks have organized special groups for LBO financing.

- To provide protection against changing interest rates, the banks have made their interest-rate protection products available to leveraged buyouts.

- To protect their own risk profiles, the banks have set guidelines for their individual commitments to transactions, selling down or parceling out the balance of the credits each leads.

Commercial banks have thereby taken a portfolio approach to the LBO market while institutionalizing their standards for supplying credit to the LBO community. This creation of an infrastructure accompanied by standards ensures the banks' participation in the business in the future.

The second development is the large expansion in equity capital that has been made available for LBOs—by some counts as much as $25 billion in 1987–1988 alone. Leveraged at 8 to 1, this base would represent buying power of $200 billion, the equivalent of all the acquisitions completed during 1986, a year when LBOs were 10 percent of the total. Lest one find this total somewhat overwhelming, it is important to note that the equity capital for LBOs is for the most part organized as limited partnerships, which are under the management of LBO sponsor groups. The capital itself is committed by the sponsor and institutional investors for an investment period that most often is five years. Therefore, if the $25 billion were invested over five years, it would suggest that LBO transactions equivalent to $40 billion a year would be completed during the next five years (not taking into account any new funds committed). This is somewhat more than twice the estimated rate of investment during the 1984–1987 period. Therefore, unless there is dramatic growth in the total acquisition marketplace, financially oriented buyers should represent a large proportion of future acquisitions.

The third development growing out of the high-yield market's emergence has been the evolution of what is being called "merchant banking." Through the merchant banking function, investment banks advise on an acquisition, commit their own capital through bridge loans (loans that are made when the permanent financing has not been finalized) to complete the acquisition, arrange financing for it, and invest their own money in it as equity partners, either directly or through limited partnerships that they advise. Under the so-called merchant banking banner, investment banks have marched considerable distance from their traditional underwriting and advisory functions, greatly expanding the market for corporate acquisitions in the process.

Interestingly, the high-yield market that made the growth of leveraged buyouts possible is also the market that should raise the most concern for the future. Following the stock market crash of October 1987, the high-yield market became illiquid for several months and the new-issue market for high-yield debt essentially vanished. Presently, the role of the high-yield market in facilitating takeovers and LBOs is under considerable potential scrutiny. Further, Drexel Burnham, with a 40 to 50 percent market share, has surely been weakened by its settlement with the Justice Department and the loss of Michael Milken.

To insulate themselves from possible future illiquidity in the high-yield market, a number of sponsor groups that are not affiliated with investment banks or commercial banks have secured, or are securing, their own capability to provide bridge capital. In addition, some have sought to develop mezzanine funds under their own management, thereby displacing the need for high-yield market access to complete their acquisitions.

Nevertheless, uncertainties in the high-yield area aside, one may conclude the following: that a capital base for LBOs has been committed into the 1990s; that risk capital is readily available for investment in this medium; and that the commercial banking system has committed itself organizationally to providing credit for leveraged buyouts.

While growth in the availability of capital has been essential to the growth of leveraged buyouts, the availability of companies to acquire has also been a key ingredient. In 1978, there were 2100 corporate acquisitions valued at $34 billion. By 1986, there were 3300 corporate acquisitions valued at $173 billion. During this period leveraged buyouts grew from 2 percent of the market to between 10 and 15 percent of the market. This happened in three ways, as follows:

First, as KKR demonstrated with Houdaille, very large acquisitions lend themselves to the form. As this became apparent, large transactions with a breakup component to their strategy became common; and the breakup activity itself contributed to new LBOs.

Second, while the early wisdom dictated that LBOs should be confined to steady, noncyclical manufacturing companies acquirable for low prices and possessing the capacity for large tax write-ups, today's wisdom suggests that almost any business has the capacity for financial leverage. This broadening of the market has come at a time when many of the tax-related benefits available to LBOs, which greatly enhanced the cash flows of some, have been eliminated from the tax code.

Third, the LBO was deemed "acceptable" by corporate sellers and by families in and of estate settlements. These private sales, which make up perhaps 90 percent of total LBO activity, have quietly fueled the growth.

The broadening of the market for LBOs was facilitated by the following developments:

- Managers became convinced that they could manage their businesses successfully while under the burden of a leveraged capital structure; and they were successful in persuading the capital markets (sponsors, banks, and mezzanine financiers) that this was so.

- The information revolution, which has coincided with the growth of LBOs, has provided managers and financial analysts alike with the tools to analyze the true financial risks inherent in their businesses. They accomplish this by analyzing the values of the operating units within a corporate structure, various capital structures appropriate to those values, and variations in operating performance that might create financial difficulties on the one hand and improve business performance on the other.

- The restructuring of the American corporation, discussed extensively elsewhere in this volume, has vastly expanded the market for corporate acquisitions. Each leveraged buyout engendered by restructuring has spawned one or more new leveraged buyouts, as companies such as Beatrice Foods Corp. have sold operating units. Many others have found the form a comfortable one in which to operate and have undertaken second and third LBOs of the same business.

- LBO sponsors are now able to compete on an even footing with corporate acquirers through the development of new "deal technology." They have understood the advantages of financial leverage in enhancing the returns to equity and cash flow and how these advantages compare to an analysis that might be undertaken by a strategic corporate buyer. While the corporation can theoretically finance a higher purchase price by leveraging its other assets, it must face such needs of its public shareholders as dividends and quarterly performance standards; and the strategic buyer, by the nature of its public ownership, is limited in its assumption of accounting-related goodwill as part of the transaction cost in ways that a private purchaser is not. Also, LBO sponsors have understood that the cost of the new deal technology made available to service them was low relative to the ultimate benefits of the LBO ownership form. Hence, LBO sponsors learned that they could compete for prime corporate properties on price; and they learned how to finance their offers (using bridge loans, "highly confident" letters, and other techniques) within the framework of the highly competitive market for corporate control and to execute cash tender offers to shorten the time needed to acquire a public company.

Thus has the LBO expanded from an acquisition form limited to businesses with predictable operating characteristics acquired in negotiated transactions to a fully competitive acquisition form.

Deal Technology

An analysis of the leveraged buyout of Signode Corp. in August 1982, and a comparison with how the same acquisition might be done today, reflects how the availability of capital and the changing technology of deals have affected the LBO market and the acquisition market in general.

Signode Corp. was founded in the early part of this century. In 1982 it was the leading international producer of steel and plastic strapping, with related systems, for a variety of industrial packaging needs. In addition, Signode's Paslode division was a leading producer and supplier of fasteners to the housing industry. The company also produced marking systems for marking industrial products and a variety of plastic bags using the Ziploc technology. For the fiscal year ended December 1981, revenues were $700 million, and operating income (before interest and taxes) was $56 million, a cyclical low point.

In 1981, Victor Posner, a well-known corporate raider, acquired a strategic position in Signode and made several indirect overtures to acquire the company. Management expressed its strong preference to remain independent, a position supported by the board of directors. In late 1981, management decided to explore a possible leveraged buyout with Merrill Lynch arranging the necessary financing and acting as financial adviser to the company. This transaction was ultimately concluded in August 1982.

A description of the process of Signode's acquisition and financing in 1982 highlights four important changes when compared to 1988 standards: (1) There have been some important changes in the law or in application of the law pertaining, first, to the interpretation of directors' responsibilities, and second, to the tax treatment of acquisitions; (2) the availability of financing, its sources, and its application in the acquisition process have changed; (3) methods of valuation have advanced, reflecting a more liquid acquisition marketplace with higher prices but a lower cost of capital; and (4) there is significantly more competition for each acquisition, which affects deal strategy and application of the new technology.

The Acquisition Process

The Signode board felt comfortable with the advice of counsel that it could negotiate solely with an investor group (which included management) as long as management excluded itself from all board deliberations, which were conducted through a committee of independent directors. The board did not feel that an auction or even solicitation of one or more alternative offers was required. Instead, they felt comfortable relying on an opinion of their investment bank that management's proposal was fair to the Signode shareholders. As it happened, the price and other terms were determined through negotiations, which at one point were terminated because the parties could not agree. Among the terms other than price was a financing condition for the benefit of the buyers.

One need only to contrast this process with the well-publicized competition in RJR Nabisco Inc. between management and KKR to know that in today's world boards feel that they must consider, indeed solicit, multiple offers; and that an auction process is the most efficient, tested means of so doing. The court decisions that have altered the selling process have thereby raised shareholder rights a notch above the considerations of other corporate constituents, and mandated that the real tests of fairness are determined only in an open process. At the same time, the protections that were afforded acquirers in the Signode era are generally not available to today's buyer, whose only true tactic for completion is speed. In today's world, an announcement of agreement is little more than an announcement of open season for hungry buyers. Hence, today's buyer must arrive at the bargaining table with all its financing arranged.

Tax-Related Changes in the Law

Signode was among the last companies to effect partial liquidations as part of its tax planning. The impact of these provisions (and subsequent IRS code interpretations that permitted transactions involving mirror subsidiaries) was an adjustment in basis for selected operations in a manner that caused the taxpayer to incur little risk of recapture assessments on the step-up in basis of already depreciated assets. Signode was also able to take an aggressive posture on its inventory, which was carried at LIFO cost. Recalling that the acquisition occurred following numerous years of inflation, and that Signode subsequently worked off considerable inventory that it concluded it did not need, the ability to make this adjustment provided considerable subsequent cash savings. By late 1987, with the end of the use of mirror subsidiaries and the final repeal of the General Utilities doctrine, all these types of benefits had been eliminated. The federal government had ceased supplying tax assistance to acquirers.

The Availability of Financing

The Signode board entered into an agreement to sell the company that was still conditional upon financing. In fact, from start to finish, the acquisition required more than eight months to complete. As shown in Table 12-1, at $430 million, the acquisition was completed at approximately six times 1980 actual and 1983 forecast earnings before interest and taxes, and eight times 1981 actual earnings before interest and taxes. This price represented a small premium on accounting book value (with appropriate adjustments; there was no acquisition goodwill), and provided the senior lenders with a strong base of assets in all lines

Table 12-1. Signode Corp. Operations

(Thousands)

	Forecast*		Fiscal years		
	1983	1982	1981	1980	1979
Operating revenues	$813,413	$736,120	$700,252	$695,504	$695,183
Earnings before interest and taxes	75,959	61,151	56,100	73,776	81,419
Depreciation	22,000	20,000	20,709	19,211	16,020
Capital expenditures	26,000	26,000	21,222	30,535	31,603

*Reflects adjustments for acquisition accounting.

of business to back up their credit. As a consequence, the investor group was able to develop a $320 million domestic and foreign credit facility.

Even with a business recession then in progress, all participants felt that there was adequate cash flow coverage of their interest. As it developed, Signode made a substantial reduction in its senior credit facility in the early phases of the LBO through materially improved management of its working capital, which it accomplished without reducing its commitments to its customers.

To complete its acquisition, the investor group arranged $79 million of subordinated notes and $34.1 million of preferred stock. Each of these security holders also purchased common stock—the notes bore interest at 19 percent, an acceptable combined rate of return for debt and equity of a Signode-quality LBO—and purchased a meaningful equity interest to enhance their total return. The preferred stockholders contracted to receive dividends of 15 percent and 15.5 percent, with proportionately more common stock. Signode's retirement fund became a meaningful owner of these securities. All these securities were privately placed with major institutional buyers. The terms were heavily negotiated, as were the intercreditor terms between the bank and the note holders, the rights of the preferred stockholders, and the shareholders' agreement. Although there were certainly precedents in all these areas, they were not well established.

In the financing world of 1988, because of the four developments cited earlier in this chapter, the market for all forms of LBO financing was much broader and more liquid; and it has evolved to accommodate purchasers who must compete in today's auction-driven environment. If Signode were seeking financing in 1988, it probably would already have managed its working capital to lower levels (four years after its LBO, Signode management had reduced total assets by approximately $100 million while sales had increased). Yet, because all parties to the acquisition would be willing to consider the value of the various parts of Signode, it would still be able to obtain senior credit in excess of $300 million.

Now, however, the purchase price would be eight times forecasted earnings before interest and taxes (EBIT)—or more, perhaps in excess of $600 million. Yet the risk capital would be a far more easily completed piece of the transaction. While management and Merrill Lynch would have been forced to win Signode in an auction, they would have done so with Merrill (or any other credible sponsor) having committed to bridge the nonsenior portion of the financing ($200 to 250 million) while committing the equity from its LBO fund (a limited partnership under its management). The purchaser then would commence a cash tender offer and, all else being equal, would purchase control some 20 business days later. The investment bank then would undertake to finance out its bridge loan with a public offering of high-yield bonds—a typical 1988 yield of 13.5 to 14 percent with a modest equity sharing.

The acquisition company would need some extra credit to cover deal costs. In 1982, it cost Signode about $6.5 million to complete its LBO. Today, with commitment fees, bridge-loan costs, and high-yield financing costs, the charges would be closer to $30 million.

Management Participation

The modern period for leveraged buyouts began with the moniker, "management buyouts," and evolved into leveraged buyouts. Nonetheless, the fundamental premise of buyouts has proven to be true: that management ownership of an operating business, generally in partnership or participation with a financial sponsor, and focused by a preponderance of contractual payment obligations in its capital structure, produces sound operations and high investment returns. Fundamentalists in leveraged buyouts want management to make a meaningful personal financial commitment to ownership, for which they will recognize management's disproportionate contribution to a favorable outcome by granting them a promoted interest. Thus did the Signode management acquire a major interest in their company.

This basic approach continues to be applied, with management's ultimate position determined by such variables as their personal capital, their importance to the success of the business, and what grasp they have on the deal. But now we also confront managements in many new postures. First, managers often have developed the transactional opportunity and seek buyout sponsors' support—Donald Kelly's involvement in Beatrice Foods being the most noted case. Second, as the buyout form matures, sponsors may wish to seek liquidity for their investment while managements may be willing to reinvest their profits. This position often enables managements to control to some degree the related sales, thereby enhancing their bargaining positions vis-à-vis LBO sponsors. Hence, management that has already created value and is desirous of having greater control often can by leading a recapitalization or a new LBO of its company.

How Are They Doing?

One would be remiss in a discussion of current developments in LBOs if one did not address the question of how well they are working. The proponents of LBOs argue that the need to service large amounts of debt forces management to create lean organizations, eliminating unneeded staff and unsuccessful divisions from a base business. With this comes focus—focus on service levels to customers, on product quality, on the people who make the business successful. The increased focus is easily communicated to the entire organization, which becomes more supportive of corporate goals. Debt is therefore repaid quickly, reducing financial risk. Further, new investment is frequently increased, as future growth is the primary means for achieving investment returns in that 90 percent segment of the LBO market that cannot rely on sales of assets, divisions, or subsidiaries.

The opponents of leveraged buyouts argue that they needlessly cost jobs; that focus on debt retirement reduces competitiveness because leveraged companies invest less in research and development and in new physical assets; and that they are designed solely to benefit "financial engineers," who reap gains at the expense of others.

There is also a body of negative opinion that the modern LBO experience does not include a business recession (the 1981–1982 experience notwithstanding). Those holding to this view believe that many present-day buyouts are too thinly capitalized and either will have difficulty meeting their obligations in a downturn or will need to cut muscle and bone along with fat in order to do so. A number of groups in the buyout field have begun to organize themselves to take advantage of these prospective events and related consequences.

There is not in fact an accurate body of information measuring the results of leveraged buyouts. Nonetheless, with notable exceptions, the form seems to have been living up to its promise as a form of governance as well as an investment form. Perhaps the best evidence of this is the continuing expansion in its application, and the continued commitment of capital to LBOs by knowledgeable investment professionals.

Looking Ahead

The leveraged buyout of RJR Nabisco for approximately $25 billion has prompted continuous questions about whether it is the first of many such megadeals. While one can only speculate, RJR Nabisco has pointed up several interesting trends:

First, while it is the largest acquisition (let alone LBO) in history by a factor of two, it has been readily financed. And, of course, all the newest deal technology has been applied in so doing.

Second, a sizable "stub" or remnant securities interest—including equity—has been left in public hands. While this is not the first time this has been done, it will be the most closely followed of such securities, and success will undoubtedly beget success while also relieving much criticism.

Third, there has been extensive participation by foreign banks in the lender group. It seems likely that these participants will also move into the risk portion of the capital structure.

Finally, RJR Nabisco has also spawned extensive scrutiny in Washington both among tax-writing committees of Congress and among those concerned with issues of ethics and fairness. As noted earlier, RJR Nabisco, as a large merchant banking transaction, is the exception—not the rule—as an LBO. Yet while the market is made up of substantially private types of acquisitions, RJR will in the end influence many of the rules by which LBOs will be governed in the future. At this writing, based on extensive discussions with public officials, one is tempted to speculate that government will accept many of the benefits of LBOs and not further increase their cost of capital by changing the tax law, but that more complete standards of disclosure will be imposed on LBOs of public companies.

To date, LBO groups have not pursued hostile takeovers. Clearly, as the "raiders" have proved, financing is not a barrier to undertaking a hostile offer. Rather, there have been two mitigating factors. First, LBOs are management-dependent. Most sponsors and most sources of financing to date have strongly preferred to support existing management groups. Therefore, management opposition has been a natural deterrent to hostile LBO offers. Second, the institutional partners of the LBO sponsors have been unwilling to support groups that wanted the right to make hostile offers, preferring to avoid the controversy and the related risks.

But while we saw many objections raised to KKR's tactics in RJR Nabisco, these restrictions to LBO-sponsored hostile offers are in fact falling away. There is an increasingly large pool of managerial talent, tested in the crucible of restructurings and LBOs, who are available—even anxious—to be called upon to manage LBOs, particularly underperforming ones. Their credentials are slowly being accepted by the financing sources for LBOs. Also, the institutional investors that object to sponsors undertaking hostile offers have found themselves at the nexus of corporate control as the result of proxy contests. Forced to make difficult decisions, institutional investors are no longer routinely siding with management and, in cases like 1988's Texaco proxy fight, are actually entering the governance process themselves. Hostile offers by LBO groups, supported and financed by institutional investors, cannot be far behind.

It is also likely that the LBO form will begin to accommodate broader employee constituents than management. While it is true that the employee stock ownership plan (ESOP) approach to LBOs has been an active component of the market for some time, there is a growing desire on the part of employees in all kinds of companies, irrespective of whether their status includes an organized union, to participate in the ownership of the companies that employ them. The more the job becomes a right of the employee or an obligation of the corporation, the more important ownership becomes in balancing the needs of various constituents. Hence, new arrangements to accommodate employee ownership seem likely to evolve.

In conclusion, the leveraged buyout as a form of organization is proving itself to be more versatile, with far broader acceptance, than had been thought likely or possible during the early phases of its modern development. While its resiliency in the face of a business downturn remains relatively untested, its appeal—the appeal of ownership—to employees at all levels of a corporation continues to grow. As it has, the technology applied to the deal process has expanded, as has the capital base committed to future transactions, ensuring its continued meaningful participation in corporate acquisitions and restructuring transactions. As we saw from the Signode example, the success of early LBOs was fostered by improved asset management and by a variety of tax strategies that enhanced cash flows. These opportunities are generally not available today. Tomorrow's LBO will need to accomplish its financial objectives by winning in the marketplace—by being a more successful competitor.

13

Employee Stock Ownership Plans as a Restructuring Option

James F. Carey

Partner, Jones, Day, Reavis & Pogue

Employee stock ownership plans (ESOPs) were designed by Congress in the Employee Retirement Income Security Act of 1974 (ERISA, codified at 29 U.S.C. SS 1001-1381 [1976]) to be a tax-effective financing technique for raising capital, in order to promote the congressional policy of equity ownership by employees in corporate employers: "The Congress, in a series of laws...has made clear its interest in encouraging employee stock ownership plans as a bold and innovative method of strengthening the free private enterprise system which will solve the dual problems of securing capital funds for necessary capital growth and of bringing about stock ownership by all corporate employees" [Tax Reform Act of 1976, Pub. L. 94-455, SS 803(h)].

The tax and financial advantages associated with ESOPs have been enhanced in almost every tax bill enacted since 1974, including tax legislation designed generally to raise revenue. Today ESOPs often play a key role in a variety of corporate transactions, such as leveraged buy-outs and going-private transactions, dispositions of unwanted business segments, and management defenses to tender offers, proxy contests, and other efforts to gain control of a corporation.

Notwithstanding the corporate purposes an ESOP can serve, an ESOP is a type of employee benefit plan that is subject to the various requirements of Title I of ERISA and that must meet and continue to satisfy various provisions of the Internal Revenue Code of 1986 ("the Code") applicable to qualified plans in general. This means that persons who have the power to control an ESOP are fiduciaries whose first duty under ERISA is to the employees participating in the ESOP and their beneficiaries, and not to the corporate managers who implement the ESOP in response to the tax and financial incentives offered by Congress. The fiduciary aspects of ESOPs often create tension and conflicts with corporate policy that are difficult to resolve, and unless these conflicts are appreciated and analyzed in advance, an ESOP may end up thwarting a corporate goal it is designed to help management achieve.

This chapter will briefly describe what an ESOP is, the special features that give ESOPs their tax and financial attraction, and how ESOPs are typically used in corporate transactions. The chapter will then discuss the key factors that should be considered by management in designing and implementing an ESOP.

What Is an ESOP?

An ESOP is a type of qualified defined contribution plan (either a stock bonus plan or a combination of a stock bonus plan and a money purchase pension plan) that provides deferred compensation benefits for employees and their beneficiaries, usually in the form of employer securities. Recent legislation has extended to stock bonus plans many of the qualification requirements that previously applied only to ESOPs, and the difference between the two types of plans has blurred. As used in this chapter, the term "ESOP" refers to a plan that satisfies all the requirements of Section 4975, so that it may borrow funds from a party in interest or a disqualified pension without engaging in a prohibited transaction under Section 406(a) of ERISA or Section 4975(c) of the Code.

The term "qualified" means that an ESOP must satisfy certain nondiscrimination and other rules of the Code that apply to all pension, profit-sharing, and stock bonus plans, including rules relating to minimum participation and vesting standards. The term "defined contribution plan" refers to the fact that, like a profit-sharing, money purchase, or stock bonus plan, an ESOP is an individual account plan: An account is established under the plan for each participating employee, and employer contributions and forfeitures are allocated to each employee's account generally in proportion to his or her compensation. The features that distinguish an ESOP from other qualified defined contribution plans are:

- An ESOP is designed to invest primarily in "qualifying employer securities."

- An ESOP is excused from complying with some of the limitations and restrictions under ERISA and the Code that are otherwise applicable to defined contribution plans.

- An ESOP can engage in certain leveraging transactions that would be prohibited under ERISA and the Code if undertaken by other plans.

Special Requirements Applicable to ESOPs

The principal requirements that a plan must satisfy to qualify as an ESOP are described below.

Designation

An ESOP must be formally designated as an ESOP in the plan document.

Qualifying Employer Securities

An ESOP must specifically state that it is designed to invest primarily in qualifying employer securities. In the Department of Labor's view, the "primarily" requirement will be satisfied if the plan provides for the investment of more than 50 percent of its assets in qualifying employer securities (D.O.L. Op. No. 83-006A). The term "qualifying employer security" is defined in the Code to mean readily tradeable common stock of the employer (or of a corporation that is a member of the same controlled group) or, if there is no readily tradeable common stock within the controlled group, common stock of the employer that has a combination of voting power and dividend rights equal to or in excess of both the class of common stock that has the greatest voting power and the class of common stock that has the greatest dividend rights.

In many instances this requirement can be satisfied only by the creation of a new class of common stock. Preferred stock will be treated as a qualifying employer security only if it is noncallable and convertible at any time at a reasonable conversion price into common stock that would meet the requirements of a qualifying employer security. Because qualifying employer securities by definition include only stock of a corporation, neither debt securities nor securities issued by an unincorporated employer can ever qualify.

Voting Rights

Voting pass-through requirements apply to employer securities held by an ESOP that are allocated to the accounts of participants and beneficiaries. If the employer securities are required to be registered under Section 12 of the Securities Exchange Act of 1934, the participant must be permitted to direct the trustee as to voting on all matters presented to shareholders of the employer for a vote; otherwise, participant voting rights with respect to employer securities acquired after 1979 are limited to major transactions, such as mergers, recapitalizations, liquidations, and the sale of all or substantially all of the assets of the employer's business. (Voting pass-through rules for securities that were acquired before 1980 and are not registered under the Securities Exchange Act of 1934 apply only to corporate matters that require more than a majority shareholder vote.) Because tender offers do not involve a shareholder vote, there is no statutory requirement to pass through tender offer decisions to participants and beneficiaries.

Distributions from the ESOP

All ESOP participants and beneficiaries must be permitted to require a distribution of their vested account balances in the form of shares of employer securities, unless the employer's charter generally restricts ownership of securities to employees and the ESOP, or the ESOP is established by a bank that is prohibited by law from repurchasing its own securities. Participants and beneficiaries may also be permitted to elect to receive the value of their vested account balances in cash.

Put Option

If the employer securities held by an ESOP are not readily tradeable on an established market, a participant or beneficiary who receives a distribution of employer securities acquired after 1986 must be permitted to require the employer to purchase all or any portion of the securities at a price determined under a fair valuation formula. The put option must extend for a period of 60 days following distribution, and, if not exercised during that period, for another 60-day period in the following plan year.

Under certain circumstances, the employer can elect to pay for employer securities acquired upon exercise of a put option in installments over five years, provided the deferred payments are secured and bear a reasonable rate of interest. The ESOP cannot be obligated under the put option but may assume the employer's obligation if the ESOP trustee determines it would be prudent to do so.

Diversification Election

An ESOP must permit participants who have reached age 55 and who have participated in the ESOP for at least 10 years to elect to diversify the investment of a portion of their account balances. Diversification can be accomplished by offering at least three investment choices (other than employer securities) under the ESOP or by distributing the portion of the account balance the participant could diversify. The diversification election applies only to employer securities acquired by the ESOP after 1986 and need not be given to a participant if the value of employer securities acquired by the ESOP after 1986 and allocated to the participant's account does not exceed a minimum cost, currently $500.

Valuation of Employer Securities

All assets of an ESOP must be valued at least once a year, and if the employer securities held by the ESOP are not publicly traded, the valuation must be made by a qualified independent appraiser.

Leveraged ESOPs

One of the significant financial and, in the context of corporate defense strategy, tactical advantages of an ESOP is the ability to acquire a large block of employer securities with funds borrowed from the employer (or a person related to the employer) or from a third-party lender with the loan guaranteed by the employer or a related person. Loans by an employer to a qualified plan, and third-party loans to a plan guaranteed by the employer, are generally prohibited transactions under ERISA and the Code and are also subject to excise taxes. Employer loans and guarantees are exempt from these prohibited transaction provisions if the ESOP and the terms of the loan satisfy certain requirements. Loans that satisfy these requirements are referred to as "exempt loans."

An exempt loan must be for a specific term, cannot be payable on demand, and must bear a reasonable rate of interest, which can be a variable rate of interest. An exempt loan must also be primarily for the benefit of ESOP participants and their beneficiaries. The primary benefit requirement does not mean that the exempt loan cannot benefit the employer by facilitating a corporate policy or goal, but rather that the loan must promote employee ownership of employer securities. This requirement will normally be satisfied if the loan meets the conditions descibed below.

Use of Loan Proceeds

The proceeds of the loan must be used only to acquire qualifying employer securities, to repay the loan, or to repay a prior exempt loan, but cannot be used to pay the expenses of administering the plan.

Suspense Account

If an ESOP acquires employer securities with the proceeds of an exempt loan, the employer securities must be credited initially to a special suspense account in the ESOP. Employer securities are released from the suspense account (and released from pledge, if pledged as collateral for the loan) and allocated to participants' accounts as payments are made on the ESOP loan. Employer securities may be released by taking into account principal and interest payments on the loan or by taking into account principal payments only.

Liability of the ESOP

The only collateral that an ESOP may give to secure an exempt loan is qualifying securities that are acquired with the proceeds of the loan and held in the suspense account. The only assets of the ESOP that may be used to repay an exempt loan are the collateral given for the loan, contributions made to the ESOP to satisfy its loan obligations, the earnings attributable to the collateral and the investment of such contributions, and dividends attributable to certain shares of employer securities held by the ESOP. Otherwise, an exempt loan must be without recourse to the ESOP.

Default Provisions

If an ESOP defaults on an exempt loan, the value of the ESOP assets acquired by a lender to satisfy the ESOP's obligation cannot exceed the dollar amount of the default. Therefore, if the qualifying employer's securities pledged as collateral for a loan have increased in value, the lender can acquire only a number of shares with a value equal to the dollar amount of the default.

If the lender is the employer or a person related to the employer, the lender can recover assets from the ESOP only to the extent of the ESOP's failure to meet the payment schedule of the loan, and the balance due under the loan may not be accelerated. The prohibition against acceleration upon default does not apply to a loan from an unrelated lender, even if the loan is guaranteed by the employer or a related person.

Other Restrictions

Employer securities acquired with the proceeds of an exempt loan cannot be subject to any put (other than the statutory put described earlier), call, or other option or buy-sell or similar arrangement. However, if the employer securities are not publicly traded, such securities may be subject to a right of first refusal in favor of the employer, the ESOP, or both, exercisable at a purchase price equal to the greater of the then fair market value of the securities or the price offered by a third party.

Tax and Financial Advantages of ESOPs

ESOPs offer corporations the opportunity to raise capital on a tax-favored basis and should be considered in conjunction with, or as an alternative to, venture capital financing and conventional bank financing for working capital or for acquisitions. The use of an ESOP as alternative financing will typically involve a leveraged ESOP, where funds are borrowed from a third-party lender and used by the ESOP to purchase securities from the employer. The funds received by the employer in exchange for the securities can then be used to achieve the restructuring or other corporate goals that caused the corporation to seek additional capital. A leveraged ESOP will result in shareholder dilution, and this dilution should be taken into account in comparing ESOP financing with other forms of available financing.

A leveraging transaction may involve a third-party loan to the

ESOP guaranteed by the employer or a related person, or a third-party loan to the employer followed by an employer loan of the same funds to the ESOP. The form of the transaction is often motivated by the conventions of the lender rather than tax or financial considerations.

The principal advantages of ESOP financing are the ability to repay borrowings through deductible employer contributions to the ESOP and, in effect, to deduct principal payments on the loan for federal income tax purposes; the ability to deduct dividends paid with respect to employer securities held in the ESOP and used to repay the ESOP loan or distributed to participants; and the availability of a reduced interest rate because, under Section 133 of the Code, qualified lenders can exclude from income 50 percent of the interest received with respect to certain ESOP financing arrangements.

Employer contributions to an ESOP are subject to more liberal deduction limitations than are contributions to other defined contribution plans. An employer may deduct up to 25 percent of covered compensation for contributions to an ESOP that are applied to repay the principal amount of an exempt loan, and may deduct an unlimited amount for contributions to an ESOP that are applied to repay interest on an exempt loan. Effective for plan years beginning after December 31, 1988, a participant's "compensation" for purposes of calculating deductions for plan contributions under a qualified plan is limited to $200,000, adjusted for increases in the cost of living.

An employer may deduct the amount of cash dividends paid on securities held by an ESOP if, pursuant to the terms of the plan, the dividends are paid in cash directly to participants, paid to the plan but distributed in cash to participants no later than 90 days after the close of the plan year in which paid, or used to make payments of interest or principal on a loan incurred to purchase the securities.

Section 133 of the Code permits qualified lenders to exclude from their income 50 percent of the interest received on "securities acquisition loans." A "securities acquisition loan" for this purpose includes a loan to an ESOP, or a loan to an employer that lends the proceeds to an ESOP on substantially the same terms, to the extent that the proceeds of the loan are used to acquire employer securities for the ESOP. The interest exclusion available under Section 133 generally permits qualified lenders to offer interest-rate savings of up to 20 percent of the rate otherwise applicable to the borrower, and this interest-rate reduction is an additional financial incentive to the use of an ESOP in corporate restructurings.

Debt Restructuring

The Section 133 interest exclusion also offers an opportunity for corporate debt restructuring through what are known as "immediate allocation loans," which do not involve any borrowing on the part of the ESOP. An immediate allocation loan includes any loan to a corporation with a term that does not exceed seven years, provided that, within 30 days of the loan, the corporation transfers to an ESOP employer securities equal in value to the proceeds of the loan and, within a year of the loan, the contributed securities are allocated to participants' accounts. Employer securities transferred to the ESOP can be authorized but unissued shares of the stock, treasury shares, or shares acquired by the employer in market transactions.

Immediate allocation loans can be used only in connection with a plan that qualifies as an ESOP. However, if a portion of an employer's plan that does not presently qualify as an ESOP is designed to invest primarily in employer securities, that portion of the plan can be designated as an ESOP and thereby qualify for the Section 133 interest exclusion.

Beyond the technical requirements of Section 133, immediate allocation loans in today's financial environment generally (1) provide for an interest-rate adjustment every 30 to 60 days, (2) are transferable by the lender, and (3) require an affiliate of the employer to redeem on demand the notes evidencing the loan. These features enable the notes to carry substantially lower interest rates than could be obtained through conventional financing arrangements because lenders treat the notes as short-term obligations, notwithstanding their stated maturity.

A series of immediate allocation loans can be structured to match the timing of an employer's otherwise required contributions to a plan. For example, an employer that sponsors a Section 401(k) plan that invests in employer securities could issue one or more promissory notes each month in a face amount equal to the estimated salary-reduction contributions by participants and the employer matching contributions for that month. The employer could satisfy its contribution obligation for the month by transferring employer securities within 30 days to the ESOP component of the plan in an amount equal in value to the proceeds the employer receives from the issuance of the notes. In this manner, the benefits associated with immediate-allocation loans can be achieved without increasing employee benefit costs.

Management Decisions Affecting ESOPs

In considering the use of an ESOP in a restructuring transaction, there are a number of key issues that should be analyzed and resolved by management before the ESOP is implemented. The most important of these issues are the feasibility of the ESOP, valuation considerations, voting and tender offer provisions, financial accounting treatment, and employee communications.

Feasibility

The ability of a leveraged ESOP to service its debt depends entirely on the employer's ability to make deductible contributions to the ESOP. As noted earlier, the amount of the employer's annual deductible contributions used by the ESOP to repay principal is limited to 25 percent of covered compensation and is therefore a direct function of the size of the total compensation of employees participating in the ESOP. Accordingly, it is important to determine whether the participant compensation base is sufficient to enable the employer to make deductible contributions in the amount necessary to satisfy the terms of the ESOP note.

To increase the size of the covered compensation, an employer may wish to provide more liberal eligibility standards than are required under ERISA or the Code (at least until the ESOP loan is repaid) and to permit new employees to participate, for example, as of their date of hire instead of after a year of eligibility service. It may also be possible to generate additional contributions for purposes of loan repayment by permitting employee contributions either on an aftertax basis or through cash or deferred contributions under Section 401(k) of the Code. These contributions may raise federal securities law and other issues that must be reviewed by legal counsel.

If the employer securities held by the ESOP are not publicly traded, the put option required to be given to terminating participants will affect the employer's cash flow projections, and the effect of the put option should be determined in advance. Although distributions to terminated participants may in most instances be delayed while the ESOP loan is being repaid, thereby deferring any obligation to repurchase shares distributed to participants who exercise the put option, the put option will continue to apply to securities acquired with the proceeds of an exempt loan after the loan has been fully paid. An employer should therefore analyze its historical employee turnover rate and the likely range of future share values in order to project the cash flow needed to honor the put option.

Valuation

Perhaps the single most important factor in a leveraged ESOP transaction is the valuation of the employer securities to be acquired by the ESOP. The valuation factor affects the ESOP transaction in two significant ways. First, the purchase of securities from the employer will not be exempt from the prohibited transaction rules of ERISA and the Code unless the purchase price paid by the ESOP does not exceed the fair market value of the securities. Second, the decision by the ESOP to purchase the securities is a fiduciary decision that must satisfy the ERISA standard or prudence, and the value of the securities will directly affect the prudence of the investment.

If the employer securities are publicly traded, fair market value normally can be determined with reference to the traded price of the securities. If, however, there is no public market for the securities, fair market value must be determined by the ESOP fiduciaries in good faith. Under proposed regulations recently published by the Department of Labor (29 C.F.R. SS 2510.3-18 [1988]), the "good faith" requirement cannot be satisfied if valuation decisions are made by management or other persons related to the transaction. It is therefore necessary that the ESOP and its participants be represented in any restructuring transaction by an independent fiduciary who is advised by legal counsel and valuation experts independent of the employer.

Also, if employer securities held by the ESOP are not publicly traded, the securities must be valued annually by an independent appraiser. This valuation is necessary for purposes of determining the amount to be paid to a participant or beneficiary who receives a distribution of cash instead of employer securities and for purposes of determining the price to be paid to a former ESOP participant or beneficiary who exercises the put option.

In a leveraged buyout of a corporation or a portion of its business, an ESOP will typically participate in the new company along with equity participation by management and venture capital investors and debt participation by banks or other institutional lenders. The ESOP fiduciary must determine the fair market value of the employer securities not only with reference to the value of the assets of the business and its historical and projected earnings and discounted cash flow but also with respect to the value and share of the equity allocated to other investors.

To satisfy the ERISA good faith standard, it is essential for the trustee and its advisers to participate actively in the negotiations concerning the acquisition and financing of the business. A failure to satisfy this standard will result in a breach of the fiduciary's obligations under ERISA and in personal liability on the part of the fiduciary for any loss to the ESOP either for paying too much for the employer securities or for participating in an imprudent investment.

Voting and Tender Offers

Another important fiduciary issue relates to voting and tender offer procedures under the ESOP. As discussed earlier, under some circumstances voting rights must be passed through to participants, and in many circumstances voting rights may be passed through, even though not required. Neither ERISA nor the Code provides any specific rules with regard to passing through tender offer decisions, although ESOPs commonly pass these decisions through to participants.

Voting and tender offer decisions, whether passed through to participants or not, are decisions subject to the fiduciary responsibility rules of ERISA for which the named fiduciary of the ESOP has primary responsibility. A named fiduciary is justified in following participant directions only if the participant is fully informed about the issues relevant to the decision, is able to instruct the fiduciary confidentially, and furnishes instructions only with respect to securities allocated to his or her account. It is advisable that voting and tender offer decisions with respect to securities allocated to an ESOP suspense account or allocated to the accounts of participants who fail to instruct the fiduciary be made by an ESOP fiduciary exercising independent judgment.

The degree of independence required by the fiduciary with residual voting and tender offer authority may depend on the significance of the particular decision. Instructions with respect to voting for an uncontested slate of directors in most instances may be exercised by an ESOP committee consisting of representatives of management, while instructions regarding a proposed transaction that is opposed by management should be furnished by an independent fiduciary to satisfy the ERISA fiduciary standards.

It is important, therefore, that the ESOP contain a mechanism that permits the engagement of independent fiduciaries who will assume responsibility for discreet matters in the event the named fiduciaries are prevented from acting because of a real or apparent conflict of interest. The appropriate mechanism will permit the named fiduciaries to interview and select the most qualified independent fiduciary for the particular matter, rather than having the decision revert by default to the ESOP trustee.

Financial Accounting
Considerations

Engaging in a leveraged ESOP transaction will have financial accounting consequences that should be reviewed with the employer's auditors and understood by management before the transaction is consummated. For example, an employer's guarantee of an ESOP loan will be reflected on the employer's balance sheet as a reduction of shareholder capital. Similarly, if an employer loans funds to an ESOP, a reduction in shareholder equity will occur because the ESOP repayment obligation is treated as a negative entry in the equity section of the balance sheet.

This reduction in shareholder equity may cause the employer to violate net worth covenants in loan agreements or other financing arrangements. In addition, securities held in the ESOP suspense account are treated as outstanding for purposes of earnings-per-share calculations, even though the employer may recover the shares in the event of a default. Employer contributions to an ESOP are treated as a compensation expense, but dividends on ESOP shares are charged to retained earnings (and not included in compensation expense), even if the dividend is deductible for tax purposes.

Employee Communications

To succeed as an employee benefit plan and to achieve a high degree of employee motivation, an ESOP must be effectively communicated to participants. In the context of a restructuring, ESOPs will often replace another type of retirement plan; and it is important from the viewpoint of maintaining employee morale and limiting fiduciary liability that employees clearly understand that their benefit is tied directly to the performance of the employer, and that in most instances employer securities cannot be disposed of to avoid anticipated losses.

In addition, an ESOP that participates in a leveraged transaction will normally be required to value securities allocated to participants' accounts at a lower value than the value at which they were acquired. This is because the annual valuation of employer securities held in the ESOP will reflect the debt incurred by the employer and the ESOP to effect the leveraging transaction. As a result, the amount of employer contributions to the ESOP to pay for the securities may exceed the value of the securities released from the suspense account during the years immediately following the ESOP transaction or until the loan is repaid.

Unless employees participating in the ESOP understand that this is a natural consequence of using an ESOP in a leveraging transaction, the ESOP may work against the goals sought to be achieved in the transaction by causing unacceptable levels of employee dissatisfaction, particularly where employee pretax or aftertax contributions are used to pay the ESOP loan.

Advisory Counsel Required

The tax and financial advantages associated with ESOPs are too great to overlook when a corporation is considering any kind of restructuring. However, because of the possible application of federal and state securities laws, the qualification requirements of the Code, the fiduciary standards of ERISA, and the financial accounting treatment of ESOP transactions, ESOPs may not be appropriate corporate financing techniques in all situations. The discussion in this chapter provides a general overview of extremely intricate and technical provisions of the law governing ESOPs. Corporations that wish to study the feasibility of utilizing an ESOP in a particular transaction should consult with advisers who are experienced in these matters.

14

Strategies and Tactics of Share Repurchases

Roberts Wyckoff Brokaw III

Managing Director,
Merrill Lynch Capital Markets

Charles J. Plohn, Jr.

Managing Director,
Merrill Lynch Capital Markets

Share repurchase programs are common today among publicly owned corporations. In 1987, approximately 1550 corporations announced repurchase programs totaling about 2.7 billion shares, with a market value of almost $86 billion, including almost 1200 announcements covering 1.7 billion shares, with a market value of $43 billion, after the stock market crash on October 19. Approximately 725 companies in 1988 announced plans to repurchase some 2 billion shares, with market value of $57.3 billion (not including the 135 million shares that four companies announced they would be repurchasing as part of an "unbundled stock unit" program, a plan that was subsequently dropped).

Buyback programs run the gamut from open-market purchases undertaken over long periods of time to satisfy normal, recurring needs (for instance, to supply shares sold pursuant to various issuer-sponsored programs, such as stock option, stock purchase, or dividend reinvestment plans), to large, one-time self-tenders using cash raised from a major borrowing and/or disposition of assets. The point between these two extremes where the reacquisition of shares is classified as a restructuring varies from situation to situation. Buybacks that are not significant on their own may be deemed part of an important restructuring when combined with certain transactions discussed in other chapters of this volume.

In this chapter we do not dwell on determining the point at which a buyback program constitutes all or part of a restructuring. Armed with the knowledge provided in other chapters of this volume, the reader's ability to recognize a restructuring may be like U.S. Supreme Court Justice Potter Stewart's capacity to perceive pornography—"I know it when I see it." For this discussion, it does not matter whether or not an announced accumulation program crosses the line. Our purpose is to present a framework to determine whether repurchases should be undertaken and, if so, to ascertain the most cost-effective tactics, with the objective of maximizing shareholder investment value.

Conceptual Differences between Share Repurchases and Extraordinary Distributions

Share repurchases and extraordinary distributions either via dividend or recapitalization are three major methods of apportioning a given amount of assets (e.g., cash) or securities (e.g., debentures) to common shareholders. Admittedly, our categorizations are a bit arbitrary. For instance, some recapitalizations may in fact use share repurchases as a means of reducing the common equity base. These three methods, as summarized in Table 14-1, entail some simplifying assumptions, to assist in ease of illustration.

A given amount of cash can be expended via either a repurchase program or an extraordinary dividend. In theory, these two methods generate equal pretax aggregate values to shareholders, and therefore a choice between the two would probably be a matter of indifference under most abstract financial analyses. However, important practical differences can result from tax and accounting considerations, dividend policy, or objectives regarding certain target blocks of stock.

Table 14-1. Comparison of Restructuring Options and Impacts

Share repurchase	Extraordinary dividend	Recapitalization
	Size Relative to Share Base	
Large, medium, or small	Medium or small	Large
	Impact on Issuer	
Reduces outstanding shares	Does not change outstanding shares	Reclassifies shares
Improves positive EPS if "earnings yield" (E/P ratio) is greater than aftertax cost of (or return on) cash, and reduces number of shares on which dividends must be paid	Future EPS not as high as under share repurchase	Alters prior-period comparability of EPS book value per share, and dividends
	Reduces book value per share	Reduces debt capacity
Increases book value per share for purchases below book value and vice versa	Reduces debt capacity	
Reduces debt capacity		
	Impact on Holders*	
Selling holders: Initially, increases shareholder investment value; "weakest" holdings removed	Pro rata distribution: Initially, increases shareholder investment value; over longer term, depends on impact that distributing corporate resources has on the company's future opportunities	Initially, increases shareholder investment value; over longer term, depends on (1) impact that distributing corporate resources has on the company's future opportunities and (2) consequences of any disproportionate reduction in share ownership
Nonselling holders: Whether better or worse off than sellers depends on future share price performance		

*Before calculating any tax impact.

Notably, of the 12 major reasons given below for corporations to acquire shares, only two or perhaps three would apply to an extraordinary dividend.

From the corporation's viewpoint, an extraordinary distribution does not reduce the share base for computing future earnings per share (EPS). If the same cash is devoted to a share repurchase, future EPS will be higher than if an extraordinary payout had been effected. This cosmetic bookkeeping advantage of the buyback could result over time in more favorable comments by analysts. The repurchase also reduces the amount of cash necessary to maintain a constant per-share dividend policy and permits absorption of shares from those most ready to sell, thereby improving the overall market for the issuer's equity.

The stock repurchase also is more tax-efficient from the shareholder's point of view. The greater flexibility of the share repurchase affords tax-sensitive investors a greater variety of ways to optimize their aftertax position. Under a repurchase, individual holders' future plans will determine whether they are better off offering their shares (or receiving the equivalent cash as a pro rata dividend) or not offering their shares. As discussed below, major holders with either a low tax basis or some other reason not to sell their shares (e.g., control considerations) can optimize their position even further with a transaction involving "share repurchase puts" (SHARPs).

For a restructuring of significant proportions, the flexibility of a share repurchase has fewer real advantages over a recapitalization that forces pro rata distribution to all holders—or, in one important variation, all holders who are not affiliated with the management group. (Public holders—those not affiliated with management—often receive mostly cash and/or fixed-income securities plus a disproportionately small amount of new shares, while the management group receives only new shares, in a disproportionately large number, but one that approximates parity value with the total package given the public.) The value premium and aggregate consideration involved usually make participation compelling, even for the most tax-sensitive holders. The changes in book value and earnings per share are so extreme that even less sophisticated analysts and investors should recognize the clear distinction between EPS before and after restructuring. In recapitalizations designed to increase management-affiliated holders' proportionate ownership via share reclassification, the distinction is especially clear. A major transaction of this variety presents a good reason to change regular dividend policy. Finally, since a shareholder vote is often mandatory or deemed advisable, certainty of a single proportionate treatment of the public holders also can make the best sense.

Should a repurchase be selected rather than an extraordinary distribution or a recapitalization, the following analysis can be relevant. While small share repurchase programs may fall short of restructuring, many of the same considerations can apply. Aspects relevant to such smaller programs are therefore also important in our discussion.

Why Corporations Reacquire Their Own Shares

Companies that reacquire their shares generally do so for one or more of the following reasons:

- To invest excess cash at a higher rate of return on equity
- To change the capital structure
- To increase earnings per share
- To increase the book value per share of the remaining shares
- To use as an acquisition currency
- To offset dilution of "issuer plans," such as stock purchase, stock option, dividend reinvestment, or similar plans for employees or security holders of the issuer
- To eliminate smaller shareholdings and thus reduce servicing costs
- To eliminate an undesirable major shareholder
- To defend against an actual or threatened takeover proposal
- To inhibit potential raiders from accumulating shares in the open market
- To remove market overhang and increase the percentage of ownership of the remaining shareholders
- To show management confidence in the company
- To create or add to an employee stock ownership plan (ESOP)

It should also be noted, however, that a repurchase program can produce adverse results, including:

- A possible decline in the stock's liquidity
- The negative implication that management cannot find viable reinvestment opportunities for surplus funds in the company's existing business
- A reduction in net worth and borrowing capacity plus an increase in the debt-to-equity ratio
- An increase in the percentage of ownership represented by a potential raider's existing share position
- No pooling-of-interests acquisition accounting for two years unless

there is strong evidence to indicate that the shares were reacquired not
as currency for a stock merger but rather for other qualified purposes

Suitability and Size of a Repurchase Program

Numerous financial and market factors must be considered in evaluating the stability and size of a repurchase program, including:

- The company's cash position and impact on future cash flow
- Debt-to-equity ratio
- Projected debt capacity
- Credit ratings
- Pro forma earnings impact, including opportunity costs
- Relative price/earnings ratio
- Stock price versus historical stock price range
- Market liquidity
- Likely tax impact on shareholders

The company's needs for future financial flexibility—for instance, to
finance expansion of its business or to make acquisitions—can limit the
size of the program. Also, the pro forma improvement in EPS can be
small or even negative for companies with high price/earnings multiples, placing practical limits on the number of shares acquired. Finally,
a more ambitious program generally produces higher average repurchase prices, meaning diminishing marginal returns.

These various factors have been considered relating solely to a share
buyback. Particularly in large repurchases or recapitalizations, cash often is raised through the sale of assets, offsetting the negative impact on
financial flexibility and drawing a clear line between operating results
before and after restructuring.

Repurchase Methods

Companies generally reacquire their own shares through open-market
purchases, self-tenders, exchange offers, and private transactions. Each
of these methods is governed to some degree by Securities and Exchange Commission (SEC) rules and regulations.

Issuers usually reacquire their shares in the open market pursuant to Rule 10b-18, which was adopted by the SEC (Release No. 34-19244) effective November 26, 1982. Rule 10b-18 provides a "safe harbor" from liability for manipulation connected with repurchases of common stock in open-market transactions by the issuer and certain related persons. The issuer and other affiliated persons will not incur liability under the antimanipulative provisions of the federal securities laws [Sections 9(a)(2) or 10(b) and Rule 10b-5] if purchases are made in compliance with the purchasing conditions of the rule, which limit the time, volume, and price of repurchases and the number of broker-dealers that may be used. Compliance with the safe harbor provisions of Rule 10b-18, however, does not shield the issuer and affiliated purchasers from the antifraud provisions of Rule 10b-5, and Rule 10b-18 repurchase programs should therefore not be undertaken when the issuer is in possession of material nonpublic information. Purchases of common stock made on behalf of an "issuer plan" by an "agent independent of the issuer" are not considered to be attributable to the issuer and are not covered by the rule.

Cash tender offers and exchange offers by issuers for their own securities are generally regulated by SEC Rule 13e-4. The rule, which was adopted effective September 21, 1979, imposes filing, disclosure, dissemination, and substantive requirements in connection with issuer tender offers in order to prevent fraudulent, deceptive, and manipulative acts and practices.

The disclosure requirements of the rule include the source and amount of funds for the offer, the purpose of the offer and, if material, certain historical financial statements and pro forma information on the effect of the tender offer on items such as the issuer's balance sheet, income statement, and book value. The substantive requirements of Rule 13e-4 cover such matters as the period of the offer, withdrawal rights, pro rata purchases, any increase in consideration, payment for return of securities, and postoffer purchases, and generally parallel the substantive provisions of the Williams Act regulations of third-party tender offers.

Private transactions between an issuer and selling holder are subject to the antimanipulative provisions of Section 9(a)(2) and Rule 10b-5. During the course of a Rule 13e-4 tender or exchange offer, all purchases must be made in accordance with the terms of the offer. Privately negotiated purchases that are made during the course of a Rule 10b-18 repurchase program may, under certain circumstances, affect the repurchase program's compliance with the Rule 10b-18 safe harbor conditions.

Choosing the Appropriate
Method of Repurchase

In Table 14-2, we set forth in a matrix format several of the consider-ations used to select a method of repurchase. The appropriate starting point is the issuer's primary objective—how many shares it wants to reacquire, within what price limits, and over what time period. Along with consideration of general stock market conditions and forecasts, this analysis would include:

- Stock price relative to general market averages
- Stock price relative to its industry group share levels
- Share price range over the past year
- Daily, monthly, and annual trading volume
- Segmented price and volume analysis (trading volume at different price levels plus cumulative totals)
- Block trading activity

Additional factors to consider are:

- The percentages of individual and institutional ownership, evaluation of recent turnover, a breakdown by size of holdings and geographic distribution, and, in some instances, the likely tax impacts for differ-ent owner segments (based on when they are likely to have purchased shares and at what prices)
- A comparison and evaluation of self-tenders of comparable size by other issuers, including the percentage of shares outstanding sought, the percentages of monthly and annual trading volume sought, pre-miums paid and stock price relative to the price range over the past year
- An evaluation of comparably sized open-market repurchase pro-grams by other issuers

In the period from January 1986 to July 1988, *open-market* programs represented 86 percent of the total number of announced repurchases, as well as 79 percent both of the total number of shares sought and of their market value; however, these programs on average represented less than 7 percent of the shares outstanding of those issuers announc-ing open-market programs, although various companies authorized more than one open-market program during the period. *Self-tenders* employing cash and those employing securities (i.e., exchange offers) as

Table 14-2. Comparison of Methods of Share Repurchase

	Privately negotiated purchase	Open-market purchase	Self-tender			
			Fixed price/cash	Dutch auction/cash	Exchange of securities	SHARPs
Strategic Considerations						
Timing	Immediate once negotiated	Completion date uncertain in advance	Expiration date specified in advance	Expiration date specified in advance	Expiration date specified in advance	Expiration date specified in advance
Market exposure/trading considerations	None, to the extent that the number of shares included in the purchase satisfies the company's needs	More flexible than self-tenders but involves market risk since there is uncertainty about the actual number of shares that could be acquired within a specified time period and price change	Less flexible than open-market purchase, but avoids prolonged market risk while providing greater certainty that the number of shares being sought would be acquired within a specified period at a specified price	Less flexible than open-market purchase, but avoids prolonged market risk while providing greater certainty that the number of shares being sought would be acquired within a specified period at a price within a specified price range; greater price flexibility than fixed price/cash tender	Less flexible than open-market purchase, but avoids prolonged market risk while providing greater certainty that the number of shares being sought would be acquired within a specified period for specified consideration	Less flexible than open-market purchase, but avoids prolonged market risk while providing greater certainty that the number of shares being sought would be acquired within a specified period for specified consideration

Table 14-2. Comparison of Methods of Share Repurchase (*Continued*)

	Privately negotiated purchase	Open-market purchase	Fixed price/cash	Dutch auction/cash	Exchange of securities	SHARPs
			Strategic Considerations	Self-tender		
Targeting of holders	Specific holder(s)	Any holder selling shares in the open market (often blocks from institutional holders)	All shareholders	All shareholders	All shareholders	SHARPs are distributed proportionately to all shareholders, but those not wishing to sell can still capture the premium by selling the SHARPs to holders who do wish to sell.
Impact on holders:						
Selling holders	Sell shares at a negotiated price with no market risk.	Sell shares at market price.	Sell shares at a premium to market price. Possible proration.	Sell shares at a premium to market price. Possible proration.	Sell shares at a premium to market price. Possible proration.	Sell shares at a premium to market price. All shares tendered with put rights are accepted.

Nonselling holders	No consideration Their percentage of outstanding shares increases.	No consideration Their percentage of outstanding shares increases.	No consideration Their percentage of outstanding shares increases.	No consideration Their percentage of outstanding shares increases.	No consideration Their percentage of outstanding shares increases.	Can sell put rights to other holders who want to tender shares, thereby capturing premium. Their percentage of outstanding shares increases.
Financial statement impact	Immediate impact of reduced number of shares	Impact of reduced number of shares spread over the purchase period	Impact immediately after expiration of self-tender	Impact immediately after expiration of self-tender	Impact immediately after expiration of exchange offer	Impact immediately after expiration of put rights
Use of securities firms	Usually no (sometimes as adviser)	Yes (as agent)	Usually yes (as dealer-manager or adviser)	Usually yes (as dealer-manager or adviser)	Usually yes (as dealer-manager or adviser)	Usually yes (as dealer-manager or adviser)
Transaction costs	Generally none	Negotiated commission	Fees for depositary, forwarding agent and information agent, advertising, printing, postage, legal and accounting. Often fees for either (1) financial adviser or (2) dealer-manager and, possibly, soliciting dealers.			

Table 14-2. Comparison of Methods of Share Repurchase (Continued)

			Self-tender			
	Privately negotiated purchase	Open-market purchase	Fixed price/cash	Dutch auction/cash	Exchange of securities	SHARPs
			Legal Considerations			
Public announcement	Generally after the transaction	Not required unless material Recommended for shareholder relations	Required	Required	Required	Required
Applicable SEC regulation	9(a)(2) 10b-5	9(a)(2) 10b-18 (safe harbor) 10b-5	13e-4 10b-5	13e-4 10b-5	13e-4 10b-5	13e-4 10b-5
State corporate law	Valid corporate purpose Within corporate power	Valid corporate purpose Within corporate power	Valid corporate purpose Within corporate power	Valid corporate purpose Within corporate power	Valid corporate purpose "Blue sky" statutes Within corporate power	Valid corporate purpose "Blue sky" statutes Within corporate power
Volume	Subject to general antimanipulative restrictions	Daily purchases subject to 10b-18 volume limits plus blocks	Number of shares specified in advance	Number of shares specified in advance	Number of shares specified in advance	Number of shares specified in advance

Price	Subject to general antimanip-ulative restric-tions	Purchases made at market prices / Average cost per share can-not be deter-mined in ad-vance	Specified price per share (usu-ally at a pre-mium)	Specified price range per share (usually at a premium)	Specified per share consider-ation (usually at a premium) of securities and possibly some cash	Specified price per share (usu-ally at a pre-mium)

When Recommended

Readily identifi-able blocks available at prices at or near market	Proportionately smaller repur-chase needs or needs spread over an ex-tended period of time, in any case where a liquid market exists	High-premium transactions where pro ra-tion is accept-able	Instances where share price is volatile or where price needed to ac-quire a given amount of stock is uncer-tain	Instances where new securities could not be readily or quickly sold to finance a cash tender; certain other special instances	Larger, higher-premium ten-ders where there are large inside and/or tax-sensitive holders

a single category represented 4 percent of the total number of announcements, more than 11 percent of the total number of shares sought, more than 14 percent of the total dollar amount, and on average 25 percent of the shares outstanding. *Private* repurchases, generally from unwanted suitors, retiring management, or institutional holders, represented 10 percent of the announcements, 9 percent of the shares, and 7 percent of the dollar amount, while representing on average 11 percent of the shares outstanding of those issuers announcing private reacquisitions.

Some Generalizations

When comparing the various repurchase methods, the following generalizations should be kept in mind.

Sizable open-market repurchase programs involve market risk because there is uncertainty about the actual number of shares that can be acquired within a certain time period or within a specified price range. Although there is not an explicit price premium, repurchases tend to support the price of the stock during the reacquisition period. Open-market repurchases are more flexible than self-tenders, and the only additional costs to the issuer are negotiated commissions, generally computed on a cents-per-share basis.

It is also important to remember that each open-market program has its own personality based on the issuer's objectives. Within the limits of Rule 10b-18, open-market programs can be as aggressive or passive as the issuer wants. For example, companies can be in the market for daily purchases (which are subject to Rule 10b-18 volume limitations), daily purchases plus blocks (which are exempt from the volume limitations), or blocks only. In addition, blocks can be solicited or unsolicited.

Self-tenders are more visible than open-market repurchases and provide an effective means of generating interest in the stock. They often provide the quickest way to repurchase a large amount of stock and allow issuers to avoid prolonged market risk, meaning greater certainty that the number of shares being sought will be acquired within a specified period at a specified price. A self-tender is the fairest repurchase method, since it results in an offer to all holders, and it can provide issuers a way to eliminate odd-lot holdings, which are costly to service.

However, self-tenders are much less flexible than open-market repurchases. They must remain open for at least four weeks, require a premium over market, and entail greater additional costs, such as fees for any dealer-manager and any soliciting dealers, the depositary, and the forwarding and information agents, as well as advertising, printing, postage, legal, and accounting costs.

Self-Tender Special Cases

"Dutch auctions" and share repurchase puts (SHARPs) are special cases of the self-tender that can be important tools to the issuer in effecting an efficient repurchase. The former is frequently employed today for tenders in which precise pricing is an important consideration. The latter now is rarely used but has potentially greater applicability. It allows major nontendering holders to benefit from the premium over market that would otherwise be effectively unavailable to them.

The *Dutch auction* technique, first used in 1981, permits the issuer to specify a range of prices within which it is willing to entertain tenders and, at expiration, select a single acceptable price payable to holders tendering at or below that price. Applicable securities regulations require that one price be paid for all shares purchased. The Dutch auction gives the issuer an inside look at the "supply curve" for its shares and efficiently accommodates market shifts during the 20-business-day minimum period that an offer must be open. After all, in light of shifting markets, even perfect knowledge of the price at which a given amount of stock is available on the day a tender is launched may be incorrect four weeks later.

Share repurchase puts are short-lived, transferable rights (distributed pro rata to all holders) to tender a given number of shares to the issuer, generally at a premium over market at the time the program is launched. SHARPs are effectively the reverse of a traditional rights offering (i.e., rights to *acquire* shares *below* market). SHARPs give all holders the ability to capture the market value premium, through either (1) participation in the tender or (2) sale of their rights to others (for an amount that should approximate the excess of the put price over the then-current share price).

This second degree of freedom is particularly important to large holders who would not sell their shares because of control or tax considerations. For a holder with a low tax basis, the receipt and sale of the SHARPs, although taxable events, can produce positive economics in situations where participation in a self-tender would not: The tax relates only to the value premium, which is represented by the SHARPs. Because only the SHARPs need to be sold to capture the premium, there is less destabilization of the shareholder base. "Weak" holders are provided a means to sell back to the company, and "strong" holders are not pressured to sell merely to capture the premium. By contrast, in a traditional single-price or Dutch auction self-tender, even those institutions that would otherwise be long-term holders might well sell their shares to arbitrageurs, who are better able to deal with the market dynamics involved.

While a full discussion of SHARPs is beyond the scope of this presentation, suffice it to say that the technique may not make sense in small self-tenders where the premiums involved are also small. The vehicle also entails certain securities and tax-law complexities beyond those of traditional self-tenders and may cause difficulties under the antidilution provisions of certain convertible securities, warrants, and options.

A final method of self-tender, which can be effected in any of the single-price, Dutch auction, or SHARPs formats, is a voluntary exchange of new securities for outstanding common stock. Because cash is simple and therefore often the more cost-effective vehicle, the exchange should be reserved for those instances in which raising the cash is not possible because of time, credit, or market capacity constraints, or possibly in which the exchange suits certain tax or market-matching objectives that are not possible with cash. Not surprisingly, exchange offers for common stock, as well as the cash form of self-tender, are used more often when the proportion of outstanding shares sought is high.

Private transactions provide a good way to very quickly eliminate large overhanging blocks or an undesirable major shareholder. However, they raise questions of discrimination in favor of certain shareholders.

Careful Review of Overall Strategy

Share repurchases are an important means to reduce an issuer's equity base via payments to holders, although other methods clearly exist. Determining whether repurchases constitute the most cost-effective way requires a careful review of overall strategy. Even after a decision to implement repurchases has been made, the most efficient tactics are by no means necessarily obvious without careful study, particularly given the legal and market constraints involved and the proliferation of new techniques now available to issuers.

PART 3

Related
Issues

15

The Contribution of Executive Search to the Corporate Restructuring Process

Hobson Brown, Jr.

President,
Russell Reynolds Associates Inc.

Steven B. Potter

Managing Director,
Russell Reynolds Associates Inc.

No management, no bid. McKinley Allsopp faced an investor's classic dilemma. The investment banking firm needed to supply management in order to bid in the 1987 auction of North American Systems Inc., the Cleveland-based maker of Mr. Coffee drip coffee makers. McKinley Allsopp had 14 days to find an operating entrepreneur who could manage for cash and growth in a highly leveraged, cash-constrained environment. It retained Russell Reynolds Associates, which in six days found Jack Eikenberg, past chief operating officer and executive vice president of Cuisinarts Inc., and past president and group vice president of the Revere Ware Division of Revere Copper and Brass Inc. The investor group, including Eikenberg as would-be president and chief executive officer, planned bidding strategy, valued North American System's assets, and performed necessary due diligence. The group bid seven times operating income, or about $72 million, and won the auction. The shift in corporate control of Mr. Coffee took just 76 days.

Corporate restructuring demands investing, financing, and operating decisions. Cash generation is critical, and return to competitiveness is paramount. Success stems from gains in operating efficiency and is measured in traditional terms of rates and ratios of profitability (return on equity), productivity (return on sales), efficiency (return on assets), and total return to shareholders.

Going outside a company to find new management can often be the key success factor in corporate restructuring strategy. As is widely observed, when a company wants to make big changes, outsiders can often be freer to deliver the necessary shocks.

A 1988 study of 80 business units at large corporations conducted by the Strategic Planning Institute, Cambridge, Massachusetts, concluded that executives recruited from the outside had a greater impact on the performance of corporations in growth and declining stages of their product life cycles than executives promoted from within. Successful outsiders exceeded their profit goals by 10 percent, whereas those promoted from within failed to meet their profit goals by an average of 15 percent. The study found that outsiders adapt better to turbulent market conditions because they have new ideas, are willing to consider alternative solutions, and are less inclined to stick with ineffective strategies and policies.

Clients who go outside to attract executive talent rely on the perceptiveness and speed of executive recruiting consultants to identify candidates who can refocus a company and hasten its return to competitive leadership. The search process becomes a stringent test of perceptiveness and judgment.

Understanding the implications of a search for a client's business is essential. Quick and thorough identification of appropriate candidates is the initial challenge. A recruiter's judgment of candidates' suitability for the client and the position is next. Then exhaustive interviews with each candidate shape perception of each individual's character, ability, and performance. After presentation of candidates to a client, thorough checks with past colleagues and personal references strengthen or weaken the client's perception of each finalist.

Need for an Operating Entrepreneur

In a restructuring strategy, the search process generally focuses on a client's need for an operating entrepreneur who can manage for both cash and growth to maximize investors' total return. Several examples in this chapter, including Mr. Coffee, British Airways, and Harnischfeger Industries Inc., will show that executive search contributes to a successful restructuring strategy by finding the strongest "outside" operating decision maker quickly.

The management goal in corporate restructuring is to enhance the future earning power of underlying assets. The objective is to convert low-return assets into high-return assets by focusing on core business and core skills.

When initiated via tender offer by investor groups with industry experience or existing managements, corporate restructuring is an investing decision subsequently supported by operating decisions (as in Mr. Coffee). When initiated by current management, it is an operating decision later fueled by investing decisions (as in British Airways and Harnischfeger Industries). In both cases each party restructures to unleash growth potential. Each perceives opportunities to own assets that are undervalued relative to perceived future cash-generating abilities.

The bid for Mr. Coffee is an example of restructuring as an investing decision. The founders of North American Systems, a company that was formed in 1968 and grew to $115 million in sales by 1987, wanted to sell. McKinley Allsopp, the interested buyer, saw an opportunity to enter the world's second-largest commodity business (coffee), a stable "smokestack" industry with predictable future cash-generating ability. The investor group also believed that it could operate and build the business by first reducing operating costs and then identifying complementary lines of business to capitalize on Mr. Coffee's brand name, its aggressive marketing and sales orientation, its three strong distribution channels, and its cohesive team management concept.

Mr. Coffee's share in the U.S. coffee maker market was about 32 percent, twice as large as the nearest two competitors. It had been able to maintain that share over a five-year period despite stiff competition. In addition, the company was dominant in the coffee filter and replacement decanter markets, had a strong sales force, and advertised heavily to promote brand-name recognition. Marketing as a percent of sales averaged about 16 percent, or $20 million per year.

Financing decisions support investing decisions in corporate restructurings. Leveraged capital structures are popular in periods of economic growth and moderate inflation because investors can control assets of potentially great future value with minimum equity investment. But this leverage carries high risk. Debt as a percent of total capitalization can rise from optimal levels of 25 to 40 percent, depending on the riskiness of corporate assets, to 80 or 90 percent, and debt-to-equity ratios sometimes rise to 10 to 1 or more (11 to 1 in the case of Mr. Coffee).

Cash becomes critical because of debt service. Management must generate sufficient cash through cost reductions, price increases, and increases in unit volume, or through asset sales, in order to both raise interest coverage *and* reduce debt. In the Mr. Coffee deal, the investor group expected to generate more than enough cash in the first year to offset its approximate $10 million annual interest expense.

At least one study of 755 companies that issued high-yield debt from 1980 through 1986 concluded that high-yield companies outperformed industry in general (Economic Research Bureau, State University of New York at Stony Brook). In both growing and shrinking industries, high-yield companies increased employment at an average annual rate of 6.7 percent, versus 1.4 percent for industry. Productivity also rose as sales per employee for these companies outperformed industry in general. Sales grew faster than industry (9.38 percent versus 6.42 percent) and new capital investment in property, plant, and equipment grew more than twice as fast for high-yield companies (10.6 percent) than for industry in general (3.8 percent).

Management and Its Assumptions

Leveraged restructurings are not always successful. They sometimes fail because investor groups are overly optimistic about the future. They may overpay, believing that overly aggressive estimates of future sales can generate enough cash to raise interest coverage. In effect, they buy assets on the basis of projected rather than demonstrated earning power. In 1988, General Electric Co. paid a 170 percent premium over the then-current share price to buy Roper Corp. Bridgestone Corp. paid a 124 percent premium for Firestone Tire & Rubber Co., and Kelso & Co. paid a 114 percent premium to buy American Standard Inc. These premiums were reasonable or unrealistic in light of future cash-generating expectations.

Optimism sowed the seeds of failure in the restructurings of both Revco D.S. Inc. and National Intergroup Inc. In just 16 months the $1.2 billion buyout of Revco, a large drugstore chain, became the biggest failure in the history of leveraged buyouts. Sales were projected to increase by 13 percent and earnings by 42 percent to $103.6 million. But cash flow estimates were too aggressive. Increased competition forced price cuts that squeezed margins. Sales rose only about 6 percent, and the company lost $59 million in fiscal 1987 and another $50.1 million in the first nine months of fiscal 1988. Management subsequently defaulted on a $46 million interest payment on its $150 million-per-year interest expense.

Although there was no leveraged buyout (LBO), National Intergroup, the nation's sixth largest steelmaker in 1980, overpaid to restructure. The company's strategy was to diversify out of cyclical steel and into perceived growth industries such as oil and drugs. However, oil prices dropped, drug industry competition intensified, and an attempt to integrate divisions resulted in expense-control problems. Debt rose to $441 million (a debt-to-equity ratio of 2 to 1), and goodwill and intangibles rose to 30 percent of stockholders' equity. Unprofitable since 1984, the company reported a loss of $21.9 million on 1988 sales of $3.36 billion.

The examples clearly demonstrate that management—by the nature of its assumptions and decisions—is the number one issue in a restructuring strategy. After investing and financing decisions have been made, management's operating decisions determine whether operating margins beat the cost of capital. Savvy investors look for exceptional management to increase profitability and returns on equity, assets, and sales.

Investor groups in restructurings either have capable operating entrepreneurs with whom to joint-venture, or they must find them. There are four scenarios:

- Investors may buy assets and keep existing management in place to operate the assets in a restructured environment.

- They may gain control of assets but have to search for executive talent to manage them.

- They may gain control and have to replace existing management.

- Or they may have access to capable operating entrepreneurs but need to buy assets for them to manage.

Investor groups retain executive recruiters to help them to find, as quickly as possible, quality outside managers who can manage for cash and growth. And investor groups use compensation structures to provide the proper incentive to improve corporate performance. Operating entrepreneurs usually take equity ownership in a restructured investment, plus cash compensation for performance exceeding previously agreed-upon targets for return on investment and on capital employed. Compensation packages align the interests of management and investor groups.

Ability to Manage Growth Profitably

In the case of Mr. Coffee, McKinley Allsopp needed an experienced chief operating officer who had the ability to manage growth profitably. This is no easy task in a restructured environment in which cash must be allocated to debt service, not to reinvestment. Russell Reynolds Associates identified Jack Eikenberg, among a dozen potential candidates, as the best suited to the entire Mr. Coffee challenge: appraisal, bid strategy, closing the transaction, and managing the acquisition.

Lengthy interviews shaped perception of an accomplished general manager with full attention to profitable growth, skill in protecting a position as a low-cost producer, concern for employee communication, and talent for developing strong customer relations. A background check revealed that Eikenberg had achieved sustainable profitable growth at Revere Ware. And through extensive reference checks, our firm also was able to advise McKinley Allsopp that Eikenberg was a relationship manager. He had been the only two-time president of the Cookware Manufacturers Association and had solid relationships within the industry as well as with retail distributors of his past product lines. We considered him very able to build Mr. Coffee successfully.

The implications of his reputation and relationships to Mr. Coffee's marketing strategy were very significant. The company had historically relied on a "pull" strategy, using Joe DiMaggio in its advertising campaigns to try to attract customers to its products. But Eikenberg represented a new marketing thrust: broadened distribution (in partnership with retailers) through new channels and volume increases in existing channels—the addition of a powerful "push" to Mr. Coffee's marketing mix.

In addition, through the interviewing and bidding process, Eikenberg revealed his thorough understanding of how Mr. Coffee could grow by capitalizing on its core skills. He saw the company as an aggressive marketing and sales organization, which had three strong, underutilized distribution channels in housewares, food, and institutions, and which had an underutilized brand name. He recognized new product opportunities and introduced a completely redesigned line of coffee makers and "hot beverage" appliances. And he changed the corporate culture to that of a company that "hates waste, demands quality, respects its employees, and loves to win." Both Russell Reynolds Associates and McKinley Allsopp believed we had found someone who would foster the competitive team spirit necessary to make Mr. Coffee a world-class company.

Our belief that Eikenberg could manage Mr. Coffee for cash was borne out. Even as paper and plastics suppliers were raising prices, Eikenberg spoke of the ability to lower the cost of sales by a greater percentage. During extensive interviews, he spoke of saving more than $2 million by negotiating common carrier and shipping container freight rates, eliminating about 250,000 square feet of warehouse space, and reducing staff size. He estimated total cost savings at about $5 million. Eikenberg also envisioned a rise in unit price of Mr. Coffee machines, without losing volume, and an elimination of about $10 million of profitless sales of Mr. Coffee filters (about one-third of total sales). He believed that the profit effect of this operating entrepreneurship would amount to about 5 percent higher operating margins on coffee makers and 5 to 7 percent higher operating margins on filters. If he could also raise productivity from about $200,000 to $250,000 in sales per employee, then he expected that operating returns on total capital would be close to 25 percent and operating returns on sales would be about 14 percent.

Need to Replace Existing Management

Another company that faced a different management challenge in its restructuring process was Hanson Industries Inc., the U.S. arm of the English conglomerate Hanson Trust PLC. Through purchase of U.S. Industries Inc. in 1984, Hanson gained control of family-managed Duke City Lumber, a $40 million lumber products company (with profits of $500,000 in 1984). Hanson needed to replace existing management and restore profitability.

Hanson retained Russell Reynolds Associates to find a new president for this unit of its building products group. The successful candidate had to be a strong general manager from the wood products industry, with lumber mill operating experience, to reduce costs, consolidate assets, negotiate timber procurement contracts, and broaden distribution channels. He had to be a leader who could change the company's corporate culture to a profit motive, a team player who could improve management skills, and a person with the stature necessary to be considered for group or corporate succession.

After researching the industry, our firm introduced Dan Dutton, past operations manager for Louisiana-Pacific Corp. His operating strengths were clear, and his profit orientation seemed particularly well suited to a company like Duke City, which had historically not focused on profitability as a clear corporate objective.

Dutton delegated responsibility and introduced accounting control systems designed to create awareness of the profit impact of employee decisions. He reduced the work force by 40 percent, expanded plant capacity by approximately 30 percent, and eliminated approximately $10 million of unprofitable business. The results: Profits rose dramatically, as Duke City earned $2.5 million on $41 million in sales in 1986, $4 million on $40 million in sales in 1987, and $6 million on $40 million in sales in 1988. Return on capital also rose, placing Duke City near the top in that category among Hanson's 120 companies in the United States.

Buying Management First

Given the success of restructurings, investor groups now frequently retain executive recruiters to identify strong operating entrepreneurs and then bid for control of assets that those entrepreneurs can manage. In other words, investors buy management first, then assets. Weiss, Peck & Greer, an investment and merchant banking firm, invested in John Mahoney first and TransLogic second.

TransLogic Corp., Denver, Colorado, was a one-product business unit of Mark Controls Corp., based in Skokie, Illinois. It had 1983 sales of about $20 million. It made pneumatic tubes to transport interoffice paperwork and lightweight materials, and did 90 percent of its business with hospitals. The parent managed the unit's narrow, mature product lines for cash, not growth. But Mahoney, president of the unit, perceived broader solutions to interoffice delivery problems using high-technology systems. He saw cash *and* growth.

After 17 years at TransLogic, Mahoney and his management team initiated a $23 million leveraged buyout of the company in 1983, using their own money. His plan was to diversify the company's product lines, its revenue sources, and its customer base, and to build sales through new product introductions, acquisitions of competing product lines, and a bigger, more productive sales force.

Weiss, Peck & Greer learned of Mark Controls' interest in selling TransLogic from the auditing firm the two had in common. Mahoney piqued the firm's interest, and it backed him. By 1987 he had transformed TransLogic into a manufacturer of computerized industrial conveyors with higher margins on annual sales of about $40 million. Sales were growing at about 15 percent per year, only 50 percent of which originated with hospitals. TransLogic's restructuring was so dynamic that if the company were to go public, Weiss, Peck & Greer expected to reap a 10-fold return on its investment.

Outsiders Who Can Strengthen Competitive Advantage

As a prelude to restructuring, managements of companies often retain executive recruiters to find outside executives who will strengthen their competitive advantage.

British Airways, Britain's state-owned airline, had to improve operations before it could restructure. The company had historically suffered from burdensome overhead, a lack of productivity, government intervention, an operations-driven versus a marketing-driven strategy, and a belief that volume more than profitability was the key to success.

Performance reflected mounting inefficiency that culminated in serious losses in 1981. The airline reported operating margins of about 5 percent, but pretax losses (excluding nonrecurring losses and extraordinary items) of about $220 million on sales of $3.7 billion. Operations began to improve in 1982 as margins rose to about 12 percent and pretax profit rose to $77 million on sales of $3.4 billion. However, the company's net worth remained negative, and debt still exceeded 100 percent of total capitalization. At that time Lord King, chairman of British Airways, retained our firm to search for a group chief executive who could improve the company's operations further.

We identified Colin Marshall, former deputy chief executive of Sears Holdings PLC, a British retailer, and past president and chief executive officer of Avis Inc. Worldwide, as the most capable manager for the company's needs, and we presented him as the strongest candidate. Marshall had a track record of managing growth profitably. It had taken him only seven years, from 1964 to 1971, to move Avis past Hertz in European sales and profits. And between 1976 and 1979 he was responsible for Avis's sales increase from $433 million with $33 million in pretax profit, to $797 million with $82 million in pretax profit.

Our interviews with Marshall revealed the fact that because of his 24 years in the car rental/leasing business he understood service industries and computer reservation and ticketing systems. The firm perceived that Marshall knew the similarities between the car rental and airline industries and considered both travel-related, people businesses with virtually identical markets.

Lord King hired Marshall. He immediately cut British Airways' staff by about 25 percent and added more fuel-efficient equipment, thus cutting its passenger-load breakeven level to less than 60 percent. Operating margins improved in 1983 to about 15 percent, and pretax income rose to about $260 million on sales of $3.3 billion. At a time when Britain's Civil Aviation Authority had begun to question the carrier's future viability and had considered cutbacks in its international route network, Marshall vigorously attacked the company's productivity problem and service image.

To further build its competitive position, Marshall began an expansion drive to establish British Airways as one of the world's few "megacarriers" able to cope with higher capacity in the face of lower fares. It outbid Scandinavian Air Systems in 1987 to buy British Caledonian Airways for $457.9 million. This restructuring gave British Airways a virtual monopoly in Britain's airline industry and a dominant position in the European travel market in which air traffic was expected to grow faster than the U.S. market, and made it the world's leading international carrier in passenger miles flown (14.5 million in 1987). To build revenue, British Airways signed a marketing partnership agreement with United Airlines Inc. that was expected to increase passenger volume by about 200 to 300 passengers per day. It also pushed to modernize its computerized reservation system.

Reflecting its improved management, the company reported pretax profits of $260 million on sales of about $5.2 billion in fiscal 1987. Prior to the British Caledonian acquisition (lifting British Airway's 1988 revenues to $7.1 billion), the company's net worth was about $650 million and debt had fallen to about 35 percent of total capitalization. British Airways went public on February 11, 1987, at 125 pence per share, equivalent to $19.69 per American Depository Receipt. Its shares were among the biggest gainers on the London Stock Exchange in 1987, appreciating by almost 40 percent before October 19, 1987.

Adding Value to a Restructuring

Harnischfeger Industries is the final example of how executive recruiting can add value to restructurings. *The New York Times* hailed the company's return to competitiveness as a "Midwestern Miracle" and "…one of the more unlikely stories of modern industrial history."

Started in 1884, the Milwaukee company was run by the founder's grandson until 1982, when its product concentration, lack of financial controls, and slow responsiveness to changing market conditions led to troubled times. Sales of construction equipment fell about $135 million to a 1982 level of about $160 million. Middle East customers stopped buying because oil prices had plummeted, and the 1981–1982 recession dramatically reduced purchases of capital goods domestically while a strong dollar attracted heavy overseas competition.

Management reported 1982 sales of $451 million, 67 percent of which was of construction and mining equipment, and a pretax loss of $77.5 million. At its 1982 low, the market value of the publicly held company had fallen to $65 million from about $225 million in 1979, its debt as a percent of total capital had risen to about 58 percent from a historic average of about 40 percent, and it omitted its dividend.

In 1982, Henry Harnischfeger retained Russell Reynolds Associates to find a chief operating officer. He needed a person who could conserve and generate cash and restore the company to competitive life—in short, someone who could save the company.

Through extensive interviewing and sourcing, the firm identified, and presented as the suitable candidate, William W. Goessel, past executive vice president–paper group and member of the board of directors of Beloit Corp., a privately held manufacturer of pulp and paper with about $550 million in annual sales. The firm learned from interviews with Goessel that he was a company man, having spent 32 years at Beloit. He certainly knew manufacturing. The firm also perceived him as a good controller, a motivator, and a tough labor negotiator, with good instincts for people and timing—two instincts he would use most. Over a three-year period as group vice president, he had reduced overhead, introduced budgeting and controls at three plants, and succeeded in expanding pretax margins from 7 percent to 20 percent.

Goessel had resigned his position at Beloit, a family-owned business in which the family had decided to tighten its control. Believing that he would not be promoted to chief executive officer and that the company was headed for trouble, he sought a better opportunity. Our firm knew of him because of his past success in improving Beloit's operations.

At Harnischfeger, Goessel conserved cash immediately by cutting costs. He reduced corporate staff, halted purchase orders not related directly to order backlog, sold corporate aircraft and employee houses, delayed payables from 30 to 60 days, shut down a crane factory, and accepted stock options in lieu of cash bonuses and pay raises. In 1983, he negotiated standstill agreements with 17 bank and insurance company creditors, in which they were to be paid interest only, while escaping any limitations on future borrowing to finance acquisitions. He also retained our firm to find a quality chief financial officer to manage the company's financing decisions and financial controls. Jeffery T. Grade was recruited from IC Industries Inc. (now Whitman Corp.). Next, Goessel generated cash by bidding and winning a low-margin, $63 million sale of heavy machinery to the Turkish government. Agreeing to a risky sale at 5 percent below normal cost, he turned a 3 percent profit on the transaction by gaining design and wage concessions.

With cash in hand and renewed competitive strength, Goessel began restructuring Harnischfeger in 1986, the year in which he was promoted to chairman and chief executive officer and Jeffery Grade became president of the company. This team sold preferred stock to fund the $175 million acquisition of Beloit Corp., Goessel's previous employer and a company bigger than Harnischfeger. The timing of the purchase was superb, as the paper and forest products industries started to boom worldwide. Beloit accounted for 51 percent of Harnischfeger's 1987 sales of $957 million and 77 percent of its operating income.

Goessel raised even more cash both by selling a 20 percent interest in Beloit to Mitsubishi Heavy Industries for $60 million (effectively valuing Beloit at $300 million), and by capturing the overfunded portion of Beloit's pension plan. Goessel restructured again in 1986 by buying Syscon Corp., a computer company with substantial Defense Department contracts, for $92 million. Syscon generated $113 million in 1987 sales and $13.6 million in operating income while raising its order backlog to $329 million. Goessel also sold 80 percent of the company's construction equipment unit in a management-led leveraged buyout.

The results of Harnischfeger's restructuring have been impressive. The company recorded 1987 revenues of $974 million, 51 percent of which were sales of mining equipment, and had a record backlog of $1.1 billion at the end of January 1988. The company employs about 11,500 persons, up from about 2500 in 1982. Harnischfeger's stock price performance has been superb. From a 1982 low of $5.50 per share, the company's shares traded to a 1987 high of $29.875 per share, a five-year compound rate of total return to investors of more than 40 percent per year. Its market value rose to $782 million, 12 times its low of $65 million. As an expression of confidence in Harnischfeger's future, management reinstituted a cash dividend of $0.05 per quarter.

The Exercise of Perceptiveness

As these and many other examples of public companies demonstrate, executive recruiting contributes significantly to the success of corporate restructuring. Executive recruiters exercise perceptiveness and prudence in the timely identification of suitable candidates who can force operating efficiencies and capitalize on investing opportunities. The "value added" of executive search is its link to corporate competitiveness and profitability.

16

Executive Compensation Issues in a Restructuring

Peter T. Chingos

National Practice Director,
Compensation/Human Resources Consulting
Services, KPMG Peat Marwick

The importance of a highly motivated management team to a company in the process of restructuring cannot be overemphasized. To implement a major turnaround without paying close attention to the reward systems that drive key players is to court disaster. People are an organization's most valuable asset, especially in a restructuring.

To some extent, the principles of executive compensation are the same in a restructuring as in any other phase of a company's life cycle: the need for competitive base salaries, for sound salary increase policies, for identifying key managers for participation in incentive plans, for proper performance measures. These principles apply in all companies, no matter what their stage of growth. Compensation objectives don't change because of a restructuring—companies must still attract, retain, and motivate—but the means to achieve the objectives often do change. This is because executive compensation is based on the ability to identify key players and to set goals and objectives that support strategic financial objectives. In a restructuring, not only may the goals and objectives shift, but the players may change as well.

This chapter will focus on some of the executive compensation issues that challenge management in three kinds of restructuring: *mergers and acquisitions, leveraged buyouts (LBOs), and initial public offerings (IPOs)*. We will also examine the role of employment contracts.

Let us begin by reviewing some of the basic principles of compensation strategy alluded to above and outline the role each element of compensation plays in an executive compensation strategy.

There are three steps in formulating a compensation strategy:

1. Identify the structure of the new organization and determine how it is likely to change in the future—i.e., what are the specific financial and performance objectives that you are trying to achieve in the near and long term?

2. Identify who within the management ranks will play a role in attaining these objectives. It is important to distinguish between those who impact on annual performance and those who impact on longer-term performance.

3. Identify the elements of the pay program and the specific role each element plays in attracting, retaining, and motivating executives. As one goes through a reorganization, these relationships become even more significant.

The Elements of Compensation

Salary

Salary serves as the cornerstone of compensation and is the element on which all other forms of pay are based. If salary is low, it is likely that benefits, retirement income, and annual and long-term incentives will be low as well.

Though salary plays an important role in attracting and retaining executives, it is less significant as a motivating factor. Since controlling fixed costs is important in a restructuring, companies usually try to control salary increases and provide additional compensation through incentives. The objective is to maximize the use of base-salary dollars, and companies are increasingly placing greater emphasis on salary administration and performance management for all levels in the organization, including executives. This is done by first identifying what are the basic responsibilities and expectations of the individual, communicating the responsibilities to the individual, and then holding the individual accountable. By doing this, companies are able to give salary increases only when they are deserved and to hold back increases from those who are not contributing at the desired level.

Annual Incentives

Annual incentives are reward systems limited typically to a 12-month period. Specific performance objectives are identified and communicated before the plan year begins. The objective is to create a stronger relationship between desired business results and variable compensation.

Companies can fund the incentive pool in a number of ways. Heavily regulated industries (e.g., banks and savings and loan institutions) often use peer performance to determine the funds used for the annual incentive plan. Start-up companies often use plans based purely on management discretion. Growth companies generally use a fixed-formula method (e.g., 10 percent of earnings above a 6 percent return on equity) because they are not yet able to forecast specific financial results. Companies with a good planning process usually favor a goal-attainment plan based on achieving specific financial results.

In restructuring, annual incentives can be a significant means of attracting and motivating management. This is why target incentive opportunities as a percentage of salary are often higher in a restructuring than what is found under normal circumstances.

The success of any annual incentive plan depends on top management's willingness to judge performance and ability to measure the desired results. The difficulty in a restructuring is that with the change in mission and business objectives comes the need to change the internal performance measures used to support the new entity. Forecasting may therefore be difficult. Also, the new organization may want to increase or reduce the number of people eligible for annual incentives.

Long-Term Incentive Plans

Long-term incentive plans (also called "capital accumulation plans") reward executives for performance beyond one year—typically, three to five years and sometimes even 10 years. These plans involve either cash payments or equity. There are basically three kinds of long-term incentive plans commonly used in U.S. companies: investment plans, appreciation plans, and full value plans.

Investment Plans.   Under investment plans, the executive is given the opportunity to purchase shares of common stock at a fixed price over a specified period. The two most common types of investment plans are nonqualified stock options and incentive stock options.

Nonqualified stock options allow an executive to purchase stock at a fixed price for a specified period of time, usually 10 years. The option price is almost always equal to the fair market value at the time of grant, though it may be less or even more than fair market value. When the executive buys the shares, he or she is taxed at ordinary income rates on the spread between the grant price and the fair market value at exercise. There is no charge to earnings unless the option price is variable or less than 100 percent of fair market value at grant, and the company may deduct income recognized by the employee, provided the appropriate taxes are withheld (see Figure 16-1).

Incentive stock options allow for the purchase of stock at a fixed price for up to 10 years, and qualify for capital gain treatment, provided certain IRS requirements are met. The option price must be at least equal to the fair market value at the time of grant. The employee receives long-term capital gain treatment (now taxed at the same rate as ordinary income) when the shares are sold, provided the shares are held for two years after the options are granted and one year after the date of

Timing	Years		
	1	5	6
Nonqualified Stock Option	Grant	Exercise	Sale
Fair Market Value	$30	$80	$90
Executive Investment	$0	$30	
Executive Gain	$0	$50	$10.00 (Capital Gain) Total Gain of $60.00
Executive Tax*	$0 $50 x 0.28	$14.00 $10 x 0.28	$2.80 Total Tax Due $16.80
Executive Net Gain (After Tax)	$0	$36.00	$7.20 Total Net Gain $43.20

* Assumes that ordinary income and capital gain rates are 28%.

Figure 16-1. Nonqualified stock options. This investment plan allows an executive to purchase stock at a fixed price for a specified period of time, usually 10 years.

Timing	Years		
	1	5	6
Incentive Stock Option	Grant	Exercise	Sale
Fair Market Value	$30 ➡	$80 ➡	$90
Executive Investment	$0 ➡	$30	
Executive Gain	$0 ➡	$0 ➡	$60 (Capital Gain)
Executive Tax*	$0 ➡	$0 ➡	$16.80 Tax Due ($60 x 0.28)
Executive Net Gain (After Tax)	$0 ➡		$43.20 Net Gain

* Assumes that the capital gain rate is 28%.

Figure 16-2. Incentive stock options allow for the purchase of stock at a fixed price for up to 10 years and can qualify for capital gain treatment.

exercise. There is no charge to earnings and the company foregoes the tax deduction (see Figure 16-2).

Appreciation Plans. Under appreciation plans, the executive receives the increase in share price, measured by fair market value or other formula, from the time of award to some specified future date. No investment on the part of the executive is required.

Stock appreciation rights are generally granted in tandem with stock options and provide an executive with the appreciation in the market value of the stock, usually in return for surrendering the option. Stock appreciation rights may be paid out in cash, stock, or a combination of both. The appreciation in fair market value is charged to earnings each quarter through the vesting schedule (see Figure 16-3).

Full Value Plans. Full value plans give the executive the full value of the shares of common stock, or a specified dollar amount. No investment is required in these types of plans. The three most common full value plans are performance shares, performance units, and restricted stock awards.

Performance share plans provide rewards for meeting specific long-term performance targets. Contingent share units are granted at the be-

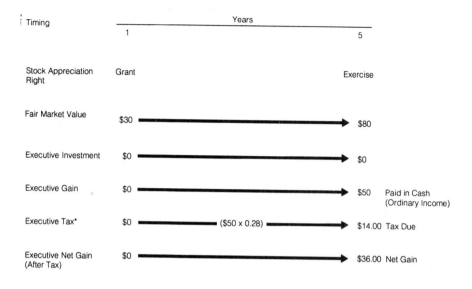

Timing		Years	
	1		5

Stock Appreciation Right — Grant → Exercise

Fair Market Value — $30 → $80

Executive Investment — $0 → $0

Executive Gain — $0 → $50 Paid in Cash (Ordinary Income)

Executive Tax* — $0 ($50 x 0.28) → $14.00 Tax Due

Executive Net Gain (After Tax) — $0 → $36.00 Net Gain

* Assumes that the executive is subject to an ordinary income rate of 28%

Figure 16-3. Stock appreciation rights provide an executive with the appreciation in the market value of the stock, usually in return for surrendering the option.

ginning of each performance period, usually every three to five years. At the end of the performance period, the executive earns a portion or multiple of the share units originally granted, to the extent that the performance targets are met. A minimum performance threshold must be met before an award is paid. Performance share units may be paid out in cash, stock, or a combination of both. The value of performance shares is charged to earnings to the extent that goals are achieved over the performance period, adjusted to reflect the value of the shares at the end of the period. At payment, the company receives a tax deduction equal to the executive's ordinary income (see Figure 16-4).

Performance unit plans are similar to performance share plans. Contingent units with a specified dollar value are granted at the beginning of each performance period, usually every three to five years. At the end of the performance period, the value of the units earned will depend on the extent to which performance targets are met. Performance unit awards may be paid out in cash, stock, or a combination of both. The value of the performance units is charged to earnings to the degree that goals are achieved over the performance period (see Figure 16-5).

Restricted stock awards are shares of stock that vest only after a specified restriction period. The executive immediately has voting and dividend rights on the shares, but if the executive terminates before the

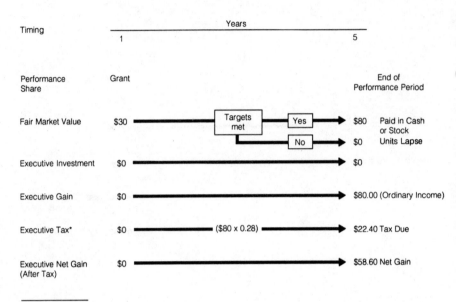

* Assumes that the executive is subject to an ordinary income rate of 28%

Figure 16-4. Performance share plans reward executives for meeting specific long-term performance targets.

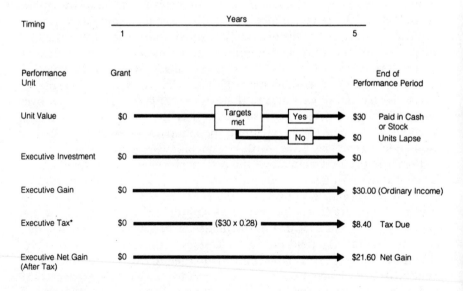

* Assumes that the executive is subject to an ordinary income rate of 28%

Figure 16-5. Performance unit plans. Contingent units with a specified dollar value are granted at the beginning of each performance period, and the value of the units earned will depend on the extent to which performance targets are met.

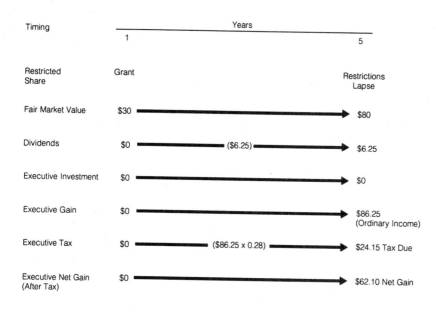

Timing		Years	
	1		5

Restricted Share — Grant — Restrictions Lapse

Fair Market Value	$30	→	$80
Dividends	$0	($6.25) →	$6.25
Executive Investment	$0	→	$0
Executive Gain	$0	→	$86.25 (Ordinary Income)
Executive Tax	$0	($86.25 x 0.28) →	$24.15 Tax Due
Executive Net Gain (After Tax)	$0	→	$62.10 Net Gain

---

* Assumes that 83 (b) election is not made and the executive is subject to an ordinary income rate of 28%

Figure 16-6. Restricted stock awards are vested only after a specified restriction period, and must be returned to the company if the executive terminates before the lapse of the restriction period.

lapse of the restriction period, the shares must be returned to the company (see Figure 16-6).

More than salary and annual incentives, long-term incentives play the most significant role in attracting, retaining, and motivating executives. Indeed, in an LBO or IPO, the size of the award is often a multiple of what is found in a typical company or what is found in a merger or acquisition. The tax and accounting rules that govern long-term incentive plans play an important role in which plans are useful or desirable in a restructuring. Obviously, one big advantage of stock options is that they don't cost the company anything because executives pay for the shares themselves and there is no charge to earnings.

Benefits, Perquisites, and Retirement Programs

Executive benefits packages usually include supplements to the core benefits of life insurance, major medical and dental insurance, and short- and long-term disability insurance. Perquisites may include company cars, tax preparation, financial and estate planning, luncheon and club memberships, and physical fitness programs. Benefits and perquisites not significant in attracting, retaining, and motivating executives.

Restructured companies generally do not reduce the level of benefits and perquisites. They often, however, consolidate individual operating unit benefits and perquisites plans into one corporate-wide program. Retirement plans can play a moderate role in a restructuring.

Let us look at some compensation issues that arise in the three kinds of restructuring mentioned above. We will focus on base salary, annual incentives, and long-term incentives.

Mergers and Acquisitions

The discussion below assumes that the business activities and personnel of the two organizations in a merger or acquisition are at least partially consolidated at the management level.

Base Salary

In a merger or acquisition, it is essential to examine the two salary systems in place. Since one group of employees is likely to be paid less than their counterparts in the other company, management will have to decide whether or not to increase the pay of those receiving less. Because jobs and reporting relationships almost inevitably change in a merger or acquisition—especially for middle and top management—the obvious first step is to review and reconcile the positions in the two organizations. Second, it may be necessary to review and modify the organizational structure to reflect changes in reporting relationships, new accountabilities, and spans of control. Ultimately, the same salary system will have to service both groups of employees, especially in a merger. This may mean throwing out both systems and starting afresh.

In the case of incentive-eligible positions, disparities may exist even though total compensation is similar. Here the mix must be examined. For example, you may find that total compensation is $100,000 for the same job in both organizations, but in one the split between base pay and annual incentive may be 60/40 and in the other 80/20.

Annual Incentives

Costs are usually considerable at the beginning of a merger, and profitability often suffers in the short term owing to extraordinary expenses.

It may take a year or more until the planning process can accommodate the merger. Thus, when corporate profitability is the principal determiner of incentive funds, it may be necessary to factor out extraordinary costs so that incentive levels can be maintained. Otherwise, incentive payments may drop and employee relations problems may result.

Also, over and above looking at the mix of salary to incentive for individuals and groups of employees, it will be necessary to compare the plan design and allocation process and take the necessary steps to establish a corporate-wide plan. One organization may use a goal-attainment plan, i.e., the amount in the bonus pool is linked directly to planned financial objectives; the other organization may use a fixed-formula approach, i.e., the bonus pool is credited with a fixed percentage of profits above a specified threshold. Problems of this sort will arise if the two organizations are in different phases of growth—for example, when an older, mature company with a goal-attainment plan acquires a start-up or growth company with a discretionary or fixed-formula plan.

Long-Term Incentives

When the merged companies have similar incentive plans, the main question is one of continuation, so that key executives are retained and motivated during the crucial period when the company is being turned around. Where possible, it is common practice to continue the plans of both groups using the stock of the new company adjusted for the new price. Naturally, the numbers of employees involved, the types of plans in place, targeted award amounts, and vesting schedules all must be examined and reconciled.

It is important to recognize that the new direction of the company may be difficult to chart from day one. Established time frames for accomplishing business results will change from what they were and will almost certainly accelerate owing to the need to get through the merger phase as soon as possible. As a result, vesting schedules for performance plans may have to be revised.

Leveraged Buyouts/ Management Buyouts

A leveraged buyout or management buyout calls for a unique compensation strategy. The relationship of debt to equity—typically about 90 percent debt to 10 percent equity—and the resulting need to refocus the company, pay off the debt (through cash flow or from the sale of assets), and take the company public (usually within five years), calls for an aggressive and fine-tuned executive compensation plan.

Base Salary

Base salary is a "low-emphasis" item in an LBO, owing to the need to control fixed expenses. Management must decide to what extent salary increases should be continued during the period when the company is saddled with significant debt. Most organizations will continue low to moderate salary increases during the early stages and resume normal increases as they pay off the debt to a manageable level.

Annual Incentives

Annual incentives are a "moderate-emphasis" item for management and are usually continued after the buyout is completed. The significant difference in incentive practice is the shift from the classic internal financial performance measures, such as earnings per share and returns on equity, investment, capital employed, and assets, to meeting specific cash flow objectives, debt reduction schedules, and disposition of assets.

Companies most frequently use a "goal-attainment" plan that links the incentive pool for management to the achievement of planned financial results. The virtue of this approach is that it is simple to administer and easy to communicate and understand. It can be applied on a centralized or decentralized basis, such as group, sector, division, or profit center. This provides the flexibility to identify performance at the organizational level that is held accountable for such results. This approach allows tailoring and measuring performance to the individual or group of individuals responsible for the desired results.

Once the incentive pool is created based on predetermined performance, amounts would then be allocated to plan participants for being on the team, or based on individual contribution to team performance, or perhaps on a combination of both. The question becomes one of where the company wants to place the emphasis, i.e., company, division, or individual performance. And it doesn't have to be all or nothing. It is typical to put greater emphasis on *company* performance for senior management, and to place greater weighting on *individual* performance further down the responsibility levels.

Special plans for extraordinary events and asset sales are also used. As management identifies the assets, plants, divisions, or operating units that are to be sold, it is necessary to adopt an incentive plan to retain key executives and employees critical to the success of that unit. These plans may use a formula to determine the amount of incentive to be paid. These formulas vary depending on the size of the asset sale. Such formulas could be a percentage of the sales price, a percentage of the net gain to the company, or a percentage of the valuation price. The bonus may be paid to the disposition team or to one individual.

"Hang-in" incentives are also used to retain employees of entities that may be sold. These plans often provide for a predetermined bonus to be paid if the individual stays with the company. The program can be structured so that the individual must stay until the unit is sold plus a period of time after the unit is acquired by the new organization. A participant will earn a pro rata portion of the incentive opportunity identified for each full month that he or she continues in the employ of the company. After the sale occurs, all the awards will be paid out. If the intent was to retain the individual after the sale was completed, a portion of the incentive would be deferred to reflect the period of future service.

In addition to using special hang-in incentives for key employees for the operating units that are positioned for sale, we also see the use of increased key employee severance benefits. This is done to retain key employees during the transition period without incurring the expense required under the hang-in incentive program. The use of severance benefits provides the ability to focus retention efforts on the most mobile employees. It also serves to improve morale by providing protection in case of involuntary termination resulting from the sale of a business unit. The key employee severance program may provide 3 to 12 months of salary, continued employee benefits, future service credits toward retirement plans and, often, outplacement assistance.

Long-Term Incentives

Long-term incentives are a "heavy-emphasis" item in a leveraged buyout where management is involved. Indeed, for the management/ owners, the most important element of pay is their equity stake in the new company. This comes from stock purchase (usually a combination of cash, promissory notes, convertible debentures, and the cancellation of prior equity plans) and stock options.

In an LBO, the number of shares reserved for options can be as much as 20 percent or more of shares outstanding, as opposed to 3 to 6 percent in most public companies. In an LBO, shares would frequently be set aside for both an immediate stock purchase and an option plan. Senior management would participate more heavily in the stock purchase plan and less in options. Middle management would participate in the less risky stock option program.

Once again, options are used over other plans because they are cost-effective and receive favorable accounting treatment. Restricted stock plans are sometimes used for key executives who are not owners because they are a powerful retention tool and their expense for accounting purposes is known at grant. Stock appreciation rights are rarely used because they carry a charge to earnings that could be significant if the stock soars. Performance plans are not used for the same reasons and because, in the case of management owners, they are superfluous.

A note of warning: Beware of adding a feature to the option plan that provides for adding or reducing shares to individuals if certain performance measures are met or not met. If this occurs, the plan may be deemed a variable plan and the appreciation in the value of the shares may be charged to earnings over the performance period. Once again, if the stock soars, the cost can be considerable.

Initial Public Offerings

Companies often use the initial public offering to adjust salary levels to the market rates of a publicly traded organization. Because of the need to control fixed costs, base salary is usually not a high-priority item when a company goes public. In general, newly public companies keep base salaries at or slightly below competitive levels and make only low to moderate salary increases. The compensation strategy is usually to supplement salaries with aggressive, cost-effective, incentive compensation plans.

Annual Incentives

Because the investing public wants to see good use of their money in a short period of time, an effective annual incentive plan that rewards short-term results is crucial for a newly public company. The difficulty lies in forecasting results and setting accurate financial performance goals during the first year the company is public. For this reason, newly public companies often use a fixed-formula plan to fund the incentive pool rather than a plan based on goal attainment. Fixed-formula plans should be seen as a short-term expediency. Once a company is able to conduct accurate business planning, it should consider funding the incentive pool through a goal-attainment plan.

Long-Term Incentives

Most newly public companies start out with stock options as the principal long-term plan because the potential gains from the plan are directly linked to that of the stockholder and there is no charge to earnings. They are often given to more employees than is typical in a company that has been public for a number of years because the award recognizes past as well as future service. Equity participation is also a very powerful incentive for the many people involved in the preparation of the public offering. The only other plan used in an IPO is restricted stock, which, like options, is a good retention vehicle and, since the cost is fixed at grant, carries no hidden surprises if the stock increases considerably. Stock appreciation rights other than for insiders are usually avoided because they carry a charge to earnings that can be considerable if the stock soars after the IPO. Performance plans are avoided for the same reason and also because of the difficulties of establishing accurate performance measures during the early days of an IPO.

Most companies will set aside enough shares for long-term incentives to last about five years. Depending on the size of the public offering, the percentage of shares set aside for long-term incentives rarely exceeds 10 percent of stock outstanding.

Employment Contracts

Since employment contracts surface regularly in a restructuring, it seems appropriate to outline briefly how they work.

Executive contracts have been around for many years, but in the recent past change-of-control agreements, commonly called "golden parachutes," have received much attention in the press. Employment contracts fall into three categories: those that are broad-based, general contracts; those that provide protection in the event of termination; and those that provide protection in the event of a change of control. The appropriate contract is a function of the type of action the company is trying to protect against. Below are the key provisions of an executive employment contract.

Term of Contract

The term of contract varies by level of management, ranging from a low of one year to a high of 10 years. For a CEO the average term of a contract is two to three years, and this is scaled down by level of management. Often there is an "evergreen" feature that automatically renews the contract if both the company and the executive agree. The term of the contract does not necessarily dictate the amount of compensation to be paid in the event of termination. Some contracts will provide for compensation in the event of termination throughout the term of the contract; others may provide for a specified amount of compensation. The purpose of providing a specific dollar amount in the contract is to prevent a situation in which an individual is terminated on the last day of the contract.

The Deficit Reduction Act of 1984 included new provisions aimed at excess golden parachute payments. If such payments are deemed excessive, the company making the payment will not receive an income tax deduction for it, and the recipient will be required to pay both ordinary income tax and a 20 percent excise tax. These provisions were designed to discourage corporations anticipating hostile tender offers from entering into defensive management arrangements to be triggered by a successful takeover. To avoid such a heavy tax, parachute payments must be kept under the base amount allowed—2.99 × a "base amount," which is the individual's average annualized compensation for the previous five years.

Duties and Responsibilities

Employment contracts typically specify the key duties and responsibilities, including reporting relationships, of the individual covered by the contract. In addition, many companies will specify a dollar amount as a multiple of salary by level of responsibility, i.e., the CEO at 2.99 × salary, the COO at 2 × salary, and the executive vice president level at 1.5 × salary.

Definition of Compensation and Benefits

The nature and amount of compensation must be clearly stated in the contract. This may seem an easy task, but as we examine the many elements of the executive pay program, we quickly find that this issue requires considerable precision and definition. Compensation is defined as salary and target incentive or, in some cases, the average of actual incentives paid over the last three years. Salary often includes an annual cost-of-living adjustment through the term of the contract.

Participation in long-term incentives, such as stock options, restricted stock, stock appreciation rights, and performance shares, should be addressed in the contract with specific reference to continued participation and contingencies in the event of termination or change of control. Other benefits should include life insurance, short- and long-term disability insurance, medical and dental insurance, and retirement plans. Some organizations provide for future service credits toward the retirement plan that reflect the term of the contract or the period and the amount of compensation to be paid. If the chief executive is to receive 2.99 × salary, these additional years of service should be added to the retirement plan. Also, we now find more and more perquisites, such as automobile use and club membership, included in the employment contract.

Payments to Executive upon Termination of Employment

It is important to identify the various types of termination that could occur, such as voluntary or involuntary termination, and what would constitute termination for cause. Also, the contract should define what would happen in the event of death, disability, or retirement, or termination resulting from a change of control, merger, or acquisition. These definitions must be clearly spelled out, and the executive's rights should also be identified.

Change of Control

If a change-of-control provision is incorporated into the employment agreement, it is necessary to define what constitutes a change of control. Generally, a change of control occurs if any of the following takes place: a 20 percent or 25 percent acquisition of the company's outstanding stock; a proportional change in the composition of the board of directors; a merger or reorganization such that the company is not the surviving entity; and the sale of more than one-third of the company's assets.

There are a number of additional provisions that could be added, depending on the specific circumstances—e.g., noncompete agreements, hiring away employees, using confidential information. It is advisable to seek legal counsel in preparing such a document.

Human Resources Issues

In the preceding analysis we have focused exclusively on executive compensation issues. Needless to say, there are also broader human resources issues that need to be addressed if a restructuring is to be successful from a human resources standpoint.

Human Resources Planning

Major organizational changes necessarily lead to new reporting relationships, management style, and cultural values. Some very important activities are to assess the management and employee talent required in the new organization, to identify what new resources may be needed, and to formulate a specific action plan to achieve desired goals within a specific time frame. In a restructuring, the more management can anticipate problems arising from potential surpluses or shortages of the right kinds of people and can take action to minimize their effects, the smoother the restructuring will be.

Skills Review

In a restructuring, a company needs more than ever to be flexible and able to cope with increasing changes in markets, products, and technologies. By analyzing the current skill "fit," a company can determine what training and development programs are required to address the staffing problems that inevitably arise in a restructuring. Since a shortage of skills can seriously affect the competitive ability of the firm to survive, a careful analysis of current talent against future needs can be crucial to a successful restructuring.

Communications and Involvement

Any type of major organizational change causes employee anxiety levels to soar. One cannot overemphasize the need to provide a high level of communication to employees in order to minimize and resolve sources of tension and to develop a clear understanding of the objectives and rationale for the change. If employees know what is going on, they will demonstrate a greater capacity for change and will be more committed to the success of the new organization.

17

Managing Corporate Culture to Achieve Growth and Renewal[1]

Michael R. Cooper
Strategy Consultant

Over the past few years, organizations have been forced to reexamine basic assumptions about how they operate. The forces of globalization, deregulation, and increasing segmentation of markets have led to reexamination of corporate mission, of the strategy required to support mission, and of the organizational culture required to support strategy.

The question of mission is the most fundamental: When a company reformulates its mission, it is, in effect, redefining the business it is in. For example:

[1]Portions of this chapter are based on the following article: Michael R. Cooper, "Managing Cultural Change to Achieve Competitive Advantage," *Handbook of Business Strategy: 1987/1988 Yearbook*. Warren, Gorham and Lamont, Boston.

- Banks that once identified their mission as deposits and lending now define it as financial services.

- Telephone companies, which once defined themselves as providers of universal dial tone, now provide total information service.

- Health-care providers, who formerly sought the best comprehensive care, now focus on cost-effective care.

As missions change, new strategies are being developed to support these missions. These changes are often as profound as the changes in mission: An aggressive approach to marketing can send shock waves through an organization populated with caretakers of a time-honored product, and a cost-reduction plan can produce disillusion in a work force whose premise has been that only quality matters. Once the challenge of redefining mission and strategy has been met, further challenges remain. Effective implementation of the new mission requires the right organizational culture.

Culture is the critical intermediary that determines whether mission and strategy will or will not be successfully implemented. Culture is never neutral—it either helps or hinders the organization as it seeks to achieve competitive advantage. As they begin to pay attention to their culture, managers find themselves asking many questions: Do we delegate authority, or does executive management sign off on everything? How high a premium do we place on performance? Do we plan, or do we react?

As they begin to learn answers to these questions, top managers inevitably wonder what to do with their new knowledge: Should we delegate more? Will planning really pay off? *Underlying these questions is a search for a culture for success.*

There are, as it turns out, *cultures* for success rather than a single culture for success. The right culture for an organization is the one that best supports its strategic objectives. The challenge for an organization is to:

- Assess the fit between its current culture and the culture required to implement its chosen strategy successfully.

- Take steps to change the organization's culture to better align it with what is required.

In what follows, this process will be explored in detail. The issues addressed are:

- *What is corporate culture?* How can culture be defined in concrete terms? How can it be measured?

- *Linking culture and strategy.* What culture is required to implement strategic objectives successfully?

- *Success in market-driven companies: managing growth and renewal.* How the culture of small, successful market-driven companies helps them achieve their objectives, and how a large company can become more market-driven.

- *Implications for restructuring organizations.* What large companies can do as they strive to adapt their culture to changing strategic objectives.

What Is Corporate Culture?

Culture in an organization can best be defined as a body of learned practices that employees share and transmit to new employees. In other words, *culture* is "the way things get done in the organization."

Most people have a sense of the culture of their organization. When asked, they can tell stories that characterize the culture for them. If one collects these stories from a number of employees, it is possible to identify patterns that provide an impression of the culture. Often, the stories focus on an individual; this may be the founder or a current leader who has had a substantial influence on the organization. Other stories may focus on incidents that illustrate the culture, such as the way employees banded together to face an obstacle, the success of a new product introduction, or the like.

This anecdotal approach does provide a picture of the culture, but the picture is a series of impressions, not necessarily complete, not readily quantifiable, and not useful for direct comparison with competitors or with other organizations of interest. To measure culture more systematically, it is possible to proceed in a more quantifiable way. *Culture* was defined above as "the way things get done in an organization." This leads naturally to measurement of culture in terms of day-to-day management practices.

For a number of years, the Hay Group has been measuring culture in what now totals hundreds of organizations. Out of this experience, a framework has emerged that produces meaningful, useful information about an organization's culture. The core dimensions examined in this culture assessment are:

- *Planning systems.* How structured is the planning process? How clearly are company goals set?

- *Decision making.* Is the decision-making process decentralized?

How quickly are decisions made? How far down is significant authority delegated?

- *Organizational integration.* What is the degree of cooperation and coordination among various units in the organization?

- *Management style.* Are initiative and risk taking encouraged? Are conflicts discussed? Is constructive criticism offered?

- *Performance orientation.* What is the degree of emphasis placed on individual accountability? Are high performance goals set for individuals? Are individual performance expectations made clear?

- *Organizational vitality.* How responsive is the organization to change? Are the goals venturesome?

- *Management compensation.* Is pay competitive? Is it performance-based? How are benefits regarded?

- *Management development.* Does the company develop talent from within? Are promotions based on capability? Are talents well matched to jobs?

- *Corporate identity.* What is the overall image of the organization with the staff? With the public? Do employees feel the organization is ethical?

Linking Culture and Strategy

Culture Measurement

The framework described above forms the basis for measuring an organization's culture. When the assessment is being performed to determine the compatibility of strategy and culture, the measurement process may include the following elements:

- Understanding the overall corporate mission and strategy, the mission and strategy of individual business units, and the corresponding objectives for major departments and functions

- Exploring the values shared by management, both what the values "are" and what they "should be"

- Assessing the current organizational culture and identifying the structure, process, and people components needed to support the strategy

Data are collected through personal interviews, observations of meetings, interactions, events, analysis of organizational charts, plans, policies, and written culture questionnaires.

An analysis framework for determining the required culture is shown in Figure 17-1. Down the left-hand side of the matrix is listed a series of critical success factors that represent the unique ways a particular organization competes or plans to compete in its marketplace. Across the top is listed a series of key organizational and managerial attributes. These include the core cultural dimensions described previously as well as additional attributes that are associated with successful implementation of the organization's business strategy.

Determining what the culture should be entails trade-offs. For example, what is the required culture for a company that has identified top-of-the-line product quality and excellent customer service as keys to its success in the marketplace? How formal should the planning process be? What role should technology development play? Is a high degree of coordination between units essential, or can it be at moderate or low levels? How much freedom to act must managers have?

Cultures for Success

A common question is whether there is a culture for success. As it turns out, there are different cultures for success, each dependent on an organization's strategy.

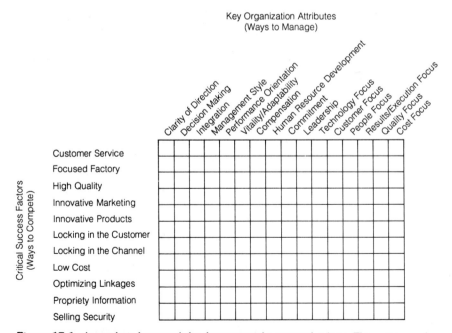

Figure 17-1. An analysis framework for determining the required culture. This matrix can be used to help determine the compatibility of an organization's strategy and its culture.

Different organizations compete in different ways. One of the great contributions made by strategists in the 1970s was getting managers to think about their operations as part of an industry. An industry has definable markets, economics, and competition. An industry is populated by competitors who make similar products. Within industries there are several competitive options open to an organization. Each option has certain characteristics in its organization/culture mix that distinguish it from others. There is a culture for success that depends on how an organization competes. Here we will focus on product-driven and market-driven organizations.

The Product-Driven Organization. Strategically, the product-driven firm competes with low costs. Cost advantage is often achieved through scale, worldwide sourcing, and "first mover" advantages that freeze out competitors before competition develops. Toyota competes very effectively with scale, precise inventory management, and careful attention to the costs of complexity, but the strategy of competing through production expertise is not limited to auto makers or even manufacturers.

The structure of the product-driven firm is usually functional. Senior management tends to have risen through production management, with brief tours in marketing. Most hiring, and the bulk of the firm's knowledge base, is in the functions of engineering and manufacturing. Many of the management practices are "hardwired" by plant design and process constraints, as are many cultural factors.

In an oil refinery, for example, the economics of refining require large facilities and 24-hour-a-day operation. Unless shifts are rotated rigorously, the refinery will tend to develop distinctive cultures on each of its shifts. The graveyard shift will always feel out of touch with management, who will be forced to rely to a greater extent on bulletins and the chain of command to communicate with that shift, when face-to-face meetings might be more effective. These problems can be exaggerated because refinery workers are typically stationed some distance from each other, creating in them a "loner" mentality. Successful product-driven companies have cultures and management systems that can overcome these difficulties while maintaining efficient operations.

The Market-Driven Organization. The market-driven organization sees its mission as profitably building share. Growth is not revered for growth's sake. Rather, the market-driven organization seeks to identify customer needs that it uniquely can fulfill. As businesses move through their life cycle, the key factors for market-driven success change. The role of distributors, for example, may be insignificant at first when the customer has a high need for education and is willing to pay high prices for the advantages of a new product. As the product matures and becomes commoditylike, distributors can play a very significant role in the marketing mix. Customers start to base their purchases on availability and price, rather than on product attributes. Similarly, savvy market-driven organizations allow for pricing and promotional flexibility to accommodate the peculiarities of each product-market segment. Successful market-driven organizations have cultures and supporting management systems that fit this range of needs, maintaining profitability while allowing diversity.

Empirical Organizational Culture Profiles

Although there is no universal "culture for success," it is possible to identify certain cultural attributes that are often found in higher-performing companies. Research conducted across a broad range of companies in the Hay Group Culture Data Base has yielded findings about the keys to success. is particularly useful to examine the culture patterns of successful companies at opposite ends of a strategy-category continuum as depicted in Figure 17-2. Successful market-driven organizations can be compared with successful product-driven organizations.

Figure 17-3 shows a profile of successful market-driven organizations. These organizations seek to be customer-driven by identifying customer needs that they can uniquely fulfill and thus build market share. The culture characteristics that are emphasized are decision making, organizational vitality, and performance orientation. In

Figure 17-2. Business contrasts: cultural patterns of successful companies at opposite ends of a strategy-category continuum.

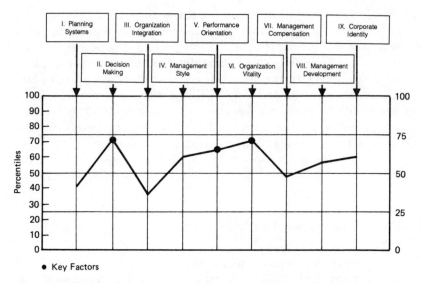

Figure 17-3. Profile of successful market-driven organizations. Cultural characteristics that are emphasized in these customer-driven companies are decision making, organizational vitality, and performance orientation.

these organizations, high focus is found in management systems designed to maintain the organization's shorter-term paybacks in dynamic marketplaces: (1) Decision making is pushed close to the customer, with managers in a position to react quickly and effectively to the marketplace; (2) pace setting for competitive advantage is reinforced by fostering a sense of urgency to accomplish venturesome goals; and (3) accountabilities for end results are clearly spelled out, well communicated, and understood.

Successful product-driven organizations evidence a very different set of common culture characteristics. For example, in successful utilities, where the strategic mission in the core business is reliability and consistency of service, high focus is found in management systems designed to maintain the organization's memory banks, as seen in Figure 17-4: human resource development, organizational integration, and planning systems. Assuring the know-how for reliable and consistent service delivery in these organizations requires: (1) the development and continuity of the next generation of management and employees for know-how transfer; (2) integration and cooperation across departments for know-how coordination; and (3) planning systems that can project and ensure long-term know-how requirements.

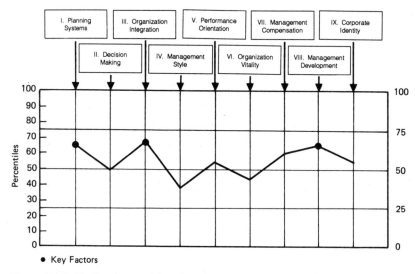

Figure 17-4. Profile of successful product-driven organizations. A very different set of cultural characteristics is emphasized in these organizations: human resource development, organizational integration, and planning systems.

Determining the Culture That Best Supports the Strategy

As illustrated in the previous section, there is no universal optimal culture that fits all organizations: It depends on mission and strategy. If a market-oriented strategy is implemented in an organization that traditionally has emphasized a maintenance-and-control decision making process, then the strategy and the culture do not fit—they pull in opposite directions.

Culture must support strategy, and, again, it is never neutral. If culture is not part of the solution, it is probably part of the problem. But when culture and strategy work together, the chances for high performance increase dramatically. As every organization has its own culture, so every organization's success depends on finding and building the best culture to support its mission and strategy. Focused management practices that deliberately reflect different business strategies are rapidly emerging as reality. The critical challenge for the 1990s is effective strategy implementations: determining the optimal culture needed and then ensuring that this culture is developed and sustained.

Success in Market-Driven Companies: Managing Growth and Renewal

In the preceding sections, corporate culture has been defined in terms of day-to-day management practices. The strength of this approach is that it facilitates moving from culture assessment to culture management.

Culture can, indeed, be managed, especially when it is understood in terms of management practice. Management systems must reflect the strategy the organization is striving to achieve: Deliberate emphasis on selective management practices is needed to close the gaps between where an organization is and where it should be.

Below, two case examples of successful culture management are examined. Both involve managing culture in successful market-driven organizations. The first involves the *Inc. 500*—small, successful companies whose market-driven approach to management has many implications for management in larger organizations. The second case involves culture change in a financial institution entering new markets.

The Inc. 500. The Inc. 500 are the fastest-growing small, privately held companies in the United States, with an average five-year growth in sales of 1328 percent. Over the same five-year period, their average work force has grown from 19 to 106 employees, and their sales per employee have more than doubled. The way these small companies organize to succeed make them a case study in culture management with implications for companies of all sizes that are undergoing change.

The Hay Group, in conjunction with *Inc.* magazine, undertook a study of these companies to identify the characteristics that make them successful and the ways they manage growth (cooper, morgan, M.B., *The Hay/Inc. Report: Managing Growth and Renewal,* Center For Management Research, Boston, 1988). Placed in the context of culture and culture change, the key findings of the study are discussed below.

The strategy of Inc. 500 companies can be characterized as market-driven. A majority of Inc. 500 CEOs say that their companies' success is due primarily to marketing. These CEOs also say that their primary strategic advantage comes from attention to quality and customer service. Contrary to popular stereotypes, a unique product or service is not a prerequisite for growth: Inc. 500 CEOs place a premium on how the product or service is marketed or positioned, not on the product or service itself. A glance at the companies on the Inc. 500 list reveals their diversity of product and service lines. The Inc. 500 includes companies in the aluminum siding, mail-order, and manufacturing businesses along with the expected software firms and high-tech boutiques.

Inc. 500 CEOs were also asked to identify the aspect of their business that gives them the greatest competitive advantage. The majority choose either customer service or product quality, while only about 2 in 10 identify innovation.

These small companies are doing what many large companies say they are trying to do: They are placing a premium on service delivery and quality, and focusing on marketing. These are objectives that many larger companies espouse while continuing to pay attention to reducing costs.

The emphases in Inc. 500 cultures are the same as those in successful larger market-driven companies. As indicated above, successful market-driven companies emphasize decision making, organizational vitality, and performance orientation. The study reveals that these characteristics, as defined earlier in this chapter, are present in Inc. 500 companies:

- Decision making is pushed close to the customer, with managers in a position to react quickly and effectively to the marketplace. Inc. 500 company employees, compared to those in larger companies, are more likely to say that they have the authority they need, are listened to by management, and have a chance to have their ideas adopted. The contrast between the Inc. 500 and larger companies is most pronounced among salespeople, who are a key to remaining close to the customer.

- Pacesetting for competitive advantage is reinforced by fostering a sense of urgency to accomplish venturesome goals. Employees consider the competitiveness of their Inc. 500 companies very high, are proud to be part of their companies, and feel challenged by their work. They are dedicated to their company's mission, and are prepared to exert the energy required to achieve the company's objectives.

- Accountabilities for end results are clearly spelled out, well communicated, and understood. Most Inc. 500 employees are closely identified with their company's mission, and most believe they are an integral part of achieving the company's objectives. Compared to employees in larger companies, Inc. 500 employees are less likely to say that poor performance is tolerated. They also say that their skills and talents are used effectively.

As these small, successful companies grow, they must actively focus on these key management practices. The study demonstrates that failure to do so results in declining employee identification and commitment, with subsequent loss of competitive advantage.

Large companies striving to be more market-driven can learn a great deal from these small, successful organizations. The Inc. 500's service

and quality orientation, their motivating employees by providing challenge, and their practice of listening to and adopting employee ideas,
can all be profitably exported to larger organizations. One key is effective management of the sales force: Any organization striving to become
more market-driven must learn to glean information and cultivate ideas
from this important front-line resource.

Managing Organization Transition.   This case illustrates the use of culture assessment and culture management in an organization in transition. The organization is a large financial institution that had responded
vigorously to the new opportunities afforded it as a result of deregulation. Its strategy called for entering many markets not previously open
to it. Some of these new ventures had already been implemented, and
others were in the planning stages at the time of the culture assessment.
Becoming market-driven and close to the customer was fundamental to
the strategy.

There were four central questions asked: (1) Where are we moving
from? (2) Where are we now? (3) Where are we going? (4) How will we
get there?

In this particular case, the CEO had the answer to questions (1) and
(3): he knew the history of the organization and where it had been, and
he had a comprehensive strategic plan to indicate where the organization was headed. What he needed to know was where the organization
stood at the present time, and what steps were *needed* to get where the
strategy called for them to be.

Figure 17-5 presents a snapshot of the culture assessment, including
the organization's profile and, for comparison, the profile of successful
market-driven companies. For one "key success factor," organizational
vitality, the organization is shown to be right where one would expect a
successful market-driven organization to be: high in venturesomeness,
responsiveness, innovativeness, and internal pace of activities.

At the same time, a number of gaps were identified where the culture
differed from that of successful market-driven organizations. In sessions with senior management it was determined that the excessively
high focus on planning systems and organizational integration was the
result of extensive time being spent by managers in planning meetings,
review sessions, and efforts to maintain coordination across units. The
low focus on decision making and performance orientation was recognized as failure to delegate significant accountabilities and to clearly define or hold management responsible for behavior required for competitive advantage.

As a result of the analysis, management was in a much stronger position to refocus the selected management systems required for the organization's future success. Management recognized that to maintain its

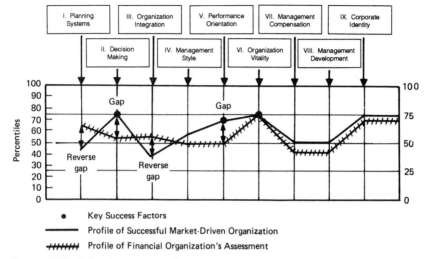

Figure 17-5. Cultural assessment of a company in transition: how one company trying to become more market-driven matched up against the success model, and identified cultural gaps that needed to be addressed.

vitality over the long haul and to become market-driven it would need to clearly define the end results expected of individual managers, and then to give them the freedom to accomplish those ends. Senior management decided to shift people and financial resources out of excessive planning and integration and into delegative decision making, freedom to act, performance clarity, and accountability.

Implications for Restructuring Organizations

Both the financial institution just described and the companies in the Inc. 500 represent successful marriages between culture and strategy. In the case of the financial institution, culture was consciously changed, with top management taking steps to make the organization more market-driven. In the Inc. 500, the CEO, often an owner-founder, is actively managing the organization to achieve strategic objectives, in effect creating and sustaining a market-driven culture in the process. Both cases demonstrate that culture can be managed. As companies restructure, management can take the steps required to align culture and strategy.

As they begin to restructure their organization, management needs to both ask and answer the following questions:

- *Where are we?* This entails an assessment of the organization's culture, structure, and staffing. And executive management needs to compare these management systems to strategic/peer organizations.

- *Where do we want to be?* Certainly, it is important for an organization to know where it currently is; but knowing where it should be is essential. Gaps between where it is and where it should be are areas that demand attention.

- *Where are the gaps?* Relative to strategic/peer organizations, executive management must agree on top-priority strengths to be sustained and selective, competitive weaknesses to be changed. This requires understanding, commitment to change, and high focus.

- *How can the gaps be closed?* What elements of the management systems need change: Strategy? Structure? Process? People?

- *How rapidly can identified gaps be closed?* What is the organization's tolerance for change?

- *Where and how do we begin to act?* Management must emphasize practices consistent with strategy objectives, and executive management commitment to change must be both visible and sustained.

- *Are we progressing?* Progress must be measured against internal trends and peer organizations to find out where and why success is occurring. Winning and losing business units within the organization should be compared.

Culture Reshaping Principles

The process of aligning strategy and culture encompasses the following basic steps, starting preferably with step 1; but practically, it is possible to start with step 1, 2, 3, or 4.

- *Step 1.* Clarify mission/strategy.
- *Step 2.* Analyze critical success factors.
- *Step 3.* Select the required culture: key organization/managerial attributes.
- *Step 4.* Assess the current culture.
- *Step 5.* Identify gaps with required culture.
- *Step 6.* Adjust the levers.
- *Step 7.* Monitor the alignment.

In step 6, the organization takes the appropriate actions to better align the strategy and culture. Levers available to facilitate change are strategy, structure, process, and people. The sequence of lever implementation typically depends on the degree of change/transition/transformation required and accepted by executive management.

Strategy. It may be necessary to rethink and revise the strategy itself. To be successful, the strategy must be in accord with external and internal realities. No matter how well the organization is geared up to implement strategy, it is not likely to succeed if the strategy is based on incorrect or incomplete assumptions about the external business environment. It is often necessary to retest the underlying assumptions about the competitive environment and the company's strengths and weaknesses in order to separate any myths from reality.

A variety of studies can be used to test the company's strategy: market analyses, industry analyses, competitor analyses, company analyses. To the extent that new insight is gleaned from these studies, a different strategic direction might be needed.

Similarly, the culture diagnostic process will have identified whether the strategy is in alignment with internal organizational realities. In some cases it is advisable to modify the business direction, if possible, rather than the culture. This is done when it becomes clear that pursuing a given strategic direction is not executable given organizational culture obstacles, and that these cannot be overcome sufficiently or quickly enough to stay in tune with the pace of change in a defined market.

Structure. Changes in organizational design can bring about changes in decision making, information flow, and management style. Functions or units may be centralized or decentralized to create new linkages to better implement the strategy. Changes in reporting levels can contribute to changing the nature of decision making. Levels may be eliminated to provide for more managerial latitude or they may be added to increase control and introduce redundancy.

Process. Management processes can be changed to reinforce the strategy. The mission and the strategic plan may not have been articulated or disseminated throughout the organization in a way that affects people who must be involved in the implementation of strategy. Or managers may not understand the real meaning or personal implications of the new values and required behaviors. There is always a gap between newly articulated values and the translation of these into required day-to-day behaviors. For example, what do terms such as "customer focus," "risk taking," and "individual accountability" mean to the veteran manager who has never been encouraged or rewarded for living up to these values?

Changes can be made in the recruiting process to attract people with a different skills base or management style. Management compensation programs can be redesigned, changing the amount, mix, and/or leverage of incentive compensation to better align it with the strategy. Performance planning can be enhanced by changes in goal-setting and performance-appraisal techniques and criteria. Systems and processes in specific functional areas can be targeted for improvement to bring about changes in cost control, market intelligence, and management information systems.

People. Many issues surface about the current management/ professional work force and its suitability for the (future) direction of the company. Does the company have enough people with the types of skills that are needed for the future? Does it have enough people with leadership potential to fill key slots? Does it have enough risk takers? Does it have enough marketers? Assessment centers, training programs, career planning, and succession planning programs are some of the actions that can be taken to address these types of concerns.

In addition to initiating change through strategy, structure, process, and/or people levers, a fundamental ingredient in all cultural change involves executive and senior leadership modeling the kinds of behaviors that are needed to shape the required new culture. Words in mission and strategy documents and corporate values statements, when not supported by the actions of leadership, can have the negative effect of causing employee cynicism to develop out of these contradictions.

The need for identifying and using organizational strengths in new and different ways for competitive advantage, as well as identifying and correcting organizational weaknesses, has never been greater. The changes occurring in business today are so monumental that organizations everywhere are overhauling their missions and strategies in an effort to survive. Changing the mission and strategy is only a part of the equation. The organizations that will be most successful are those that achieve mission and strategy and culture compatibility.

18

The Impact of Technology on Restructuring

John Sifonis

Vice President,
Temple, Barker & Sloane Inc.

Since 1981, more than 12,200 companies have been restructured in this country, at a capital cost of $490 billion. Restructuring, in this context, is defined as a merger, acquisition, or divestiture. Given this amount of activity, it is interesting to note that approximately 70 percent of the restructurings failed to live up to expectations of senior management, approximately 50 percent were outright failures, and divestitures accounted for more than 40 percent of all restructuring activity. Although the track record of restructuring has not been exceptionally good, it appears that this trend will continue, unless it is abated by changes in antitrust and takeover legislation at the federal level that create a more stringent climate than has been in effect for most of the 1980s.

Although the failure rate for restructuring is high, companies continue to pursue this course of action for two primary reasons: financial and strategic. In the case of the financial factors driving restructuring, companies, as well as individuals, are pursuing mergers and acquisitions for capital gain—that is, a high rate of return. Vast amounts of capital have been made available for this type of activity. The ultimate objective of financial restructuring is to sell assets of the acquired organization to pay down debt and to receive a return on the capital employed. It appears that there is neither a long-term nor a strategic incentive for this type of restructuring from the participating companies' perspective.

In the case of restructuring for strategic reasons, the objectives are to better position the company for competitive reasons. Some of the reasons are to increase market share, to acquire products and services, and to have the capability to compete in a global marketplace. Under this scenario, senior management's outlook is on the long term. The intent is to restructure for purposes of building the corporate entity to survive and prosper for the future.

Let us focus our attention on those companies that restructure for strategic purposes. As stated previously, there are a number of reasons why a restructuring fails. These include incompatible product lines and distribution channels, the inability to structure the operations of the new entity, differences in corporate culture, the inability to merge human resources, inadequate study of the financials of the restructured company, and a view of the future that is not shared by all members of senior management. Of the reasons stated in the literature as well as personal experiences by the author in dealing with restructured organizations, the most common and devastating failure is the inability to focus and to come to an agreement on shared values and a common view of the future.

Role of Information Technology

Based on my experiences, another important factor for this high failure rate is the inattention given to the implications of technology in the consideration of restructuring.

Information technology is a significant factor contributing to the failure rate of restructured organizations. Traditionally, senior management is comfortable with and basically understands the manufacturing, marketing, distribution, sales, financial, and human resources functions of the business. What they do not understand, in most cases, is the information technology aspect of their business—also known as the management information systems (MIS) function. Consequently, that aspect of the business very rarely enters into the restructuring equation. Senior management will analyze the other functions mentioned above but, in most instances, not only do they not understand the MIS function, they will not involve the MIS executive in the company's plans for restructuring. The consequences of this can be disastrous: If the MIS functions are incompatible or if there is no shared vision as to how these groups will work together in the future, I believe that the restructuring will not be successful.

There are a number of elements regarding the MIS function that should be taken into account by senior management when a restructuring is being considered. These elements are: hardware, applications, communications, human resources, and data. Although this is not intended to be an exhaustive list, these five elements tend to be the critical elements that make or break a restructuring from an MIS perspective. It is incumbent for senior management to take these elements into account when planning a restructuring. I am not stating that they should be experts in these areas, but merely suggesting that they need to involve MIS management in the planning and evaluation phases of a restructuring to avoid significant risk of failure as the restructuring is implemented.

Hardware

One of the considerations in examining a merger or acquisition is the type of hardware currently in use by the target company. If the acquiring company and the target company have the same brand of equipment, the restructuring effort tends to be less complex due to the inherent degree of compatibility in dealing with the same vendor. If the mainframes are from different vendors, consideration should be given to studying:

- Whether it is feasible to run a two-mainframe installation
- The cost associated with this approach
- The cost and technical implications of sharing networks or attempting to establish a communications link among and between the two mainframes
- Analyzing the cost of the embedded technology of the target company
- The strategic implications of operating a dual-vendor environment.

Although there are numerous installations that do run a dual-vendor environment, they tend to support diverse operations or different functions of the organization. For example, in some energy companies, the processing of geological and geophysical applications is processed on a mainframe vendor different from that used in processing traditional financial applications.

Only rarely does senior management consider these factors when examining the total cost and business structure implications of a restructuring. It should be noted that in some instances, the cost of the embedded technology of the target company can be substantial and may cause long-term detrimental effects on the integration of the technology of the acquiring and target companies.

Another factor for senior management to consider with respect to hardware is whether the target company operates in a centralized or decentralized business environment. If the acquiring company is decentralized and the target company is centralized, there may be significant problems associated with business operating philosophies in addition to the differences in hardware philosophies.

If the company is divesting an operating unit or a division, senior management should consider the degree of integration the operating unit has with the hardware applications currently in place. It may not be as easy to uncouple the systems from the operating unit once it is divested.

Applications

Another key element in analyzing the impact of technology on restructuring is the application portfolio of the target company. On the positive side, the target company may have a strategic system that can be of significant benefit to the acquiring company. In some instances, the existence of a strategic application may enhance the value of the target company's MIS function. However, if the application portfolio of the target is old or is incompatible with the acquiring company's portfolio, it is highly likely that a significant dollar and labor investment will have to be made to upgrade and integrate the applications after restructuring. Again, senior management should study the implications of:

- The target company's portfolio in the context of the strategic implications of the restructured company

- The age and operating cost of the company's applications

- The estimated cost to significantly enhance or redevelop the applications if they are key to supporting the target company's operations

- The estimated cost of maintaining these systems "as is" if resources and time are not immediately available to redevelop these systems

Communications

Business trends indicate that there will be increasing efforts to establish global markets. Business in general, and the world of diversified financial services in particular, are dependent on establishing communications on a global basis or, at a minimum, having access to networks on a global basis. Investments in communications technology and software are significant; but more important, there is a very limited set of expertise in any organization that is truly conversant in this technology, how it functions, and how it can be leveraged. All too often, senior management does not have a very good feel for the strategic importance of a communications network, nor do they have a good understanding of the immense technical problems and costs involved in attempting to merge disparate communications systems. The element of communications is intrinsically tied to the vendor's computer hardware. Consequently, the acquiring company should study the cost of the network, the support personnel cost, market access implications from a merged network, and the capability, feasibility, and cost of integrating diverse networks.

The network capabilities of a target company can yield significant benefit to the acquiring company if they are compatible or if the cost of integrating the networks is not prohibitive. For example, there is strategic advantage to be gained by offering an extended network, as in the case of merging two financial institutions' automatic teller machine (ATM) networks. As another example, a merged network may offer the restructured company increased market access and share as well as the potential, from economies of scale, to drop into the network an enhanced set of financial products and services that may not previously have been possible.

Human Resources

"Human resources," as used in this context, refers to MIS function personnel. There are several critical issues involving the human aspects of a restructuring within the MIS function.

All too frequently, senior management does not deal effectively with the MIS director, let alone understand the culture and egos of the MIS staff. In most organizations, the MIS executive is privy to the strategic plans of senior management, especially as they apply to potential restructuring. As a result, the MIS function hears "through the grapevine" that something is about to happen. This uncertainty and fear of the unknown tends to exacerbate an already difficult situation: a normal turnover rate of 15 to 20 percent. Anticipation of a restructuring amplifies the concern associated with an impending change and tends to accelerate the rate of turnover within the organization, either of the acquiring company or of the target company.

Another aspect of this problem is that the good people tend to leave first. Consequently, the task of integrating the MIS groups becomes more difficult because of the compressed time frames and the lack of sufficient talent to address a difficult and complex problem. One of the considerations of senior management should be not only to assess the talents of the target company, but to ensure that sufficient rewards are offered to the target company personnel to induce them to remain through the restructuring. Although the cost associated with this course of action may appear to be high, the risk of not accomplishing the integration of the MIS functions is even more significant.

Senior management should be cognizant of the fact that data processing professionals do have different egos and that the acquired company personnel do have a sense of pride in their accomplishments. A restructuring does not have to be a "win–lose" proposition for the parties involved. The acquired company's MIS group is one of the most valuable assets for ensuring that integration is accomplished.

Another major consideration is to act fast once the situation has been analyzed and the restructuring has occurred. Senior management should avoid taking action based on a consensus mode of operation. With respect to the MIS functions, one individual should be named at the outset to have full responsibility for implementing the integration of the merged organizations.

An often-missed element of the human resources side of restructuring is the role that MIS has within the company. If the target company views information systems as part of their strategic planning, and the acquiring company views information systems as a necessary evil, the likelihood is that the MIS group of the target will resign. There should be a large degree of compatibility of views among and between the MIS functions of the acquiring and the target companies. If there isn't, the likelihood of a successful restructuring will be remote.

Data

This is the last of our five critical elements but is possibly the most important. With the exception of the company's personnel, a corporation is essentially one vast data structure. This is particularly true for financial institutions—in essence, the MIS system *is* the financial institution.

For the past 25 or so years, the concept of data integration for information resource management has been pursued by MIS functions and organizations, but with very limited success. Data has traditionally been organized around individual applications rather than shared, corporate data bases. These types of data structures tend to become static and are difficult to leverage when companies merge or are acquired. However, one of the first requests that senior management makes of the MIS function is to produce a set of integrated financial statements, or the integration of customer information, with the acquired company.

To me, this is an obvious contradiction. Most companies cannot relate product, market, and customer data within their own organization, let alone trying to integrate an acquired company's product and customer data bases. Yet this is the expectation level of senior management once the restructuring has occurred. One of the most inhibiting factors in a successful restructuring is the inability to integrate, for example, customer, product, or sales data bases. With respect to financial institution mergers and acquisitions, one of the critical information needs is product, customer, and organization profitability. However, this is difficult to do because the acquiring and target companies' definitions for customer or product data may not be exact or precise. One clear lesson that can be learned from failed or less successful restructurings is that a corporation must first get a unified view of its own data before it can successfully merge or acquire another organization.

If we assume that mergers, acquisitions, divestitures, and other forms of restructuring will continue into the foreseeable future, unless senior management has a better understanding of the implications of information technology on restructuring, I believe that the success rate in the future will not differ significantly from that of the past. It is becoming more apparent in today's environment that information is a major driving force within the vast majority of companies. To ignore this and the associated information technology aspects of mergers and acquisitions is to increase an already high risk of failure.

I do not advocate that senior management study the problem to death before taking action, but rather, involve MIS management in the preliminary assessment of a target company and set into place a rational plan that is reasonable and can meet the expectation levels of senior management.

19

Accounting Considerations in a Restructuring

Duane R. Kullberg

Senior Partner,
Arthur Andersen & Co.

"Change" is a word that is becoming increasingly prominent in the business executive's vocabulary. Though change has always been with us, its pace is accelerating. As it does so, many in the business community are finding that piecemeal solutions are less and less effective. Faced with new and different kinds of challenges, executives are becoming aware of the necessity to respond on a more fundamental level than they may have in the past. This can often be done within a company's existing structure. Sometimes, however, the challenges are so complex or profound that a restructuring of the company may be essential to carrying out those changes.

Of course, restructuring itself is an enormous change. It may mean altering both operations and financial status. Operationally, restructuring may make a difference in the products offered, markets served, production capacity, and cost structure. Financially, one can expect changes in the amount and type of both debt and equity.

Practically all restructurings include the acquisition and disposition of business or facilities to accomplish one of the following objectives:

- Affect industry capacity.
- Improve market share.
- Improve focus.

Properly managed, the restructuring of a company through acquisition or disposition of a business can be easier and cheaper than establishing a new business or expanding an old one. It can provide additional equity or other long-term capital quickly, and can improve a company's competitive position against increasingly large and sophisticated rivals.

But the pitfalls are numerous. There are complex issues arising from the transaction itself that must be considered in planning a financial strategy to complete the transaction—regardless of whether it is combining businesses, selling a business or facility, divesting a subsidiary, or undertaking some other form of restructuring. The rules applying to these transactions have never been simple, and the pace of change in the business environment has rendered them even more confusing.

Tax rules provide an example. Changes in the Internal Revenue Code, revised regulations, new rules, and other legislative, administrative, and judicial actions continue to complicate the tax considerations in acquisition and divestiture transactions. The Tax Reform Act of 1986, which was supposed to simplify, did nothing of the sort. The tax rules need to be considered in all phases of a planned transaction, including the choice of the medium and the terms of payment, the method of sale, and the computation and amount of the sales price. Although stock becomes more popular as the medium of payment when market values are high, acquisitions for cash and/or debt gain favor when stocks are down. The stock market, therefore, has a significant impact on both the structuring and the taxability of business combinations.

Accounting rules can also be perplexing. For example, Accounting Principles Board (APB) Opinions No. 16 and No. 17, issued in the 1970s, have led to many arbitrary rules and situations whereby new cases do not fit previous interpretations. Changing views on certain key issues, changes in tax law and in the regulatory environment, and the emergence of transactions never contemplated by the Opinions (e.g., leveraged buyouts and recapitalizations) have all muddied the waters.

Business transactions involving the transfer of a business, division, or subsidiary often account for the main part of a restructuring. This chapter will focus on some of the general accounting considerations involved in such transfers—whether the object is acquisition or merger, on the one hand, or divestiture on the other.

Accounting for Divestitures

The accounting method for divestitures in the financial statements of the divesting company depends on whether the unit being divested qualifies as "a segment of a business"—i.e., a component of an entity whose activities represent a separate major line of business or class of customer. If it does, the results of operations of the divested entity should be retroactively deconsolidated and reported separately from income from continuing operations as a component of income before extraordinary items. The actual or estimated gain or loss from disposal of a segment should be included in the reported results of operations of the segment in the year in which the divestiture plan is adopted. Discontinued-operations treatment should not be applied to the disposition of an operation when the risks of ownership have not, in substance, been transferred.

Costs and expenses associated directly with the decision to dispose of a segment, which may include severance pay, additional pension costs, employee pension expenses, and so on, must be charged to income as part of the results of operations of the discontinued business.

When shares of a subsidiary (or a segment of a business that is subsequently incorporated) are initially sold to the public or spun off, or when debt securities are initially sold to the public by a subsidiary, the Securities and Exchange Commission (SEC) requires that the financial statements of the subsidiary in the prospectus include all expenses incurred by the parent on the subsidiary's behalf. The SEC's policy also applies to credits allocable to the subsidiary (e.g., management fees to the subsidiary in excess of the underlying cost of the services rendered).

If the divestiture does not qualify as a "segment of a business," the results of operations, assets, and liabilities are still deconsolidated, but prospectively rather than retroactively. In addition, results of these operations cannot be reported separately as a discontinued business. Instead, they must be reported as part of income from continuing operations. If material, these results of operations should be disclosed separately as a component of income from continuing operations (e.g., as gain/loss on the sale of a business).

Mergers and Acquisitions

Twenty years ago, merger and acquisition activity generally resulted from small- to medium-size companies acquiring companies in unrelated industries—"conglomerate mergers," as they were called. The number of merger and acquisition announcements peaked in the late

1960s—yet the size of the typical transaction has since grown tremendously. The billion-dollar transactions of today are a far cry from the more modest combinations of yesterday. A stable economy, a favorable regulatory environment, a growing emphasis on being competitive, and the increased availability of financing through both traditional and highly innovative techniques have all affected the types of merger and acquisition transactions of recent years.

But entering the merger and acquisition process hastily may result in small gains and large injuries. External pressures notwithstanding, the increased size and scope of the participants make it more important than ever to conduct thorough planning and investigation prior to making or accepting any offer.

In accounting for business combinations, one of two methods may be used—purchase accounting or pooling of interests. For any given business combination, these methods are *not* alternatives; *only one* will be appropriate to the circumstances.

Purchase Accounting

Under the purchase method, the combination is viewed as one company acquiring another. So, from an accounting standpoint, the target company is regarded much like an ordinary business asset. The purchase price of the acquired company is allocated to the net assets obtained. A difference between the cost of an acquired company and the sum of the fair values of tangible and identifiable intangible assets, less liabilities, is recorded as goodwill (the "residual"). The incomes of the entities are combined only for periods after the acquisition date; and the income of the acquired company is adjusted to recognize depreciation and amortization on the revised net asset values.

Purchase accounting applies whether the acquisition involves an entire entity or just a portion; whether stock is acquired or assets are purchased; and whether the buyer is offering cash, other assets, debt, equity securities (unless pooling-of-interests conditions are met), or a combination. There are three basic steps in the purchase method:

- Determining the acquirer
- Determining the cost, or purchase price, of the acquired company
- Recording the assets acquired and the liabilities assumed (or allocating the purchase price)

To many people, determining the acquirer would seem to be easy—"It's the entity that is making the offer." This assumption is accurate when nonstock consideration (e.g., cash, other assets, or debt) is being offered. But it is not *necessarily* true when stock is issued; depending on other factors, the acquiring company might *not* be the one whose shareholders own the majority of voting stock. And the determination of the acquirer can have a dramatic effect on the resultant financial reporting.

Determining the cost of the acquired company is the second step in purchase accounting. This determination should normally be made as of the date the business combination is consummated (though there are permissible exceptions). The cost of the acquired company generally should be measured by the fair value of the consideration surrendered. In the rare cases when this is not evident, the acquired net assets should be valued instead.

Any additional consideration that is contingent upon future events or transactions should be included in the cost of the entity at the acquisition date. If the consideration is not determinable beyond a reasonable doubt, it should be included in the cost as soon as the contingency is resolved. This usually creates additional goodwill, which should be accounted for prospectively, not retroactively.

Other items that should be recorded as part of the entity's cost include additional securities issued to provide a guarantee of market price and direct acquisition costs (finders' and investment banking fees, legal and accounting fees, etc.). Indirect costs (such as those incurred internally by an acquiring company) must be recorded as expenses, and financing fees and expenses should be deferred and amortized to expense over the life of the related loans.

The third step is to allocate the acquisition cost. First, all tangible and intangible assets acquired in the transaction must be identified and valued individually. This process includes considering items such as overfunded pension plans, favorable or unfavorable debt, leases and other contracts, inventories undervalued due to LIFO (last-in, first-out), undervalued fixed assets, and other unrecorded assets and liabilities. Then, the purchase cost of the acquisition, plus the fair value of liabilities assumed or incurred, must be allocated to these assets based on their individual fair values.

If the aggregate purchase cost is greater than the total fair value of the identifiable assets acquired, less liabilities assumed, that excess or "residual" amount must be allocated to goodwill. Conversely, if the purchase cost is *less* than the fair value of assets acquired, negative goodwill is recorded for any excess fair value that exists after *first* reducing the values assigned to noncurrent assets (e.g., land, buildings, machinery and equipment, intangible and other assets, but excluding long-term investments in marketable securities). Negative goodwill should normally be amortized in the same manner as goodwill.

In many cases, the final amounts assigned to individual assets or liabilities will differ for accounting and tax purposes due to the differing valuation and allocation practices that are prescribed for each purpose. These allocation differences will themselves be considered an inherent part of the accounting valuation process. However, as a result of recent requirements set forth by the Financial Accounting Standards Board (FASB Statement No. 96), the "net-of-tax" approach that accountants have used as a part of this process will be replaced by the "liability method." This new method will normally not, by itself, change net income, goodwill, or net assets (except to the extent that deferred tax assets are not considered to be realizable). However, it will change the individual financial statement accounts affected (e.g., property and equipment, inventory, cost of sales, depreciation, and provision for income taxes). The liabilities that are assumed with the acquisition should be recorded at the present value of amounts to be paid, determined by using appropriate current interest rates.

Additionally, the fair value of any preacquisition contingencies (e.g., unsettled litigation, contractual disputes, renegotiation proceedings, and contested tax assessments) should be included in the allocation of the purchase price when determinable. However, if this determination is made generally beyond one year from the acquisition date, the difference between the estimate used in allocating the purchase price and the actual amount of the contingency should be included in net income for that period. (The same holds true for changes in other estimates used in allocating the purchase price.) Therefore, care should be taken in identifying and estimating the impact of contingent matters.

The goodwill and other intangibles that may result under purchase accounting must be amortized over a period not exceeding 40 years. They cannot be written off in the period of acquisition. Intangibles should be amortized over their estimated useful life if less than 40 years. The length of the amortization period is subjective and should be reviewed periodically to determine if events warrant a revision in the original period. It is usually required, however, to use the straight-line method of amortization.

Complete details of a purchase transaction should be disclosed, and summary pro forma results of operations should be shown for the current period (and for the prior period if comparative statements are issued) as though the companies had combined at the beginning of the period.

There are additional purchase accounting issues that may also need to be considered:

- *Acquisition of minority interests.* Acquisitions of minority interests should be accounted for under the purchase method. The consideration paid should be allocated as previously discussed.

- *Push-down accounting.* When substantially all of the common stock of a company is acquired in one or a series of purchase transactions, the SEC generally requires that the purchase price be "pushed down" to the acquired company's (subsidiary) financial statements if those statements are included in an SEC filing (e.g., an initial public offering). When push-down accounting is required in an SEC filing, the financial statements required normally include both the historical financial statements through the acquisition date as well as those reflected on a push-down basis.

- *Leveraged buyout.* If it is determined that a particular leveraged buyout transaction constitutes a purchase (i.e., shareholders controlling the new company are different from those who controlled the old company), that transaction is accounted for using the purchase method as discussed above (except to the extent that shareholders of the old company are part of the controlling group of the new company). If, however, the transaction constitutes a recapitalization (distribution to existing shareholders of cash and stock, without any real change in control), historical basis would carry over and any cash distribution would be treated like a dividend.

Pooling of Interests

Under the pooling-of-interests method, the transaction is viewed as a merger (pooling) of the ownership interests into a single entity as though that entity and its combined shareholder groups had always existed. This is effected through an exchange of the majority class of voting securities. Since the transaction occurs solely among the shareholders, neither assets nor liabilities are added or withdrawn from the companies themselves, and no revaluation of the assets or liabilities of either company is reflected in the combined financial statements. Historical financial statements of companies qualifying for this accounting treatment are combined as though the two companies had always been commonly owned. Shareholders prospectively share risks and rewards in the company as they had previously done in the separate companies. The pooling method is applicable to combinations involving partnerships or proprietorships as well as corporations.

Under the pooling method, when the "purchase price" exceeds the historical carrying amount of the net assets acquired, the excess of the fair market value over this carrying amount does not have to be recorded. Therefore, the surviving company can continue to amortize the historical cost amounts without recognizing depreciation or amortization related to this excess of fair market value.

The other critical difference regarding pooling is that the surviving company reports the results of operations of both businesses combined for all periods presented in its consolidated financial statements, including preacquisition periods. In contrast, purchase accounting permits the results of operations of the acquired company to be included in the surviving company's financial statements only from the date of acquisition.

Pooling of interests is designed only for a merging of the respective shareholder interest. However, there are many actions that can change the shareholder groups in a way that would prevent a true merging— e.g., the use of cash, alterations of equity interests, redemptions, treasury stock transactions, extraordinary dividends, asset disposition, or other changes in the merged entities. Such actions disqualify the use of pooling of interests. In order to use this method, therefore, numerous conditions must be met. They can be classified as (1) preacquisition attributes, (2) combining attributes, and (3) postcombination attributes.

Preacquisition attributes are as follows:

- Another company cannot have owned more than 50 percent of either company within two years before the pooling is initiated. (Exceptions to this rule include a new company incorporated within the two-year period that is not a successor to another company and a subsidiary or division being divested to comply with an order from a governmental authority.)

- Each of the combining companies must be independent of the other. Neither may hold more than 10 percent of the voting common stock of the other at initiation or consummation of the pooling (or at any time in between).

- Either of the companies involved in the pooling can "alter the equity interests" of the voting common stock or of their relative shareholder interests in contemplation of the combination, either within two years before the plan is initiated or between the dates when the combination is initiated and consummated. There are numerous rules governing this. In particular, there are significant limitations regarding the acquisition of treasury shares, within two years preceding the combination, by either party to the transaction.

Combining attributes are as follows:

- The acquisition must be effected in a single transaction or in accordance with a specified plan's initiation. The period may be longer than one year if the delay in completing the transaction is beyond the control of the companies because of litigation or proceedings of a governmental authority. A substantive change in the terms of a merger agreement is considered a new plan and, in that case, a new one-year term applies.

- The acquiring corporation can issue only common stock with rights identical to those of the majority of its outstanding voting common stock in exchange for substantially all (90 percent or more) of the voting common stock of the acquired company. No pro rata distribution of cash is permitted, but cash may be used to purchase fractional shares or shares held by dissenting stockholders, provided that 90 percent test is met. If the company to be acquired has outstanding equity or debt securities other than voting common stock, the acquiring company normally can exchange cash, substantial identical securities, or its common stock for those securities, or can retire the securities for cash or debt. Warrants, options, and other securities deemed substantially equivalent to "voting common stock" must be exchanged for common stock or comparable securities.

- Each individual common stockholder who exchanges his or her stock must receive a voting common stock interest exactly in proportion to his or her relative voting common stock interest before the combination.

- Certain types of contingency agreements are permitted in a pooling as long as they relate to a condition at consummation and not to a postcombination contingency (e.g., they are not in effect earnings or market-price contingency agreements). The most common types of contingency agreements that are not prohibited in a pooling are those related to specific contingencies, such as litigation and income tax disputes, and "general management representations," which are present in nearly all business combinations. In general, contingency agreements related to specific contingencies may extend for the period during which the underlying contingencies are unresolved, while general management representation contingency arrangements should normally not extend beyond one year.

Postcombination attributes are as follows:

- There must be no planned transactions on the part of the combining companies to (1) agree, directly or indirectly, to retire or reacquire any of the common stock issued; (2) enter into any financial arrangements for the benefit of stockholders of the acquired company that in effect negate the pro rata exchange of equity securities, such as a guarantee of loans secured by stock issued in the acquisition; or (3) intend or plan to dispose of a significant part of the assets of the combined companies within two years of the combination, other than by disposals in the ordinary course of business or in order to eliminate duplicate facilities or excess capacity of the acquired company. Treasury stock transactions can occur subsequent to combination. However, to avoid the presumption that these transactions are considered "planned transactions," a waiting period of 30 to 90 days is suggested.

Other considerations include the following:

- Pooling accounting is precluded if the sum of (1) intercorporate investments (up to 10 percent is normally allowed), (2) "tainted" treasury shares (expressed in equivalent shares of the acquired company), (3) shares acquired for cash (dissenter or fractional shares), and (4) minority interests of the acquired company remaining after the combination exceeds 10 percent of the voting common stock of the acquired company.

In a pooling, the historical carrying amounts of the net assets of both entities must be carried forward without change. Adjustments to conform the accounting practices of the combining entities are acceptable if these changes would otherwise have been appropriate for the separate entity. These adjustments should be made retroactively. Costs incurred to effect a pooling of interests, or to integrate the continuing operations and to eliminate or mitigate existing inefficiencies, should be charged to expense as they are incurred.

Among other requirements, revenue, extraordinary items, and net income of each company should be disclosed separately for the period from the beginning of the year to the date of combination. A reconciliation of revenue and earnings previously reported by the acquiring corporation to the restated combined amounts currently presented in financial statements and summaries should be provided.

Both accounting and tax rules governing business combinations set forth specific requirements that must be met to achieve a pooling of interests or a tax-free reorganization. Those transactions that do not comply completely with the specified rules are to be accounted for as a purchase for accounting purposes and as partially or fully taxable transactions.

Usually, a pooling of interests will be a tax-free transaction, as opposed to a taxable transaction, which is normally reported as a purchase for accounting purposes. But there are exceptions. It should not be assumed automatically that a tax-free transaction qualifies as a pooling or that a purchase is necessarily a taxable transaction.

Furthermore, a sound understanding of the advantages and disadvantages of taxable purchases, as contrasted with those of tax-free poolings, is necessary in deciding which method is better for any given transaction. Companies must consider all factors—tax, accounting, and others—together with the objectives of individual buyers and sellers to arrive at the most appropriate structure for a combination transaction.

Joint Venture Accounting

Accounting Principles Board Opinion No. 18 applies to investments in corporate joint ventures, investments of 20 percent to 50 percent in the common stock of an investee company (foreign or domestic), and investments reported in parent-company financial statements when those statements are prepared for issuance to stockholders as the financial statements of the primary reporting entity.

The equity method of accounting is used for such joint ventures. In this method, the carrying value of an investment in another company is adjusted to reflect the investor's share of any change in the investee's net assets. Thus, the carrying value is increased proportionally to the investee's earnings, and decreased proportionally for dividends received.

To apply the equity method to 20 percent to 50 percent investments in the common stock of investee companies (consolidation is generally required when an investment exceeds 50 percent), the investor must be able to exercise "significant influence" over operating and financial policies of the investee. To achieve a reasonable degree of uniformity in application, the Opinion states that investments from 20 percent to 50 percent in the voting stock of an investee are presumed, in the absence of evidence to the contrary, to indicate that an investor has the ability to exercise significant influence over such investee. An investor's voting-stock interest percentage in an investee must be based on currently outstanding securities that have present voting privileges.

If an investment in voting stock of an investee carried on the equity basis falls below the 20 percent level of ownership, or if for any other reason an investment no longer qualifies for the equity method, an investor should discontinue accruing his or her share of an investee's earnings or losses. Investment accounts should not be adjusted retroactively under these circumstances, but dividends received by the investor in subsequent periods that exceed his or her share of earnings for those periods should be applied as a reduction of the carrying amount of the investment.

An investment that was previously accounted for under the cost method but that currently qualifies for the equity method should be adjusted retroactively. The investment balance, results of operations (current and prior periods presented), and retained earnings of the investor should be adjusted retroactively in a manner consistent with the accounting for a step-by-step acquisition of a subsidiary.

Continually Changing Regulations

An executive confronted with the myriad accounting ramifications of a business combination might feel the same way Mark Twain did when he tried to learn to navigate a riverboat down the complex, ever-shifting Mississippi. Twain observed two things: "One was, that in order to be a pilot a man had to learn more than any one man ought to be allowed to know; and the other was, that he must learn it all over again in a different way every 24 hours." Since tax and accounting regulations are continually changing, the advice of tax, accounting, and legal professionals should always be sought in matters that relate to *specific* proposed combinations.

20
Tax Implications of Restructurings

Albert A. Remeikis

Principal, National Tax Services Office,
Price Waterhouse

The federal tax implications of corporate restructurings fall into three categories: (1) asset acquisitions, (2) stock acquisitions, and (3) recapitalizations or internal restructurings. Each can be accomplished by methods that will render the transaction totally taxable, partially taxable, or wholly tax-free. Moreover, the several parties to a transaction may receive diverse tax treatment, some being currently taxable and others not.

We have recently experienced massive and complex changes in the tax law. This, coupled with the glacial pace at which guidance is provided through income tax regulations and judicial interpretations, often leaves both tax practitioners and corporate executives in the difficult position of uncertainty. Frequently hard judgments must be made on which substantial tax differences will turn. This chapter briefly highlights the principal tax considerations and uncertainties associated with restructuring.

Asset Acquisitions

Taxable Asset Acquisitions

The acquisition of a target ("T") corporation's assets may be accomplished directly via cash purchase or indirectly by merging T into the acquiring corporation with T shareholders receiving cash, notes, or other property in exchange for their T shares. In either event, T will be fully taxable on all gains or losses realized by virtue of the disposition of its assets, and the T shareholders will recognize a capital gain or loss as a result of liquidating their stock. This imposition of two layers of tax is a consequence of repeal of the *General Utilities* doctrine. Corporate-level taxation previously might have been avoided by electing Section 338.

Section 338 elections remain available today. The tax consequences differ from prior law in the important respect that old T is now fully taxable on the gains and losses that it realized as a result of the deemed sale of its property. In most situations the present value of the future tax benefits to inure from T's stepped-up asset basis is not worth the current tax cost. This observation might not be true if old T has a sufficient amount of net operating losses (NOLs) or tax credits, or if T is a foreign corporation.

There is an exception to two-layer taxation if T is a controlled subsidiary of a parent corporation. T will be fully taxable upon the sale of its property, but distribution of the proceeds to the parent will not result in taxation to the parent. The same results would obtain if the order of the transaction were reversed. T could liquidate and distribute its assets in kind to the parent, with the parent thereafter selling the property received from T. Under these conditions, T would not recognize any gain or loss upon the distribution of its assets, and the parent would take over T's basis in the property received. The subsequent asset sale by the parent would be a taxable event. In both scenarios the tax attributes of T, such as NOLs, would survive and would be transferred to the parent.

The Section 338(h)(10) election is available only when the T stock is purchased out of a consolidated group of which T is a member. Unlike the normal Section 338 election, a 338(h)(10) election must be made jointly by both buyer and seller. The tax consequences flowing from such an election closely parallel those described above, where T sells its assets and distributes the proceeds to the parent.

Because Section 338(h)(10) produces the same one-layer tax consequence without the necessity of cumbersome asset transfers, it has become the technique of choice whenever a purchaser wishes to acquire a member of a consolidated group. In addition, as demonstrated by an example discussed below in connection with unwanted assets, Section 338(h)(10) affords a solution to the problem of disposing of unwanted T assets without an immediate tax cost.

Nontaxable Asset Acquisitions

Corporate reorganizations provide for the tax-free acquisition of T's assets (as well as stock) and are defined in Section 368. The rationale for allowing nonrecognition treatment for reorganizations is that they do not represent an appropriate time to tax the parties because the transaction works for a mere change in form. Hence the definitional requirements for reorganization treatment together with relevant case law are designed to ensure that (1) the assets of T remain devoted to the conduct of a business in corporate solution within the acquiring corporation; and (2) the shareholder's investment in T remains substantially unliquidated by taking the form of a stock interest in the acquiring entity.

The following example demonstrates the tax consequences that result to the various parties as a result of a tax-free reorganization.

T, a publicly traded corporation, plans to merge into the acquiring corporation ("A"). The plan of reorganization contemplates that each shareholder of T will receive in exchange for each share of T stock a package of consideration, which will consist of one share of A stock and $10 in cash.

On the surface, this appears to meet one of the reorganization definitions set forth in Section 368(a)(1)(A) (dealing with mergers). However, two nonstatutory, judicially created tests must also be satisfied. These are the continuity of interest and the continuity of business enterprise tests.

The continuity of interest doctrine sets forth the view that literal compliance with this reorganization statute is not sufficient. Continuity requires that a substantial part of the total consideration to be furnished to the T shareholders, in the aggregate, must consist of a stock interest (whether common or preferred) in the acquiring corporation. There is no precise formula as to what portion of the total consideration must be stock. Relevant case law indicates that 38 percent will suffice but that 16 percent is inadequate. Tax advisers will want stock to represent 40 to 45 percent of the mix in order to render an opinion. In our example, reorganization status would not be available if the A stock had a value of only $1 per share. Further, some courts have taken the view that a transaction will be taxable if the T shareholders had a clear plan to dispose of the great bulk of their A stock as soon as possible following consummation.

With respect to continuity of business enterprise, the regulations state that reorganization status will be denied unless A either (1) continues a significant amount of T's business, or (2) retains a significant amount of T's operational assets for use in any business.

There is no specific guidance as to what constitutes a "significant" amount; however, the regulations contain an example that indicates that retention of one-third of T's operating assets should suffice for this purpose. Assuming that our hypothetical merger of T into A qualifies as a reorganization, A will recognize no gain or loss upon its receipt of T's assets in exchange for A stock and the assumption of T's liabilities. A will also assume T's historical tax basis in the assets received, and T's tax attributes will be integrated with A's. Assuming that T's shareholders own less than 50 percent of A's total equity after the transaction, the limitations of Section 382 discussed below will be applied to any NOLs and tax credits of T that survive in A. T will likewise recognize no taxable income as a result of the transaction.

The tax consequences to T's shareholders are measured by first comparing the value of the total consideration (A stock plus $10 for each T share) with their tax basis in the T stock surrendered. No loss can be recognized. If a shareholder realizes a gain, such gain would be recognized, but not beyond the amount of the cash (or fair market value of other property received). Thus, if we assume that the value of the A stock is $10, a T shareholder would receive a total of $20 in value. If that person had surrendered a T share with a tax basis of $5, no more than $10 of the realized $15 gain would be taxable.

Uncertainty prevails as to whether this gain should be treated as a capital gain or as a dividend (assuming that T had sufficient earnings and profits to support such a dividend). Corporate shareholders typically will prefer dividend treatment. As of this writing, the Supreme Court has agreed to hear a case in which this issue is squarely raised.

By comparison to the great merger movement of the 1960s and early 1970s, the tax-free reorganization is not as widely used today. The chief reasons for this appear to be (1) a reluctance to accept the potential dilution in earnings per share that may result from issuance of a large block of the acquiring corporation's stock; and (2) the relative attractiveness of the interest deductions available when the assets of a target are acquired via a leveraged buyout. Nevertheless, tax-free reorganizations remain an important option in appropriate situations.

Stock Acquisitions

Taxable Sales

From the point of view of the selling shareholders, acquisitions of the stock of T are relatively simple events. Unless a tax-free mode is chosen, they will be subject to capital gain or loss. As a result of the elimination of preferential rates for long-term capital gain, these shareholders will pay tax at a maximum rate of 28 percent for individuals and 34 percent for corporate shareholders.

A special situation worthy of note involves the sale by a parent corporation of stock in a subsidiary that joins in filing a consolidated return with the parent. Pursuant to the regulations, the parent's basis in the stock of its subsidiary does not remain static at historical cost. Annual adjustments are mandated instead to take into consideration the results of the subsidiary's operations.

A 1987 revision requires that the earnings and profits of the subsidiary member of a consolidated group be reduced by the full amount of tax depreciation deductions and other special earnings and profits at the time it becomes necessary to determine the parent's stock basis for purposes of computing its gain or loss on such stock. This new rule generally became effective for all stock dispositions occurring after December 15, 1987; and as a result, parent corporations will typically experience a larger gain upon disposing of subsidiary stock in taxable transactions. This rule has the concomitant effect of narrowing any tax distinction to the parent company between selling the stock of its subsidiary and causing the sale of the subsidiary's assets.

In all cases where stock of T is purchased and a decision is made that neither of the Section 338 elections will be made, it is important that the purchaser make a *protective carryover election*. This election ensures that the IRS can never impose a deemed step-up with its attendant tax liability, and avoids the unfavorable-basis consequences imposed by the regulations if assets are also acquired in addition to stock of T.

Nonrecognition Transactions

Shareholders seeking to dispose of their T stock without recognition of gain have two basic methods available. First, all T shareholders have nonrecognition if the acquiring corporation is willing to make the exchange solely for its voting stock (whether common or preferred), or for voting stock of A's parent corporation. Immediately following the exchange, A must be in control of T. Control is the amount of T stock that possesses 80 percent of the voting power of all stock entitled to vote, and 80 percent of the number of shares of each nonvoting class of stock. Such a reorganization, described in Section 368(a)(1)(B), will be strictly interpreted by the Internal Revenue Service to ensure that each and every T shareholder received *solely* voting stock as consideration for their stock. A number of court cases have denied nonrecognition treatment to all exchanging shareholders of T for even minor amounts of nonstock consideration being delivered to a few individuals.

Greater flexibility can be achieved if the T shareholders surrender their stock in a transaction structured to qualify for complete or partial nonrecognition under Section 351. Section 351 provides that no gain or loss will be recognized to persons who transfer property (including the stock of T) to an acquiring corporation solely for stock (whether voting or nonvoting) or securities of the acquiring entity, provided that immediately following the exchange the transferers of property control the acquirer. Control has the same definition as set forth above with respect to a Section 368(a)(1)(B) reorganization.

When T's stock is widely held, an acquiring corporation will frequently choose to effect a transaction of this type by forming a new subsidiary for the sole purpose of merging into T. In this manner (assuming a favorable vote by the requisite number of T shareholders), all shareholders of T will have to either participate in the exchange or exercise their statutory appraisal rights as dissenters.

As an example, P wishes to acquire a controlling stock interest in T. T's management is agreeable to the terms offered by P and, accordingly, a plan is devised whereby P will form a new corporation, S, by transferring to S cash in exchange for an amount of S voting common stock, which will ultimately constitute 80 percent of the S stock measured by vote and value. S, in turn, creates a new wholly owned subsidiary (Mergerco) with a nominal amount of capital. P, S, Mergerco, and T adopt a plan whereby Mergerco will merge into T pursuant to applicable state statutes. The shareholders of T will receive a package of consideration, which consists of S stock, debentures of S, and cash (originally received by S from P). The plan will ordinarily allow T shareholders to choose among the various classes of consideration offered but will provide for pro ration if any category of consideration is oversubscribed.

In this transaction, the transitory existence of Mergerco will be disregarded for federal income tax purposes. Rather, P and the shareholders of T will be deemed to be transferers of property to S who have control of S. The T shareholders will recognize no gain or loss to the extent that they received S stock and/or debentures of S. Those T shareholders who receive cash and stock will recognize their gain (but not loss), but only to the extent that such gain does not exceed the cash received.

Stock Acquisitions from the Buyer's Perspective

Typically an acquiring corporation is not faced with any potential for immediate recognition of gain or loss as a result of its receiving the stock of T, regardless of the tax treatment to the selling shareholders. Although the buyer will take either a cost or a carryover basis in the T stock depending on this tax treatment, this may be of little importance if the buyer has no plans to dispose of the acquired entity. As a result, the buyer's willingness to consider nonrecognition-type transactions will be driven by nontax considerations such as the earnings-per-share dilution resulting from issuing buyer stock or the possible attractiveness of pooling-of-interest accounting. Some tax considerations for the purchasing entity are discussed below.

1. *The tax history of T.*   Since T remains in existence following the acquisition, it will continue to be responsible for any underpayment of tax liabilities for years prior to the transfer of its stock to the buyer. This potential liability may be especially large if T was formerly a member of a consolidated group, since each member remains severally liable for any federal income tax obligations arising from consolidated-return years. In all events, the buyer should obtain a warranty to the effect that all tax returns of T have been properly filed and an agreement to indemnify the buyer if T's tax liabilities for prior years exceed stipulated levels. In some situations a holdback of a portion of the purchase price may be appropriate to secure this warranty.

2. *T may retain tax attributes that benefit buyer.*   The acquiring corporation may have NOLs available to offset future operating income. The Tax Reform Act of 1986 enacted a new approach designed to limit their use after the bulk of the loss corporation's ("Lossco") equity has been acquired by new shareholders. These rules are triggered if, during any three-year period, any shareholder or group of shareholders who own a 5 percent equity interest in Lossco increase such stock interest by more than 50 percent of the total equity. If an ownership change occurs, then Lossco's ability to offset future income with its NOLs will be subject to a limitation. This is computed by multiplying the fair market value of all Lossco stock on the day before the ownership change by the federal tax-exempt bond rate (published monthly by the U.S. Treasury Department). The product represents the maximum amount of annual taxable income that can be offset by the old NOLs of Lossco.

Potential ownership changes are not always easy to identify, since they may arise from virtually any transaction that affects share capital. Thus any number of transactions, such as stock issuances, stock sales, redemptions, split-offs, recapitalizations, and mergers, may in the aggregate combine over a three-year period to produce the requisite change.

3. *Deductibility of interest on acquisition indebtedness.* The buying corporation will want to be sure that it can deduct all interest expense accrued on debt incurred to acquire T. This deduction will normally be secure unless the debt falls within IRS Code Section 279. If this occurs, then interest on corporate acquisition indebtedness (CAI) will be nondeductible to the extent that it exceeds: (*a*) $5 million, or (*b*) reduction by interest paid on non-CAI debt incurred to purchase the stock of another corporation or more than two-thirds of the assets of another corporation.

Subordinated debt should not be convertible, and convertible debt should not be subordinated. When creditors insist on having an equity interest, it should be limited to an investment unit consisting of straight debt and common stock.

4. *Disposition of unwanted assets.* T frequently will have assets the purchaser does not find desirable, and that could be reduced to cash in order to pay down acquisition debt. Prior to repeal of *General Utilities,* numerous options existed that allowed for the disposition of expendable T assets at a zero or minimal tax cost. Sophisticated planners devised a number of techniques, some of which produced comparable results even after 1986. These techniques took on fanciful names such as "mirror transactions" and "son of mirror." Unfortunately, widespread publicity regarding these devices led to specific reactions by Congress and the Treasury. Today, divesting T assets is difficult to achieve without recognition of a full, current tax liability upon the appreciation in the disposed property. Section 338(h)(10) offers one technique that remains valid today.

As an example, assume that P owns all of the stock of T. P and T file a consolidated return. Acquiring corporation A is interested in owning T, but would prefer that the tax basis of the T assets be stepped up to current value. Additionally, T owns all of the stock of subsidiary S, an asset that A would rather not obtain. P and A reach an agreement under which T will distribute the stock of S to P. Thereafter, A will purchase the stock of T, and P will file a joint 338(h)(10) election with A. As a result of the election, P will not be taxed upon its sale of T stock. Instead, T will be deemed to have sold all of its properties. Old T's deemed sale will be included in the consolidation return of P, and may be offset by any consolidated NOLs or credits available. The distribution of S stock from old T to P is considered a distribution independent from the hypothetical asset sale. This distribution is eliminated and produces no current taxable income to P. T would recognize gain on the distribution, which is deferred until such time as P chooses to dispose of the S stock. Any unused tax attributes of T would survive and would be transferred to P.

Leveraged Buyouts and Recapitalizations

Leveraged buyouts and recapitalizations are tools used by investors, management, and shareholders to restructure equity into debt. Leveraged buyouts are generally initiated by investors or management who are interested in privately owning a corporation that is currently publicly held. In contrast, management and shareholders initiate leveraged recapitalizations because they want to increase their ownership or control of a corporation. Leveraged buyouts and recapitalizations are similar in the methods used to accomplish the intended results. Significant debt is incurred by borrowing, and the proceeds are used to fund distributions to the shareholders. The interest expense can be a financial burden unless there is a significant cash flow from operations to service these payments. The corporation may sell assets to repay the debt.

Leveraged Buyouts

A tender offer and a cash merger are the two most common vehicles used to enable investors to acquire all the outstanding stock of a public corporation from its existing shareholders. The investors believe that all the pieces of the corporation are worth more separately than the corporation is currently valued as a single entity. The investors will sell off unwanted assets to reduce acquisition indebtedness. In a tender offer, the investors or a newly created entity will borrow money or issue debt securities to purchase all the stock from its shareholders. In a cash merger, the investors will create a holding company and subsidiary to implement the purchase of a corporation.

In a leveraged buyout, the tax consequences to T's shareholders will in most situations satisfy the requirements of a redemption. The shareholders receive money or debt in exchange for their stock. These shareholders will recognize capital gain or loss on the exchange and can reduce the amount taxable by their basis in the stock. If the shareholders cannot satisfy the redemption requirements, the amount of money received is taxable as a dividend.

Leveraged Recapitalizations

Leveraged recapitalizations are defensive maneuvers used to prevent hostile takeover attempts. The additional debt incurred makes the corporation less desirable to a hostile raider.

A stock recapitalization is a general restructuring of the equity of the corporation. The corporation issues a new class of stock to its shareholders in exchange for their existing stock or issues a new class of securities in exchange for existing securities. The stock or securities issued can have different privileges or terms. The corporation can also distribute cash along with the stock.

There is no gain or loss to the corporation on the issuance of its stock, securities, or distribution of cash pursuant to the recapitalization. The shareholders do not recognize gain or loss on the receipt of new stock in exchange for their old stock, but do recognize dividend income on the receipt of cash.

A dividend recapitalization is comparable to a stock recapitalization except that no stock is issued. The corporation will distribute a large cash payment to all shareholders. The corporation will recognize gain or loss on any sale of assets to fund the dividend, but not on the distribution of cash. The shareholders will treat the cash as a dividend, since no shares of stock were surrendered.

A partial reduction in shareholder interest arises when management or a group of shareholders desire to obtain a larger or controlling interest by having part of the stock redeemed. The remaining shareholders increase their equity interest without using their own money. No gain or loss is recognized by the corporation upon purchasing its own stock for cash. A shareholder who tenders enough stock to meet the requirements for redemption can treat the money received as a distribution in exchange for the stock and will be entitled to capital gains treatment and basis offset. Otherwise the distribution is a dividend.

Spin-offs of Subsidiaries' Stock and Securities

In certain situations, it may be necessary or advantageous for a corporation to distribute to its shareholders stock or securities of one or more of its subsidiaries. This might be undertaken to satisfy employee demands, to obtain financing, or perhaps to defend against a takeover attempt. Since the repeal of *General Utilities,* any distribution of appreciated property, including stock of subsidiaries, will generally result in a gain being recognized to the distributing corporation and dividend treatment to the shareholders to the extent of the distributing corporation's earnings and profits. One exception to this general rule is provided in Section 355 of the IRS Code, which deals with stock distributions referred to as spin-offs, split-offs, and split-ups.

Section 355 imposes numerous requirements that must be satisfied in order for the distribution to qualify for nonrecognition treatment. The major requirements include the following:

- There must be a valid, non-federal-tax corporate business purpose for the distribution.

- The distributing corporation must hold at least 80 percent of the voting stock and 80 percent of each class of nonvoting stock (i.e., "control") of the subsidiary (i.e., a "controlled" corporation).

- The subsidiary's stock must have been held for five years before the distribution or it must have been acquired in a transaction in which no gain or loss was recognized.

- The distributing corporation must distribute "control" of the controlled corporation, and any retention of stock or securities of the controlled corporation must be approved by the IRS.

- Each of the distributing and controlled corporations must be engaged in the active conduct of a trade or business immediately after the distribution, either directly or by having substantially all their assets consist of stock of other active subsidiaries.

- The businesses of the corporations must have been conducted for five years by the distributing or controlled corporations or acquired in transactions in which no gain or loss was recognized.

- There cannot exist any plan or intention for any 5 percent-or-more shareholders to dispose of their stock in the distributing or controlled corporations after the distribution.

Many of these requirements are subjective, and taxpayers frequently seek a private ruling letter from the IRS stating that it is satisfied in order to virtually eliminate the risk that the distribution will be treated as taxable.

If these requirements are met, the distribution will not be taxable to either the distributing corporation or the shareholders. The shareholders will either allocate their basis between the stock of the distributing and controlled corporations based on the relative values of each or, in the case of split-offs, the controlled stock will have the basis of the stock surrendered in the exchange. The earnings and profits of the distributing corporation are generally allocated between it and the controlled corporation (or between the two controlled corporations in a split-up) based on fair market value.

As a final example, D has owned all the stock of C for more than five years. Both D and C have been engaged in the active conduct of a trade or business for each of the past five years. For valid business reasons (e.g., D or C needs financing that is unavailable under the current corporate structure; key employees of C or D wish to acquire an interest in C or D, respectively, without having to acquire an interest in the other corporation; or to take C public as a stand-alone company), D distributes all the stock of C pro rata to its shareholders. One of D's shareholders is individual A, who holds as a capital asset 100 shares of D stock with a basis of $100 and who will receive 100 shares of C stock in the distribution. At the time of the distribution D has earnings and profits of $1000, and C has no earnings or profits. Immediately after the distribution the D and C stock are equal in value.

No gain or loss is recognized to D, and no amount is included in the income of D's shareholders. Immediately after the distribution, D and C will each have $500 in earnings and profits. A will hold 100 shares of D stock with a basis of $50 and 100 shares of C stock with a basis of $50. A will be considered to have held the C stock for as long as A held the D stock. If D and C were part of a consolidated group, additional computations would be required under the consolidated regulations to allocate consolidated tax items and to make other required adjustments.

21

Director Liability: Protections and Loss Prevention Suggestions[1]

Sean M. Pattwell

President, Professional Liability Division,
National Union Fire Insurance Co.

The evolution of increased director liability, which began in earnest during the 1960s, mushroomed to crisis proportions during the 1980s. The explosion of litigation against corporate directors, with its accompanying judicial analysis of director conduct and applicable standards, has created a tenuous legal environment in which directors are expected to make major corporate decisions that may be subsequently critiqued by courts with little if any business acumen.

One of the most important and far-reaching decisions a board can make is one involving a fundamental change in the corporation's own-

---

[1]Any views expressed herein are those of the author and may or may not reflect the views of National Union Fire Insurance Co. of Pittsburgh, Pennsylvania, or American International Group Inc., or any affiliated companies thereof.

ership, structure, or operations. Such divisions invariably benefit some corporate constituents and adversely affect others. Because of the typical magnitude of these transactions, there is a high probability that the adversely affected constituents will be sufficiently motivated to seek recourse for the perceived harm that they suffer. Accordingly, directors face a tremendous potential for liability exposure when making corporate restructuring decisions.

As demonstrated throughout this volume, a corporate restructuring may take any number of different forms. Each type has different legal issues and implications. It is not practicable to address all those different legal issues in this limited discussion. Rather, the fundamental legal concepts common to the process of evaluating and approving any type of corporate restructuring will be summarized.

Historical Analysis

A common thread that unites all types of corporate restructuring is the fact that the corporation's directors are the persons primarily responsible for evaluating and approving the transaction. It is not surprising, then, that when a dispute arises with respect to the restructuring, the directors will likely become parties to that dispute.

When analyzing the conduct of directors in this context, courts will directly or indirectly determine whether the directorial conduct was consistent with the three basic duties applicable to directors:

- *Duty of diligence.* Directors must act with the care that a reasonably prudent person in a similar position would use under similar circumstances. They must perform their duties in good faith and in a manner they reasonably believe to be in the best interest of the corporation. Prior to making a business decision, directors must inform themselves of all material information reasonably available to them.

- *Duty of loyalty.* Directors must refrain from engaging in personal activities that would injure or take advantage of the corporation. They are prohibited from using their positions of trust and confidence to further their private interests. This duty requires an undivided and unselfish loyalty to the corporation and demands that there be no conflict between one's corporate duty and self-interest.

- *Duty of obedience.* Directors are required to perform their duties in accordance with applicable statutes and the terms of the corporate charter. Directors may be liable if they authorize an act that is beyond the powers conferred upon a corporation by its charter or by the laws of the state of incorporation.

Business Judgment Rule. If the business judgment rule (BJR) applies, directors are presumed to have acted properly and to have satisfied these three basic duties. The BJR recognizes that not every decision of the board will result in benefit to the corporation and that directors will be personally liable for loss to the corporation only if the BJR defense is not available.

To obtain the benefit of this important defense, directors must act in good faith and with a reasonable basis for believing that their conduct is in the lawful and legitimate furtherance of the corporation's purposes. They must also exercise their honest business judgment after due consideration of what they reasonably believe to be the relevant facts. The BJR is not available if, when making the decision, the director was not disinterested and independent, did not make a reasonable effort to ascertain and consider all relevant information, did not act with the best interests of the corporation in mind, or made a decision that cannot be supported by some rational basis.

Historically, the courts applied the BJR defense to claims against directors arising out of corporate restructuring transactions. Unless the director's "sole or primary motive" was self-motivated, the courts deferred to the director's business judgment in analyzing, adopting, or rejecting such transactions. Because of the dramatic increase in the size, frequency, and complexity of restructuring transactions in the 1980s, courts began questioning the wisdom of applying traditional BJR principles to these unusual transactions. Directors were frequently perceived as having a direct or indirect personal interest in the transactions, particularly when control of the corporation, and thus their own positions with the corporation, became subject to change.

As a result, the BJR in recent years has been substantially eroded by the courts in those situations where the directors are perceived to have an inherent conflict of interest, such as in a proposed takeover of the corporation. The judicial analysis of director conduct and thus the potential exposure for that conduct varies depending on whether the restructuring is independent of or related to an actual or threatened change of control.

Restructuring Unrelated to Change of Control

A director's decision to approve or oppose a restructuring transaction that does not involve a change in control should be subject to the traditional BJR, provided the director is perceived to be independent and disinterested. In this context, the primary issue is whether the director made an informed decision. The case of *Smith v. Van Gorkom* (488

A.2d 858 [Del. 1985]), serves as a good "reverse primer" to demonstrate how not to evaluate a proposed restructuring transaction.

In that case, J. W. Van Gorkom, president of the Trans Union Corp., reached a tentative agreement to sell Trans Union to an acquirer at approximately a 50 percent premium over the market value of the Trans Union stock. The perceived adequacy of that price was based solely on calculations by Trans Union's chief financial officer. Van Gorkom hastily called a meeting of the Trans Union directors to approve the transaction. The directors were not given the merger agreement before or during the meeting, and only three of the 10 directors reportedly knew the purpose of the meeting in advance. After a 20-minute oral report on the terms of the transaction by Van Gorkom and a two-hour discussion by the directors, the transaction was approved. The merger agreement was executed later that day without having been read by any director.

The Delaware Supreme Court held that the Trans Union directors were grossly negligent for making an uninformed decision. The court particularly noted the following deficiencies in the directors' actions:

- The directors relied on an oral presentation and had no written documentation with respect to the proposal.

- The board acted hastily, without prior consideration of the proposal.

- The premium over market price was accepted without sufficient valuation information (the market price of the stock was found to be an insufficient basis on which to measure the appropriateness of the offering price).

- The directors did not sufficiently provide for competing offers to be obtained.

- The directors did not make sufficient inquiry of management concerning the transaction.

- The shareholders' overwhelming approval of the transaction did not preclude liability because the shareholders had not been appropriately informed of material information.

This case demonstrates the need for objective evidence to demonstrate that the directors critically evaluated all information relevant to the transaction. By itself, a subjective belief by the directors that the transaction is in the best interest of the corporation and its shareholders is insufficient to protect directors from personal liability.

Directors may also be liable for approving a restructuring transaction that does not involve a change in control if the transaction "squeezes out" minority shareholders to the benefit of the controlling shareholders. In this context, the BJR may not be available and directors may be required to show that the transaction is entirely fair to the minority shareholders. In determining fairness, courts will examine not only whether the price was fair, but also whether the minority shareholders were dealt with fairly. Relevant to this latter inquiry are questions such as the timing of the transaction, how it was initiated, structured, negotiated, and disclosed, and how the stockholder approvals were obtained.

Restructuring Related to Change of Control

When the restructuring transaction constitutes or is related to an actual or threatened change in control, the directors are faced with an inherent conflict of interest. In addition to owing separate duties to the corporate entity and the shareholders, directors are also perceived to have a self-interest of remaining in office and preventing an outsider from obtaining control of "their" corporation.

Because of the appearance that the board may be acting primarily in its own interest, some courts have concluded that the board's duties are enhanced in the change-of-control context and that the traditional BJR should be modified. The trend of the decisions is in that direction. Where the restructuring transaction is considered a defensive response to an actual, threatened, or possible takeover bid, courts generally apply a modified BJR to evaluate the propriety of the board conduct. The following two inquiries are made in these situations:

1. Did the directors have reasonable grounds to believe that a danger or threat to corporate policy and effectiveness existed?
2. Was the defensive restructuring transaction reasonable in relation to the threat posed?

The "threats" that may justify some type of defensive action to a takeover bid include inadequacy of price, inappropriate nature of timing of the offer, questions of illegality, risk of nonconsummation, quality of securities offered, and the impact on corporate constituents other than corporate shareholders (i.e., creditors, customers, employees, and perhaps even the community generally).

A board cannot always take comfort in the fact that the approved restructuring transaction has basically the same or a somewhat better effect on the corporate entity than does the takeover bid to which the restructuring relates. Tax consequences, short-term investment goals, and other considerations may justify a raider's takeover bid but may not justify a similar restructuring by the corporation, because in the long term the best interests of the corporation or its shareholders would not be satisfied. By approving a restructuring transaction, the board may be voluntarily accepting without justification adverse consequences to the corporation and shareholders in order to defeat a takeover bid with comparable adverse consequences. Unless the restructuring transaction is a reasonable response to the threats posed by the takeover bid, director liability may result.

The potential liability of directors in approving restructuring may be particularly acute if the transaction is forced on the shareholders without their approval. Because defensive use of a restructuring transaction to thwart a hostile takeover bid can deny shareholders the opportunity to realize a significant premium and may entrench management, shareholder approval should be obtained whenever possible, following complete disclosure of all material information to the shareholders.

Once the directors conclude that a change in control of the corporation is inevitable, the directors are required to become "auctioneers," with the sole duty of obtaining the best price possible for the benefit of the shareholders. As auctioneers, directors are not required to remain completely neutral, so long as any preferential action taken is in the best interests of the shareholders. This duty to auction does not arise if the restructuring does not involve the sale or change in control of the corporation. Thus, a parent/subsidiary merger or cash-out of minority shareholders should not require the directors to auction the company, although the minority shareholders are entitled to an intrinsically fair transaction.

Because of the unique and sensitive role played by directors when dealing with restructuring transactions in the takeover context, courts, like the directors themselves, continue to struggle with how to evaluate those decisions. The articulated judicial standards are still being defined and refined. As a result, it is virtually impossible for a board to act in this context with any certainty and safety.

Disclosure and Misuse of Nonpublic Information

Disclosure Obligation

It is essential that directors properly handle nonpublic information relating to a restructuring transaction. Premature or delinquent disclosure of that information or use of that information for personal gain can create personal liability exposure.

In the absence of the corporation buying or selling its own stock or mandated disclosure under the securities laws, the corporation does not have a general duty to disclose material nonpublic information. Courts recognize that full, absolute, and immediate disclosure of crucial corporate developments may impede corporate success and therefore, absent statutory or regulatory requirements to the contrary, the decision to disclose should be protected by the BJR.

At least with respect to merger transactions, directors must weigh the probability that a merger will occur and the magnitude of the effects of such a merger when evaluating the appropriate time for disclosure. When assessing the probability that the merger will occur, it is appropriate to examine the interest in the transaction at the highest corporate levels, as evidenced by board resolutions, instructions to investment bankers, actual negotiations, and the like. To assess the magnitude of the effects of the merger, such facts as the sizes of the companies involved and the potential premium over market value should be considered. It is probable that no particular event or factor short of the closing of the transaction necessarily renders the merger discussions material.

When inquiries to the corporation are made before disclosure is mandated, a "no comment" response by the company may be an appropriate response, although stock exchange rules, prior corporate practices, and other considerations may render this type of response inappropriate. If the corporation chooses to speak, it must do so truthfully. Therefore, it is essential that the corporation adopt well-defined and widely understood corporate procedures with respect to handling public statements and inquiries from the news media and others. All corporate statements and inquiries should be handled by one person or department, and competent legal counsel should be consulted when deciding what should be disclosed, when, and how.

Insider Trading

Few areas of director and officer conduct have received as much collective attention in recent years from administrative agencies, the courts, Congress, and the news media as the misuse of inside information by directors, officers, and others. The state of the law involving insider trading is currently in flux, but it is clear that corporate directors and other insiders may be personally liable if:

- They personally trade in the shares of their corporation without first disclosing all material inside information known by them.
- They breach a fiduciary duty by directly or indirectly benefiting personally from disclosure of material inside information to another.

In defining this latter liability, based on tipping information to others, courts have liberally construed the requirement that the "tipper" benefit personally from the tip. For example, the requisite personal gain has been found when the individual conveys the information to a relative, friend, or professional colleague without any monetary consideration. The tip and subsequent trade are viewed as equivalent to trading by the insider followed by a gift of the ill-gotten profits to the relative, friend, or colleague.

To help minimize the risk of personal liability in this area, directors should adopt comprehensive procedures to prevent leaks of confidential information and trading on the basis of material nonpublic information. The procedures should be set forth in policies or guidelines that are distributed to all appropriate employees and should clearly and explicitly define the obligation to safeguard the information and prohibit trading thereon. Compliance with these procedures should be closely monitored. Punishment for those who violate the policies and guidelines should be swift and certain.

In addition, confidential information and discussions relating to that information should be limited to those persons who need to know the information. The likelihood of leaks, rumors, or misuse of that information increases with the number of persons who have access to that information. Confidential documents should not be left in plain sight. It may be appropriate to protect the identity of parties to the transaction by using code names in draft documents.

Loss Prevention Suggestions

Because of a director's inherent conflict of interest and the widespread impact of many restructuring transactions, it is impossible to fully satisfy the interests of all corporate constituents interested in the transaction. It is thus impossible to avoid claims being asserted against directors in this context.

However, certain director conduct may reduce the likelihood of claims being made and improve the likelihood that claims may be successfully defended. The following summarizes some loss prevention suggestions in this context.

Competent Advisers

Perhaps the most important loss prevention step that directors can take is to surround themselves with qualified and competent advisers. Directors are entitled to rely in good faith on experts, officers, committees, or agents of the corporation when making board decisions. When evaluating restructuring transactions, qualified and independent legal counsel, investment bankers, and accountants are essential.

The various legal, financial, and business issues relating to a restructuring transaction can be quite complex, and the applicable standards change rapidly. Therefore, where possible, the corporation should use advisers who deal with these issues regularly.

Reliance on any outside adviser or expert should satisfy each of the following elements:

- The adviser should be reasonably viewed as competent, experienced, and reputable in the area of advice.
- All relevant facts known to the directors must be disclosed to the adviser.
- The advice relied on must be rendered within the scope of the adviser's expertise.
- Directors must follow the advice in good faith and with due care.

Board Composition

Directors should be selected based on their ability to contribute meaningfully to the quality of the board's decision making process. Only qualified persons with sufficient time and interest to perform the responsibilities of a director properly should serve.

Particularly with respect to restructuring transactions, a significant portion of the board should consist of members independent from management. Persons who merely rubber-stamp the recommendations of executive officers serve no function on the board and should be avoided. If the restructuring transaction is perceived to benefit certain directors or officers, they are interested persons and should not take part in the board decision or discussions relating to the transaction. A committee composed entirely of independent, disinterested directors should thoroughly analyze the transaction and make recommendations to the full board.

Proactive Planning

Boards should periodically evaluate the corporate structure and identify advantages and disadvantages that structure has over alternatives. By delaying the consideration of a restructuring transaction until a takeover bid is submitted or threatened, the directors reduce their ability to evaluate proposals in a relatively pressure-free environment and probably subject their decisions to greater scrutiny and higher standards of care. Directors should try to be proactive rather than reactive.

Thorough Analysis

When analyzing a restructuring transaction, directors should adopt procedures and methods that allow for the identification and examination of all relevant factors. The conclusions and recommendations of independent experts and special committees of the board should be reviewed closely before being relied on. Directors should attempt to determine whether apparent deadlines are real and should use the time that they have as effectively and efficiently as possible. Copies of all proposed agreements, or at least accurate summaries thereof, should be available for review prior to the board meeting if at all possible. Reasonable inquiry should be made into the basis of the price or values assigned to the transaction and the extent of negotiating with respect to the terms of the transaction.

Directors must be willing to devote the time necessary to conduct such a thorough analysis. Although the quantity of time spent evaluating a transaction does not necessarily equate to quality of time, directors must schedule adequate time to perform their responsibilities. The recent reactions of some courts to the duration of challenged board meetings involving restructuring transactions have been as follows:

- Directors were found liable for approving the merger of the corporation during a two-hour board meeting without sufficient information concerning the transaction and without advance notice of the purpose of the meeting.

- Directors were found not liable for adopting a "poison pill" following a board discussion that was considered by one outside director to be the most extensive discussion of any single topic in his 12 years on the board.

Documentation

A complete and thorough analysis of all relevant facts will not shield directors from liability unless the directors can prove the analysis in fact occurred. Documentation is therefore one of the most important and perhaps neglected areas of a loss prevention program. Through documentation, directors should be able to identify long after the transaction what actions they took, what matters they considered and relied on, who participated in the process, and why the decisions were made.

Board minutes and other relevant documents should be carefully reviewed by directors to assure that they accurately reflect the director's understanding and intent. Where possible, the documents should also be reviewed by legal counsel with the expectation that the documents will be closely scrutinized in the future for evidence of wrongdoing. Ambiguous, inflammatory, vulgar, or other inappropriate language should be deleted.

Most important, the board minutes should accurately reflect each director's participation and decision with respect to the restructuring transaction. Each director who voted against the transaction should be identified. Mere abstention from voting is considered an implicit acquiescence in the decision and therefore is not a legally recognized defense.

Maximize Legal Protection

Directors should create a legal environment consistent with maximizing protection against personal liability. Applicable state statutes that permit the limitation or elimination of certain types of director liability should be examined and, where necessary, approximate shareholder action should be sought to obtain the fullest elimination of liability permitted by law.

To ensure maximum financial protection in the event that liability is established, the corporation's indemnification provisions should be reviewed in the light of applicable state law to assure that they provide the maximum protection permitted by law. In addition, directors and officers liability insurance should be obtained when available to help assure directors that they will be financially protected to the fullest extent practicable.

When the restructuring transaction involves a merger or other change in the legal existence of the corporation, continuing director indemnification and insurance protection should be closely reviewed. The surviving entity should be contractually obligated to indemnify the directors of the preexisting corporation. Trust funds, letters of credit, surety bonds, or other arrangements may be considered to secure this indemnification obligation.

Because director liability insurance covers only claims made while the insurance is in effect, it is crucial that continuing coverage be afforded after the date of the transaction even if directors leave office on that date. The surviving corporation may be contractually obligated to maintain this insurance coverage for a specified period, or a special "run-off" policy may be purchased.

Even if the board remains intact after the restructuring, the insurance policy should be reviewed prior to the transaction's closing date to ascertain the need for notice to the insurer as a condition for maintaining coverage after the transaction.

22
Corporate Recovery and Renewal: The Restructuring of Scott Paper Co.

Philip E. Lippincott
Chairman and Chief Executive Officer,
Scott Paper Co.

The nature of the restructuring process that took place in Scott Paper Co. is rooted in the company's history, heritage, and culture. The company was founded in Philadelphia in 1879 by two brothers, E. Irvin and Clarence Scott. The Scott brothers' original business was "coarse" paper goods, such as wrapping paper and bags. Soon, the introduction of sanitary plumbing and the rising standard of living of late nineteenth-century America sparked a new awareness of personal hygiene. The Scott brothers saw this as an opportunity to produce and market a product known as "toilet tissue." At first, Victorian niceties made it impossible for the company to advertise its products; however, public attitudes and the Scott brothers matured, and the company prospered.

The brothers could not afford a factory of their own until 1910, when an abandoned mill was purchased in Chester, Pennsylvania. From these humble beginnings, Scott grew to be the worldwide leader in sanitary tissue paper products, with manufacturing operations in 20 countries and its products sold in many more. Scott is also a major competitor in the U.S. printing and publishing papers business via its subsidiary, the S. D. Warren Co. Today, the Scott family includes more than 37,000 employees around the world.

For most of its 100-plus year history, Scott was a leader in the U.S. consumer tissue market; however, by the 1970s, the company had lost its competitive edge. Market shares eroded during the decade, and profitability slipped just as badly. The business portfolio that existed at that time was the result of unrelated diversification based on financial rather than strategic considerations. Managers tried to reconcile such varied businesses as foam manufacturing, graphic/arts materials, outdoor furniture, lighting fixtures, and paper products. In the period 1965–1970, Procter & Gamble Co. entered the U.S. consumer paper products market with two strong entries: Charmin bathroom tissue and Bounty kitchen towels. Both achieved significant market shares, a good bit at Scott's expense.

In short, the competition became innovative and aggressive, but Scott did not. The way that Scott had been thinking of its markets, its customers, and its employees no longer served the best interests of the company. Scott's business methods and culture were traditional and principled; the only problem with them was that they no longer worked. Both employees and shareholders lost confidence in the company's ability to compete effectively, and the viability of Scott as a company came into question.

During this period of decline, a number of plans were formulated to stop the downward trend. Some of the plans filled three-ring binders several inches thick. All were greeted with some enthusiasm, but most ended up on shelves. The plans we did put into action failed to achieve their goals mainly because they attacked symptoms, not the problems. We continued to increase our sales dollars during this period, but market share and profit margins continued to erode.

In late 1980 and early 1981, with the problem obviously acute, Scott senior management recognized that a major change was needed in the way that we managed the business. This change came from the executive committee, who developed a recovery strategy that shifted the strategic direction of the company. The strategy was simple in nature, but its effects were to reach every corner of Scott's businesses. Emphasis was placed on implementation and results, not on elegance of language or style, and not on the thickness of planning manuals. In effect, we rolled up our sleeves and got to work.

Adding to our concerns, Brascan Ltd. of Canada purchased 13.06 percent of Scott's shares in March 1981. By the end of October 1984, Brascan owned 24.9 percent of Scott's common stock. This was close to the maximum percentage specified in the "standstill agreement" reached with Brascan in March 1981. The agreement stated that they would acquire no more than 25 percent of Scott's common shares through December 1985. This gave us time to implement our 1981 strategy, and demonstrate our ability to create value for our key stakeholders. Commensurate with their percent of ownership, Brascan placed four members on Scott's board of directors. The situation was resolved through an agreement negotiated with Brascan in 1985 whereby the company repurchased Brascan's interest in Scott at about the then-market price along with Scott warrants.

Recovery Strategy

The recovery strategy had four prongs, which were implemented simultaneously across the business:

- Concentrating resources
- Eliminating drags and drains
- Changing culture
- Improving financial performance

The first prong identified Scott's strengths, and then concentrated on areas where those capabilities would most benefit the company and generate the greatest returns. In order to determine which areas would provide the most benefit, rigorous criteria were developed to evaluate the value of new and existing businesses. These criteria are still being used today:

- Scott must have real or perceived competitive advantage in the business.

- The markets and/or geographies in which the business competes must reward those competitive advantages. Being the leader in a market where the best competitors generate only marginal returns on investment is not a desirable option.

- Scott must be able to manage the business as well or better than anyone else.

- The business must earn a satisfactory return—risk-adjusted return that exceeds the cost of capital and places the company's return on equity (ROE) in the top quartile of U.S. industry.

The second prong of the strategy concentrated on strengthening our good businesses and shedding our weak ones. It involved focus and simplification as we sought to make our business more cost-competitive. This was accomplished by shutting down older, inefficient paper machines and mills; eliminating unprofitable brands; reducing freight and distribution expenses; divesting country affiliations and businesses that were not in alignment with the long-term direction of the company or that did not meet the strict criteria mentioned above; streamlining work flows; reducing head count; and lowering manufacturing costs.

During this period, most of our strategy focused on the recovery of the business. However, two growth initiatives, wet wipes (e.g., Baby Fresh) and industrial wipers, begun in the 1970s were carried forward into the 1980s, and one major growth initiative was undertaken in the early 1980s. Our research and development team had developed a significantly advantaged lightweight coated paper for the printing and publishing papers market that was clearly superior to available products. The lightweight segment was an area in which Scott did not compete at that time; however, in conjunction with volume commitments from our distributors, we invested $215 million to install a new lightweight coated-paper machine alongside a state-of-the-art pulp mill in Skowhegan, Maine. With the amount of capital we were investing to make our U.S. tissue business competitive again, the coated-paper machine decision raised capital spending to very high levels, with the corresponding risks associated with it.

Our decisions worked out well. A second lightweight coated-paper machine has been added to the first at Skowhegan, and the product from both machines has been sold out virtually from the time that they became operational. In fact, late in 1988 we announced plans for a third machine at our Maine location.

Culture Change

With returns in the 4 to 5 percent range, and an urgent need to increase our returns to above the cost of capital (in the 11 to 12 percent range), it was obvious that we were not going to "sneak up" on our goals. Success was going to require not just changes in strategy, but in attitudes, behavior, and the way that we ran the business.

The Scott work environment had always been a "family" affair, with lifetime employment practically guaranteed. It was becoming obvious that despite the company's difficulties, complacency was an overriding cultural characteristic. There was nothing wrong with our employees. Scott has always been staffed with extremely competent people, but absence of a successful strategy as well as the culture simply did not foster stretching and extending personal and professional goals.

This work environment needed to change to an atmosphere in which each employee is encouraged to reach his or her full potential. The emphasis is now on performance with a strong commitment to results. The number of management levels has been reduced and spans of control broadened, with a corresponding redefinition of individual roles and responsibilities. Responsibility for decision making has been placed at the lowest possible levels of the company, and incentive programs have been modified to support expectations of increased performance.

As a result of these significant changes in culture, employees changed their perceptions of the company and their relationship to it. Some of these changes were accomplished with considerable pain, but out of the process evolved a leaner, more committed, and stronger work force.

The fourth and final prong of the recovery strategy was designed to improve financial performance by realizing significant growth in earnings, cash flow, and return on equity.

The recovery strategy was announced in February 1981, and implementation began immediately. Although 1982 showed a decrease in overall earnings due to machine and plant shutdowns that resulted in volume reductions, the year provided strong indications of progress to come with commitment of a $1.6 billion capital spending program and strong U.S. earnings. The first Somerset paper machine, located in Skowhegan, was started in December 1982, and provided the base for S. D. Warren's growth in the lightweight coated-paper market. In short, 1982 laid the foundation from which later progress was created. In 1983, all financial indicators showed definite improvement, and in 1984, earnings per share established a record (the fist of five consecutive annual records) for the company.

Development of the Scott Vision

By mid-1985, the recovery process was well under way and survival was no longer the issue. The questions before the executive committee related to what we wanted Scott to become in the future, and what long-term goals that "vision" of the company implied. In essence, we realized that doing more of the same thing and doing it better were not enough to ensure the continued health of the company. Recovery and cost-savings measures could take us only so far.

As we thought about the future, we realized that we needed a clear statement of the company's purpose, the principles on which it operated, and its long-term direction. These statements were needed by the executive committee, by our employees, by the investment community, and by our other publics. Whatever we developed at the executive committee level had to be communicated to, and understood and internalized by, our employees because they would be the people to make that future a reality. We called this statement of "what we wanted to be when we grew up" the "Scott vision."

What is a "vision"? A vision is the shared view of all employees of what the company wants to be in the future. We believe that a vision is important because we can have the best strategy in the world and invest large sums of capital (and we had), but if we do not have our people working together toward common objectives at levels approaching their full potential, we will not be fully successful. Implementation of this shared vision requires that employees:

- Understand the company's objectives.
- Understand how they fit in.
- Believe that their roles are essential.
- Believe that they will be fairly rewarded and recognized.
- Believe that they will be given the opportunity to develop to their full potential.
- Believe that the company is committed to excellence.
- Believe that their personal ownership of and alignment with company objectives are essential.

Scott's vision, simply stated as the corporate purpose, is: *to continually improve the health and value of the company by creating wealth for all key stakeholders.* This is a broader idea than creating value for just shareholders, because it extends to all key stakeholders of the company—customers, employees, communities, suppliers, etc. The wealth created is defined differently for each stakeholder, since each group has different values and objectives in its relationship with Scott.

We believe that if we succeed in this wealth creation Scott will be recognized, inside and outside the company, as healthy, growing, prosperous, dynamic, and responsible—in short, the best at what we choose to do. "Choose" is the key word because the resources of any company are limited and must be focused on selected endeavors for optimal success. We are focusing our thinking and behavior on the achievement of: stakeholder alignment, human resource excellence, and growth.

Stakeholder Alignment

A stakeholder is any individual or group of individuals who can affect, or is affected by, the success of the company. There are a number of stakeholders: shareholders, lenders, the government at all levels (local, county, state, as well as federal), suppliers, communities, employees, etc. The strategic importance of these stakeholders shifts over time. For example, during the development of the Tax Reform Act of 1986, the government was a most important stakeholder.

However, we believe that there are four key stakeholder groups who are always of primary importance to the company: our customers, our employees, the communities in which we operate, and our shareholders. We strive to achieve a win/win relationship with all groups, but we must achieve it with these key stakeholders.

Stakeholder alignment is not merely a philosophy. We have taken specific actions to improve our relationship with each of our key stakeholders. For our customers, we have improved product quality and the service systems with which we support them. Our customers are critical to us because if they do not buy our products, everything else we do is academic.

We have become involved in the communities in which we operate through financial contributions, cause-related marketing programs, and through supporting the volunteer efforts of our employees. We are committed to improving the quality of life in our communities and focus on two main areas of interest: the needs of families and the disadvantaged.

Our shareholders have benefited from the results of our recovery plan. Scott's growth in earnings and improved returns have resulted in dividend increases and appreciation in the value of Scott stock.

Human Resource Excellence

We have singled out our employees as one of the stakeholder groups most critical to the success of the company. We believe that the quality of Scott people, and how we develop, support, manage, and utilize their capabilities, can be our single most important and most enduring source of competitive advantage. We are institutionalizing in our thinking and behavior the driving belief that people are valued assets, not expenses.

This is a relationship with mutual obligations. The company must create an environment characterized by:

- Open, two-way communications
- Mutual trust and credibility

- A bias toward teamwork
- Opportunities for personal growth and development
- Reward and recognition systems that support our vision
- An owner/stakeholder mentality
- Excellence in everything we do

Employees should:

- Feel good about themselves.
- Strike the right balance between work and other interests in their lives.
- Share the same values and vision.
- Develop the necessary skills.
- Possess uncommon desire.
- Have a bias toward teamwork.
- Be motivated by results and new levels of achievement.

Our biggest challenge with our employees has been establishing mutual trust and credibility. Because we are human and sometimes tradition-bent, our behavior has not always been consistent with our commitment to, and belief in, the achievement of a win/win relationship. To correct this situation, we are having more open, honest, two-way communications with employees and opening up more feedback mechanisms. We are also moving toward more equitable sharing for all employees in the successes and disappointments of the business with the introduction of variable compensation for all U.S. salaried employees.

Growth

As we use the term, "growth" is defined as the net result of consciously and continuously strengthening our base, adding related new businesses, and shedding weak or unrelated businesses, processes, and behavior. It is the engine that drives creation of wealth. Our recovery strategy focused on the shedding and strengthening dimensions of the growth cycle, and established a solid platform on which the company could obtain additional sources of growth and wealth creation.

We decided that new growth areas must meet the business criteria explained earlier, build on Scott strengths, and fit emerging trends in the external environment. At the time that this framework for growth was established, we were still "majoring" in recovery and focusing on our base businesses. It was almost four years before we were ready to move out of a predominantly recovery mode and to concentrate on growth in our current and new businesses.

We evaluated the value, role, and potential of each of our current businesses and looked at areas of potential growth through related diversification. Through this process, we came to view our business from a global perspective. The U.S. tissue market is fairly mature, whereas market growth rates outside the United States are much higher. We also expanded our view of the markets in which we compete. We had always thought of ourselves as a paper company, but now we have broadened our thinking about our markets and realized that we really participate in two major businesses: worldwide personal care and cleaning, and U.S. quality coated papers. Future growth will come from within these two areas.

Communicating the Vision

Scott's executive committee developed the vision, but organizational alignment and "buy-on" is key if a vision is ever to become reality. We first shared our ideas with senior managers of the company from around the world, and then cascaded the message throughout the organization. In 1987, I sat with six employees representing all parts of our organization and discussed the Scott vision with them. The results of this conversation were then shared with all U.S. personnel and a large portion of our international work force. We are always looking for ways to reinforce the basic message.

In spite of the length of time it took to develop the vision and the hard work involved in that process, that has turned out to be the easy part of the job. What has proved to be most challenging has been making the vision a reality: changing behavior (our own as well as others), changing the work culture across the organization, establishing win/win as the criterion for managing relationships, and most of all, establishing credibility—convincing employees and others that this was not another management fad, soon to fade away—that we were serious and committed to making the vision work.

Results of Recovery and the Vision

Over the past eight years, we have continued to implement our recovery strategy and begun to raise our concentration on the expanding aspect of growth. The success of our endeavors speaks for itself. We have made significant progress since the dark days of 1981. For the past six years (1983 through 1988), we have achieved record sales. For the past five years, we have established record earnings per share, moving from a low of $0.81 in 1982 to $4.01 in 1988. In the period 1982 through 1988, our return on investment increased from 4.3 percent to 10.3 percent (still below our goal of 11 to 12 percent), and return on equity rose from 5.3 percent to 18.1 percent. Also, we increased our dividend 60 percent on a quarterly basis. The 1988 figures quoted above exclude a nonrecurring gain of $1.22. In March 1988, Scott stock was split two for one, and all figures above reflect this split.

The results of our consistently improved performance have been rewarded by the investment community, with Scott stock appreciating 287 percent compared with the 103 percent appreciation in the Standard and Poor's 400 from year-end 1982 through year-end 1988. We are pleased with the success of our recovery and vision work.

Scott is now beginning to reach the financial and strategic goals that we set for ourselves. The company is now a solid and respected performer; however, our vision recognizes that this is not good enough. We realize that, to be truly competitive in the 1990s and beyond, we must exceed our own previous expectations for ourselves. By insisting on nothing less than excellence in everything we do, we will become the best in the areas in which we elect to compete and in satisfying the needs of all our stakeholders. We call being the best at what we choose to do "preeminence." There are financial measures of this goal, but the objective is more than financial: It embraces the entire vision. We must be the best at creating wealth for all key stakeholders through human resource excellence and our management of the growth cycle.

We have come far from the company struggling to survive in 1981. In a few short years, we have weathered financial difficulties, an attempt to obtain control of the company without the offer of fair value to the company's shareholders, and difficult market conditions in the United States and elsewhere. We have emerged a stronger and more significant company. I have the privilege of presenting Scott's success story to this audience and to investment communities around the world, but the credit for Scott's success is with our employees. The executive committee developed a recovery strategy and the vision that restructuring made possible, but our employees' dedication and enthusiasm made us successful.

It has been said that our business in life is not to get ahead of others, but to get ahead of ourselves; that a loser believes he is not as bad as a lot of other people, but a winner believes that he is not as good as he could be. At Scott, we believe that our future challenges are not in exceeding our accomplishments of yesterday but in exceeding our expectations of tomorrow.

Index